Advance Praise for Ann Meyers Drysdale

"A stunning portrayal of one of today's legendary women's basketball treasures. Ann Meyers Drysdale provides a candid look at the courage, faith, and determination that it takes to be a champion on the court and in life."
~ **Alana M. Glass, Esq.**, Forbes.com SportsMoney Contributor

"A fascinating and inspiring story, and so relevant today! Many of the obstacles Ann Meyers Drysdale overcame decades ago are still alive and well and her courageous story can help us all to triumph."
~ **Vera Tweed**, *Newsmax* Contributor

"Annie was one of the greatest players ever. I didn't say male or female, I said ever."
~ **Bill Russell**, Celtics great

"Ann always stayed one step ahead of the competition in terms of preparation. It made her strong on the courts and it's what makes her so strong as an executive today."
~ **Julius Erving**

"She was the only woman to sign a no-cut contract with the NBA. She was mad good and she had so much heart, that it didn't matter what size she was."
~ **Jamaal Wilkes**

"She's a legend."
~ **Robin Roberts**, host *Good Morning America*

"She's a modern-day Babe Didrikson Zaharias."
~ **Jim Brown**, Hall of Fame running back

To my sons, DJ (Don Jr.) and Darren,
and my daughter, Drew,
Who Inspire Me Every Day

In Loving Memory of My Love,
my late husband, Don Drysdale

To my Mom, Pat Meyers,
and all my siblings and relatives
who have ALWAYS
been there for me.

Best Wishes

you let some GIRL beat you?

The Story of Ann Meyers Drysdale

by
Ann Meyers Drysdale

With
Joni Ravenna

Foreword by Julius Erving

Behler
PUBLICATIONS
California
USA

Behler Publications
California

You Let Some GIRL Beat You?: The Story of Ann Meyers Drysdale
A Behler Publications Book

Copyright © 2012 by Ann Meyers Drysdale
Cover design by Yvonne Parks - www.pearcreative.ca.

Some of the names have been changed and some conversations have been condensed in order to retain the flow of the narrative.

Library of Congress Cataloging-in-Publication Data
Meyers Drysdale, Ann.
   You let some GIRL beat you? : the story of Ann Meyers Drysdale / Ann Meyers Drysdale with Joni Ravenna ; foreword by Julius Erving.
      p. cm.
   ISBN 978-1-933016-78-8 (pbk.) -- ISBN 1-933016-78-7 (paperback) 1. Meyers Drysdale, Ann. 2. Basketball players--United States--Biography. 3. Women basketball players--United States--Biography. I. Ravenna, Joni. II. Title.
   GV884.M48A3 2012
   796.323092--dc23
   [B]
                                2012008330

FIRST PRINTING

ISBN 13: 9781933016-78-8
e-book ISBN 9781933016-87-0

Published by Behler Publications, LLC
Lake Forest, California
www.behlerpublications.com

Manufactured in the United States of America

Table of Contents

Foreword by Julius Erving

1. A Woman in A Man's World, *1*
2. Chasing What I Loved, *16*
3. The Man Who Was Not Intimidated, *24*
4. Let The Race Begin, *31*
5. You Let Some GIRL Beat You?, *38*
6. Learning to Harness the Fire Within, *47*
7. UCLA & That Old Nemesis: Change, *58*
8. The Olympics – A Dream Come True, *66*
9. "Precious Medals", *78*
10. The Championship, At Last, *86*
11. A League of Our Own, *94*
12. The Right Strategy Equals Success, *114*
13. Burning Up the Courts Like Lava, *120*
14. Waiting It Out, *129*
15. Gal's Got Game, *143*
16. My Big Broadcasting Break, *153*
17. Goodwill Toward All, *162*
18. Juggling It All – Life With Don and Our Children, *167*
19. Any Other: Loss, *178*
20. Fly Me to the Moon, *189*
21. Moving On, *196*
22. A Single Mother, *208*
23. The Road to the Boardroom is Through the Locker Room, *217*
24. Where We Go From Here, *228*

Acknowledgments, *234*

Awards/Halls of Fame, *232*

FOREWORD BY JULIUS ERVING

Annie and I met at the Dewars Sport Celebrity Classic at the Riviera Hotel in the 70s, where we were both asked to compete. I had followed her career at UCLA, and of course, I was also familiar her brother, David Meyers, because he'd been playing in the NBA for the Milwaukee Bucks.

I knew Annie had come from this amazing family of athletes, but there was something about her that drew both me and my wife at the time, Turquoise, to her. She was a sweetheart, but there was also this fire that burned in her.

Annie had grown up one of eleven kids, and I imagine she did what she could to earn her parents' attention the way I once collected coke bottles in the projects just so I could have some pocket change.

That weekend in the 70s at the Dewars charity event, Turq and I both adopted Annie as our own, but for different reasons. Turq wanted to get her into makeup and purses. She took Annie out shopping, hoping to 'girlie' her up. But Annie wanted to hang out with me to play ball . . . any kind of ball—softball, basketball and tennis.

Playing pickup basketball with the guys, I'd always want Annie on my team because I knew that she had the I.Q., the physical talent, and the drive to win.

When you play pick-up basketball, if you want to stay on the court you have to win game after game after game. Sometimes one wrong play means the difference between winning and losing, but with Annie, there was very little losing.

When I was growing up in the projects, there were two girls who I played regularly with up through 8th grade; Debra Chow and Juanita Hayden, so I was unfazed by playing hoops with girls. Either you could play or you couldn't. I expected Annie to get knocked down and to get back up. I also expected her to set picks, hit her shots, and to be able to drive to the basket and take the contact. The only time I became a little bit protective was when we had some of the football players like Walter Payton and Joe Washington, who were better blockers and tacklers than they were basketball players, and I wanted to make sure they didn't get too crazy. I didn't need to worry, though. Annie could handle them all.

We also had guys like Rick Barry and Calvin Murphy playing with us. These were guys who knew how to play the game and they were pretty shocked to see that Annie could not only play with the guys, but that she could score.

In the years that followed we've become tight friends, like family. There was a bond created back in the 70s, and it's only grown stronger over the years. We've started growing older together and sharing our experiences as parents. While we were brought together by circumstances, we've remained close by choice.

When I reflect on what made Annie a great player on the courts, the first thing I think of is how physically gifted she was. She could run, she could jump, she was quick as a cat, and had these great hands. Annie was also mentally as tough as anyone I've known and always seemed to find a way to deliver when the pressure was on. Beyond that, Annie was always a smart player. She always stayed ahead of the competition in terms of preparation. That's why she later became a great broadcaster and a great front office executive for the NBA and WNBA with her posts at both the Phoenix Suns and Mercury. She always does her homework and comes in ready to go.

Annie used to come visit me and Turq at our home on Long Island. We would play tennis, golf, and pick-up games. She would beat me at tennis and beat me at golf. The only thing she couldn't beat me at was basketball, but I would've loved to see how that went if Annie was 6'6" rather than 5'9". There was always competition between the two of us, but along with it was a genuine friendship and mutual respect. I don't remember once in my life ever introducing Annie to anyone who didn't immediately say, "Wow, she's such a nice person. I can see why you're friends." Everyone is impressed by the kind of person she is. I like to think that nice people are attracted to other nice people. But underneath that sweetness, there's this strength.

A lot of people know about her but they don't totally know her story, the challenges she had with Don dying and raising her three young children by herself and making it work. Annie had become the first woman to do so many things that it's hard to list them all. She could have let the tragedy of losing Don change her, but she didn't. Her attitude has always been so positive, so strong.

Annie doesn't let difficulty overcome her. She's a fighter. How she can be thought of as so kind on one hand, and such a fighter on the other, I'm not sure. I guess that's what makes Annie, Annie. There's no one like her.

I think that's part of our bond, hers and mine, that we've both known great personal loss. Annie knows that I'm the last surviving member of my immediate family. I've lost my mother, step-father, my sister, and my brother. Annie lost one of her sisters, one of her brothers, and her father in addition to losing Don. I think we can look at each other, and though we know we're changed by those losses, we didn't allow them to dictate what we had to get up and do the next day. They don't hold us back from doing those things we must do. I think I'm an encouragement to her and there's reciprocity there.

When Don died, I could immediately relate to having someone so significant in your life suddenly not being there. What are you going to do about it? It's not, *how did this happen to me? It's what am I going to do about it?* Annie just rolled up her sleeves, picked up the mantle and said, "Okay, I have to be mother and father here." She had so many offers to coach or manage this or that team, and there were some big NBA teams that were after her, but while the kids were little she, put them first. Finally, when the kids were old enough, she said, "I have to get up and go out there and be productive and, in doing that, I'm going to be a motivator, inspirer, and role-model for my family. Hopefully they won't have to go through what I've gone through, but if they do encounter that kind of loss in the future, they'll be prepared."

Certainly, her daughter will be prepared for the challenges that women face because there's still so much gender bias out there. I never had that bias, probably from having played with Debra and

Juanita every day. The projects were a three-story housing project in Nassau County, Hempstead, Long Island called Park Back Gardens, but there was nothing garden-y about it. There was a park next to us called Campbell Park and that combination was my life until age 13. That's where I learned the fundamentals of the game and the street. At 13, my father passed and my mother remarried, and we moved to another community where I had a very different life. But the foundation was laid in those first thirteen years. Other people may have considered it underprivileged, but we were proud of who we were. It wasn't until much later that I realized it was the other side of the tracks, and there were people living a better life.

Annie grew up differently than I did, but there was never that sense of entitlement from her. Annie is so far removed from that. She knows that talented athletes come from everywhere. They come from the streets, the suburbs; they come from hard-scrabble, inner city schools, and from elite prep schools. It's a melting pot, and once you've reached that level of athleticism that it takes to become the first woman to receive a full ride to a Division I school like UCLA, the way Annie did, you're in that place where everybody's treated equal. You step on the court and if you can't play, you're going to get your butt kicked, regardless where you came from. But not Annie; she didn't get her butt kicked at UCLA because there was no woman anywhere who could play the way she did. She became an All American and a Champion. She was so impressive that, in his later years, Coach Wooden said in an interview that Annie was the one who really got women's basketball going in this country.

What she did at UCLA was more than just impressive; it was a door-opener. When Annie went out for the Pacers, I ran a basketball camp that was open to girls. But again, I was more liberal than others might have been at the time. I also have three daughters (and four sons) and my youngest, Julianna, who's six and very athletic, met Annie this year.

A couple of months ago I took Julianna down to a Mercury practice. My daughter and I got a chance to talk to the women about basketball and their boss, Annie. The players couldn't say enough about her. "She's just a wonderful person," they all said.

Later that season, Julianna and I were at a shoot-around for the Phoenix Mercury when they played the Atlanta Dream in Atlanta. Annie and I were sitting on the side talking while the girls were practicing. Julianna was at the other end of the court running back and forth from one side of the bleachers to the other. Annie and I both looked at her and smiled. Nobody had told her to do it.

Maybe Annie will be the one to inspire Julianna the way Babe Didrikson inspired Annie when she was little. Maybe Annie will be the one to inspire your daughter, too. I can't know this early if I have a daughter who is as driven as Annie, but I hope so. The world could sure use a lot more like her.

~ Julius Erving

1

A Woman in a Man's World

"Whatever women do they must do twice as well as men to be thought half as good."
~ Charlotte Whitton

"I've played against Calvin Murphy, Wilt Chamberlain, Julius Erving and other male pros in pick-up games, and I've always held my own," I shouted back at the hoards of reporters, hoping to give as good as I got.

"The *Detroit Free Press* called you the butt of a cruel joke. Any comment?" I didn't recognize the face, but his microphone had an NBC flag. *The Today Show* was preparing to run a segment with the heading: "Ann Meyers' NBA Bid: Hype, Hope, or Hoax?" to compete with my upcoming appearance on ABC's *Good Morning America.*

"It's a free country." My voice reverberated across the vast banquet hall of the Century Plaza in Los Angeles. Wednesday was L.A., Thursday would be New York. The Indiana Pacers had just signed me to a three-year contract after I'd been chosen as the number one draft pick by the Women's Basketball League, or WBL, and it was big news.

"Minnesota Fillies owner, Gordon Nevers, says you're betraying your own gender going out for the NBA," another voice called out. "At five-foot, nine-inches, and 134 pounds, wouldn't you be better off in the WBL?"

"I'll let the way I play next week answer that."

I hadn't made the decision lightly. Signing with the Pacers meant forfeiting my chance to compete at the 1980 Olympics. It also meant angering some people in the Women's Basketball League. The last thing I wanted was to upset anyone. I'd been flattered when the

WBL chose me as the overall first draft pick the previous year, but the timing wasn't right. I still had a few classes to finish up at UCLA in order to get my Sociology Degree. And there was the big question of whether I wanted to play professional women's basketball enough to give up my amateur status. I'd played on the first U.S. Women's Olympic Basketball team in 1976, where we'd taken the Silver, but nothing compares to taking the Gold, to hearing your national anthem as they raise your flag. I'd experienced that at other International basketball events, and I believed the U.S. women had a good shot at Olympic Gold in 1980.

Now Sam Nassi, the new owner of the Pacers, was giving me an amazing opportunity to play in the NBA and, suddenly, the stakes had changed.

"Come on, Sam, isn't this just a gimmick to sell tickets?" Sam was sitting to my right, while the Pacers head coach, Bob "Slick" Leonard, was to my left. They were also on opposite sides when it came to my bid.

"We're as serious as a heart attack," Sam shot back. "Ann's a great athlete. Have you ever seen her play tennis? She can blow 90% of the guys right off the court. If we didn't think she had a chance, we wouldn't have signed her."

Slick felt otherwise. He had flown out early to California to persuade me not to try out. "Annie, are you sure you really want to do this?"

I chalked it up to generational differences more than anything. While Slick's wife was the GM of the Pacers team, a female *player* was something else. Slick Leonard came from an era unaccustomed to seeing women suited up in athletic uniforms, much less those belonging to a men's team, and I don't think he was too happy about what my bid meant for the Pacers. Larry O'Brian, the commissioner at the time, had already green-lighted it, saying in an official statement, "The NBA does not discriminate against athletes on any basis, including sex." Slick must have wondered what the world was coming to.

"Annie, there's no way someone your size is going to make this team," he told me. But the more he tried to talk me out of it, the more determined I was to do it. That's a failing of mine, or maybe it's a strength. Either way, if you want me to do something, just tell me I can't.

I had always played with the guys, and learned to arch the ball over my brothers, who were a foot taller. I realized early on that the winner wasn't always determined by size and strength, just as later I would realize the single characteristic distinguishing an outstanding athlete from a Hall of Famer was not always physical ability, but desire. The capacity to dig deep down and come up with that little extra when others felt like their tanks were empty was, in my mind, the greatest ability an athlete could muster. It was my passion to win that had set me apart, and which had now landed me this invitation to try out for the NBA.

I was born loving athletic competition, especially if it was against the guys, and each time I did something that had never been done before, I wanted to find new frontiers to conquer. I had been the first high school student to make it onto the US National team before going on to lead UCLA women's basketball to their only National Championship after winning a Silver Medal on the first Olympic Women's Basketball Team.

During college, I played pick-up games with guys like Magic Johnson, Mark Eaton, and Marques Johnson at Pauley Pavilion, and with Calvin Murphy and Julius Erving in Vegas. They were fast, but so was I. They had size, but I had quickness. They had strength, but I had heart.

Some said my ability to play at the men's level was taking women's basketball in a new direction. If that was true, it was because the good Lord put me in the right place at the right time. John Wooden had been coaching the UCLA men's team to stratospheric heights for years before my older brother, Dave Meyers, stepped foot on campus and helped lead the Bruin men to their final championship under their beloved coach. I benefitted from having the support of both my brother and Coach Wooden during that period. And there's no doubt the national attention Dave and I received as UCLA's sibling basketball players spilled over onto women's basketball at a time when the country was coming to view women in a very different light. I didn't need my newly earned sociology degree to realize that. You'd have had to have been blind not to see it.

The 70s had given birth to Title IX, which allowed young women more equitable access to school funding. Title IX affected me, in particular, when I became the first female athlete to receive a full athletic scholarship to a Division I university. Culturally, the decade had ushered in the likes of *Maude* and *Mary Tyler Moore,* replacing TV stereotypes like Harriett and Lucy. Now at the decade's close, Patty Hearst, whose automatic-rifle-wielding image was emblazoned in the public eye four years earlier when she robbed a bank with the Symbionese Liberation Army, had her sentence commuted by President Carter, in part, due to pressure from the ACLU, NAACP, and various women's rights organizations.

The image of the fairer sex as hiding behind an apron in the kitchen was definitely being replaced, if not by that of a woman with an itchy trigger-finger, then by that of a woman with a naked ring-finger throwing her hat up in the air to the lyrics, "You're going to make it after all." If ever there could be a female NBA player, it seemed 1979 might be that time; and it looked like I might be that player.

The press wasn't so sure. Some thought it was just a publicity stunt on the part of Nassi. While I was well aware of the Bill Veck story, the baseball owner who had hired a midget in the hopes of upping attendance, I never believed Sam wanted me as a side show. Sure, there was publicity involved, but not for me. I just wanted to compete, and I'd been given an opportunity to compete with the best. I knew it would be at a price.

Leading women's magazines accused me of slighting my sisters at a time when it looked as though there might finally be a viable women's basketball league. Others implied that the NBA might be trying to dishearten the new league out of existence rather than take a chance on sharing even a slice of ticket revenue. "Shame on you, NBA, for crossing the sex barrier and letting the Pacers sign Ann Meyers when the WBL has been drooling over her for over a year now," wrote *Mademoiselle*. Sportswriters said I didn't stand a chance. "I am five-foot-nine and weigh 175 pounds, and haven't shaved my legs in thirty-eight years. I have a better chance of dancing with the Radio City Music Hall Rockettes than Ann Meyers has of playing basketball in the NBA," one *Washington Post* reporter wrote.

"It won't be a joke when they see her play," Denver Nuggets coach, Donnie Walsh, told the press. "I've seen her play against David Thompson, Wilt Chamberlain, and Quinn Buckner. She's good. From far away, you couldn't tell it was a girl."

My biggest supporter was the owner of the team himself, Sam Nassi.

It was early August when the phone rang in our home in La Habra, California. I'd just returned from the Spartakiade Games in Russia on the heels of playing in the World Championships in Korea, where we'd won the Gold. That summer we'd also taken Silver in the Pan Am Games. I was team captain and recently named overall first draft pick of the WBL Houston.

"Ann, how would you like to try out in the NBA with the Indiana Pacers?"

"Who is this?" I had taken the call upstairs in my mom's room. I was home just long enough to unpack before heading off to train at the Squaw Valley Camp for the upcoming USA Basketball World University Games in Mexico, and whoever this was, he was lucky to catch me.

"This is Sam Nassi, owner of the Indiana Pacers, and I'd like you to try out for the team."

Sam who? I'd never heard of him, but he seemed to know me. He'd followed my career and seen the publicity I'd generated for UCLA. To me, Sam Nassi was simply a voice on the phone offering me an outrageous proposition.

The Pacers, however, I knew very well. They were an ABA team who had recently moved to the NBA. Though the conversation was brief, it was long enough for me to see that Sam was serious. I was flattered and excited but I wasn't about to let it show.

"Well, I'll have to speak with my family first." We exchanged further pleasantries before signing off. I bolted downstairs and slid into the kitchen to tell my mother, practically knocking her over onto the cold linoleum.

I then made several calls. One was to my older brother, Mark, who had just become a Personal Injury attorney. I realized I would need legal representation, and at twenty-four, the difference between a sports lawyer and a PI lawyer meant about as much to me as the difference between a German Shepherd and a Doberman. All I knew was that my brother would look out for me. Mark negotiated a three-year personal service contract for $150,000. Whether I made the cut or not, for three years I would be with the organization in some capacity. At that time the minimum annual salary for an NBA player was $50,000, a lot of money back then.

Another call was to Julius Erving, whom I had played with in various celebrity tennis tournaments, and was a very close friend. Julius was already a legend in the ABA and the NBA. He was one of the most celebrated basketball players of his time. I knew Julius would be supportive and happy for me, and he was.

But the most important call I made from Mom's kitchen was to my older brother, Dave. His opinion had always mattered more than anyone's. If anybody could advise me, it would be Dave. The Bucks had nabbed him in a trade with the Lakers four years earlier, after he'd led UCLA to two championships and been chosen as the NBA's 2nd overall draft pick. Dave had been there, and he'd know what to tell me.

"That's really great, Annie," he began. "But there's no one in the NBA who is 5'8" and 134 pounds."

"5'9"," I reminded him. "And you said there's a kid in Atlanta who is only 5'8"."

"Charlie Criss, and he weighs 165 lbs. and he's the lightest guy in the NBA."

The conversation wasn't going where I wanted.

"Well, don't expect any special treatment. After all, you're potentially taking some guy's job."

It seemed it always came down to this; the right of men over women to have a job, to get the promotion, to be nominated the party's presidential pick. But Dave? He didn't subscribe to this sexist theory of the world. No, my guess was Dave was more concerned for my physical welfare than anything else. I assured him that I didn't expect to be treated any differently than any of the other contenders, and that I could take care of myself. All I wanted was to go out there and show them I could play.

The truth was, while I wanted Dave's advice and my entire family's input, deep down I think I'd already made up my mind, or at least my heart. God had given me another opportunity, and this time I wouldn't be held back. Five years earlier—while in high school—I'd chosen not to play on the boys' team. Now, I had that chance again, but on a much bigger stage. This time, I wasn't going to allow anyone to talk me out of it.

I headed up to Squaw Valley and let two days of training with the USA team pass before I worked up the nerve to tell them I wouldn't be going to Mexico to compete in the World University Games, nor would I be eligible for the '80 Olympics. It was one of the most difficult things I've ever had to do.

When I returned home to La Habra, there were three weeks remaining before the trials. I trained every day, all day, often with my brother Jeff. We played as many as fifteen pick-up games a day. When we weren't playing, he drilled me with shots, conditioning, and mentally helped me prepare.

"You'll never get a shot off like that," he'd say.

He knew what I'd be up against, and he wanted to toughen me up as much as possible. I'd run the stairs and keep my hands fast by using a speed-bag. I may not have been able to do anything about my height or bulk, but I could compensate with speed, quickness, and my shooting ability. I was a pretty good outside shooter, and with the then newly-implemented NBA 3-point rule for field goals from beyond a 23'9" arc, that talent was in great demand.

It goes without saying that I was about to go up against a lot of good outside shooters, and all of them would be bigger and stronger, but none of them could have loved the game any more than I did. Desire and talent don't discriminate between male and female anatomy. I hoped Slick wouldn't either. I wanted to show him that I could play. And for three days, that's exactly what I did.

Holed up at an Indianapolis Ramada Inn at night and Butler University during the day, the Free Agent/Rookie training camp took place inside Hinkle Fieldhouse, the same gym made famous in the movie *Hoosiers*. The tryouts lasted three days in September, and were held in the morning and again in the late afternoon. At night, I would phone my mom, steering clear of the television and newspapers. I'd hoped to avoid all the negativity surrounding my bid, but in one phone conversation I learned that Veteran Pacers player, Mike Bantom, had been quoted saying that if I was going after his job, then he was going after me whether I was a girl or not, and he hoped I didn't get hurt. My brother, Dave, had been right.

Every morning, I rode over to the gym with my trainer, Davey Craig, and the top two draft picks, Tony Zeno and Dudley Bradley. At 6'8", Tony Zeno had played for Arizona State as a forward, and he would go on to play for the Pacers for a year before playing in Italy, where in a game against Poland, he broke a backboard with a slam-dunk. Dudley Bradley had played for the University of North Carolina and was called "the Secretary of Defense" for his prowess at forcing turnovers. He would go on to set an NBA rookie record with 211 steals.

But for now, both men were simply competitors with whom I would share a ride and the court—all three of us sporting the same Pacers practice gear, complete with knee-high socks and Adidas high-top Superstars.

During the first scrimmage, a defensive player came up behind me and set a hard screen. I recovered, pivoted to the left, and sprinted down the length of the court. I cut into the lane on the break, received a chest pass from the wing and made a left-handed lay-up. It wasn't much different from what I had done thousands of times before, whether on the courts of UCLA, or the playgrounds and high school gyms, or at the Olympics or the Pan Am Games. But now the stakes were much higher; a place in the greatest league in the world.

As a little girl, my siblings and I would huddle around the television every Sunday, consumed by the plays of our idols Bill Russell, Jerry West, and John Havlicek. We'd wait for that one NBA game all week and when it was over, we'd go outside and try to emulate their moves. In my mind, I was John Havlicek. Looking back, I don't know who my brother, Dave, pretended to be, but he'd grown up to make the dream come true. Now, incredibly, there was a chance it might happen for me, too.

However, from the sidelines, I believe the press saw something entirely different: a woman amidst a dozen guys a foot taller and as much as 100 pounds heavier. They never thought I stood a chance.

A microphone was jammed into my face by someone with one of the local stations. "A lot of people say you're in over your head, literally and figuratively." I immediately wondered if a question would follow his comment and why there weren't any women covering the tryouts. There were easily ten cameras and a couple dozen reporters in the Hinkle Fieldhouse, and not a woman among them.

"What about taking a charge from Bob Lanier?" he persisted. "How are you going to do that?"

"Who in the NBA is going to take a charge from Bob Lanier?" I asked back. It was a stupid question.

"The WBL is saying you should promote women's basketball rather than shame yourself. How do you feel about that?"

"People can say what they want," I said on my way out. Rather than use the women's locker room, I headed toward the ladies' bathroom, where I knew I couldn't be followed.

On the way, I overheard one of the players talking to the press. "She's good, but she doesn't deserve to be here."

Certainly, he had a right to his opinion, and I appreciated his honesty, but I didn't agree. While everyone on the court could play, some of them just didn't seem to fully understand the game. On defense, there was a guy who would get lost, another couldn't read a pick. One didn't understand how to run the floor on a fast break. I still liked my chances, regardless what this guy thought; what any of them thought.

I'd long developed the ability to brush off comments made by my male opponents. I'd heard them all through the years, whether from boys, young men, or seasoned pros. I'd seen them express every emotion possible, from awe to exasperation, heard every type of remark, from nasty to admiring, and I'd learned long ago not to let their feelings affect me. Now more than ever, though, I had to make certain nothing got inside my head. I had to play my best.

Was I knocked down? You bet. But I knew how to fall and get back up because I'd done it so many times before. When a 6'10" center went up for a rebound, he brought the ball down below his waist, which gave me the chance to sneak in close, turn up my palm, and pop the ball loose in order to stop the fast break.

I had learned throughout my years playing that the majority of guys would bring the ball too low on a rebound. At UCLA, we were taught to bring the ball to our chests. Because of my size, I could sneak in there and give a little jab, and the ball would pop out of their hands. We both went for the ball, and in the scramble, he knocked me to the ground. I jumped right back up. I needed them to see it was no big deal because, to me, it wasn't. I had done my job, was he trying to do his. That's just part of basketball, and I needed both the coaches and the players to realize that I didn't require special treatment; the latter for their sake, as well as mine.

John Kuester, who was a free agent guard from North Carolina and played for Dean Smith, showed up for tryouts. Everybody called him "Q" because his last name was pronounced Q-ster. Q and I were in a one-on-one drill, and as I hustled back on defense, we collided and I went down. I was fine, but John's natural instinct was to worry that he'd hurt me.

He bent down next to me. "Are you okay, Annie?"

He was such a good guy and, like most of the players there, he'd been conditioned his whole life to take it easy on girls, not to play too rough. Now he was being asked to do just the opposite. We were both playing our hardest at what is a very physical game. We were going to get knocked down, but John wasn't prepared to knock a woman down. After his playing days, he became the head coach for the Detroit Pistons before going on to become an assistant coach for the Lakers.

Seeing John check to make sure I was okay brought on the ire of Jack McCloskey, Indiana's assistant coach. "That's it! Everybody over here!" Jack was running practice while Slick watched from the sidelines. He had been with the LA Lakers, and became the GM of the Detroit Pistons in the 80s during their heyday. But he was far from happy that day watching us practice. "You're gonna stop this bullshit now!"

He lit into all of us with the longest, saltiest tirade I'd ever heard. Cursing was a collateral skill developed on basketball courts the world-over, but Jack's pointed list of superlatives effectively worked to shake the reticence out of every player there and replace it with an unbridled determination to play at full throttle. By using the most over-the-top language imaginable, he didn't just give the other players permission to behave ungentlemanly around a woman, he demanded that they go out there and play without constraint of any kind.

"Forget about the cameras and the reporters, and the fact that they're here because of Annie. She's no different than any of us. Now get out there and play!"

His words got through, and I saw an immediate change in the players. It became a turning point in the tryouts. I could sense the relief. There was a freedom to the movement after that. The drills had more energy, more focus. From my perspective, it meant I was one of them. Jack had called me into the circle and spoke the same way to all of us. From that point on, I felt that I had Jack on my side.

"Fundamentally, she's better than half the guys out there," he told one of the reporters at the break.

During the afternoon scrimmage, the opposing team made a lay-up on a fast break. Jack had been urging us to push the ball up the floor as quickly as possible. As I took the in-bounds pass, I looked up the court to see my teammate streaking down the wing. I wanted to fire him an outlet pass so we could put pressure on the opposing defense before they had a chance to set up. But he didn't even turn his head. On the next offensive possession, I was dribbling with my left hand at the top of the key and looking over the defense. I called for a pick from one of my forwards, planning to use the screen to either pull up for an open jump shot or hit him with a pass as he rolled to the basket, but he didn't move an inch from the block. He just sort of went "Huh?" After Jack's directive, it was impossible to believe that these guys were just playing dumb, knowing that it would jeopardize their own standing.

"How do you feel you played this afternoon?" one of the reporters asked me later that day. I told him I'd played well, but was a little slower at one point than I could have been. The following day the headline read, "Meyers Finds NBA Tougher Than She Thought."

I wouldn't have seen it had the paper not been left open near the bench where our trainer, Davey Craig, taped my ankles every morning.

My interaction with the press in college had always been so positive. *People Magazine, Sports Illustrated, TIME,* whichever outlet it was, whenever I had been asked a question, I answered honestly. Though I wasn't big on reading about myself, the press had always been very kind, glowing even. Now I worried that no matter what I said, it would be misconstrued. If there was anything I was sure of, it was that I had never been better prepared; mentally, emotionally, or physically. I believed I had as good a shot as anyone. It surprised me that many sportswriters had made up their minds before the trials had even begun.

After all, it had only been three years since Billie Jean King beat Bobby Riggs on a national platform, and the press seemed to rally around what was the most widely anticipated tennis match of the year. There were His and Hers camps. Regardless of which side of the court you sat on in that battle of the sexes, there was almost universal support for the concept. Billie Jean became the face of feminist women everywhere. Why were things so different in this situation? Was the skill set really so different when it came to basketball? Sure, men can run faster and jump higher, but there were always exceptions to the rule.

If I found some of the press comments demeaning, the other players likely found them humorous. I was certainly not unaccustomed to feeling like an outsider. In fact, I was used to it. But these circumstances magnified my sense of isolation. Never once did I regret being there, though. It was the opportunity of a lifetime, and I was playing my heart out. While it was difficult having cameras come within inches of me out on the court, I realized they were just doing their jobs.

Late in the afternoon of the second day, someone shouted out a question at me. "Miss Meyers, I wonder, do you ever feel like Jackie Robinson?"

I was humbled by the comparison. He and I had both played several sports and held several records at UCLA, but my name didn't deserve to be used in the same sentence with Jackie Robinson's. He had opened doors for millions who had been shut out for too long. I wish I could say that I had had some greater plan, some burning desire to make inroads on behalf of all woman-kind, but that would be a lie. My only thought was making the team. Still, I appreciated that someone was acknowledging the historic aspect of what I was trying to achieve. I'm proud to be on the Board of Directors of Jackie

Robinson's foundation, which generates millions of dollars worth of scholarships for minorities every year.

Pride and historic attributes aside, my body was aching by the afternoon of the second day, and I iced whatever hurt. Mentally, I stayed focused and willed myself to the next practice. By the afternoon session of the third day, the Hinkle Fieldhouse smelled of war; of the raw combat that had been the domain of men, of battlefields where women existed only as sweet distractions, and it was inconceivable that one might actually consider herself a competent warrior. Yet, there I was. Only I was no Joan of Arc; I simply wanted to play basketball, and I wanted to play with the best. In my mind it was a question of ability, of potential, of seizing the ultimate opportunity. Was I exhausted? Yes. Was I aching? Yes. Did I believe that I'd make the cut? Yes.

During a two-on-two drill, I had the ball when a defender reached in. I ripped the ball through, pivoted away, and blew past him. I got to the hoop, made a reverse lay-up, and scored.

Later in the session, Dudley Bradley stole the ball and exploded down court on a two-on-one fast break. I thought he was going to get all the way to the hoop, but the defender cut him off, and Dudley passed the ball back to me. I pulled up and hit a jumper from the top of the key, just as I had done hundreds of times before.

In the final scrimmage of the day, I pulled down a rebound and drove the ball quickly up the court. I faked a pass to the corner and then stepped into a three pointer, knowing it'd be difficult to get a shot off amongst the big trees inside. It looked good when it left my hand, but it went in and out.

When the session ended, Slick Leonard called me over. I followed him into one of the Butler University classrooms adjoining the gym. He pulled up a chair and sat with his back to the door so that the photographers, who were on the other side vying for a space in the small window of the door, couldn't see his face.

I sat on the desk across from him and watched the press jockey for position. *Location, location, location,* I thought. It seemed whether you were an investor, a photographer, or a basketball player trying to get a shot off, it always came down to real estate. At least that's what I kept telling myself. I was trying to think of anything to stay cool. I realized it could go either way.

2
Chasing What I loved

"When one door of happiness closes, another opens; but often we look so long at the closed door that we do not see the one which has been opened for us."
~ *Helen Keller*

"Annie you did a great job."

Badabing, Badabing, Badabing. The way my heart raced I was afraid it might explode right out of my chest. Adrenaline. Great if you had something to do with it, lousy if you were just sitting there, waiting for test results. I exhaled slowly. *Was this really happening? Was I really about to become the first woman to make it into the NBA?*

Then I heard Slick mumbled something about wishing those guys had my heart.

I was so naïve. I still thought I'd made it. I didn't realize that some people like to prop you up before they lower the boom.

"I wish you had their height," he said next.

Everything after that was just a jumble of sounds, the wonky-talk of Charlie Brown's teacher. He never said the words *you're cut*. But that was all I heard from that point on. I put my head down, and stared at the floor. I didn't ask why they weren't afraid to draft Charlie Criss at 5'8". Why bother? We both knew what Slick was really thinking: *Hey you got your shot, now get lost.* I felt sick, it was hard to breathe. I could feel my throat tightening and the sting of tears forming around the backs of my eyes, tears that would spill over onto my cheeks if I blinked, confirming Slick's bible-like conviction that no woman, anywhere, was tough enough to play in the NBA. I kept looking straight down at that scuffed-up classroom floor, breathing through my mouth, eyes wide-open the whole time. There was no way I'd cry in front of Slick, and I refused to give the press the satisfaction. I waited until I got back to my hotel room to cry, where it was hard to stop.

I believed I had what it took to make it in the NBA, not as a starting player, or even a sixth player, necessarily, but as a team member. I couldn't justify Slick's decision. I knew I'd played hard, run the offense efficiently, and hit plenty of shots during the tryout. Had he not seen them? Sure, he'd have gotten all sorts of flak from the press and probably would have taken some nasty remarks from fans who thought the whole idea of a woman playing in the NBA was preposterous. But we both knew I had the support of the owner. It was doubtful Slick had missed the newspaper quote from assistant coach, Jack McCloskey, saying I was fundamentally better than half the players out there.

I had spent the last three days playing my heart out against the top NBA players in the country, and everything from my sneakers to my forehead showed the wear and tear. Yes, they were bigger and stronger, but I had played smart, the way any good, small player must. I had given it everything I had. I had forfeited my chance to play in the '80 Olympics (none of us knew then there would be no '80 Olympics), and I'd trained like never before. And I had prayed. I had done everything within my power to prove that I could play among the best. But none of it was enough to convince Slick. I felt empty, discarded, spent. I was devastated.

I realize now that it would have taken a Bill Veck, the owner of the Cleveland Indians who hired a midget named Eddie Gaedel to bat, or a Phil Esposito, or a Charley Finley to have made my dream happen. It would have taken someone who was willing to try something unusual and say "to hell with the flak" — a Barnum and Bailey kind of guy who realized that sometimes you have to shake things up to get people in the stands. And at that time, the Pacers were having trouble filling up the seats. Sam Nassi was exactly that guy. He believed in me. He knew I could get the job done. It was unfortunate his coach couldn't get beyond my size and plumbing. Of course, back then it didn't feel *unfortunate*, it felt like I'd taken a wrecking ball straight to the gut. I sank into my hotel bed that night and eventually drifted off to the sounds of metal springs and sobbing, and descended into a world where basketballs, coaches, and the Hinkle Fieldhouse didn't exist.

The next morning, I took a cold rag to eyes mercifully too young to fully reveal the previous night's anguish, then slipped into a beautiful crimson dress. Gazing at my reflection, I knew I looked pretty, which was a personal sticking point with me for this day. I broadened my shoulders, lifted my chin and forced the corners of my mouth to turn up. "Let's do this thing."

The Pacers were hosting a luncheon for the sponsors, and I was expected to speak. Crestfallen as I was, I'd never let it show. And in this dress, anyone who suspected otherwise would have their proof that beneath the basketball jersey, I was 100% female.

When I walked into the room, heads turned, and I'll admit I was glad. *Let them see that I'm not some freak. Let them understand that I'm a basketball player who just happens to be a woman.*

Bob Lamey, the play-by-play radio announcer for the Pacers games, was the first to congratulate me on my brief talk at the Pacers luncheon. "Nice speech, Ann."

Giving a speech was okay, but what was next for me? Since I'd signed a three-year contract with the Pacers, it took several weeks for the organization to decide what they were going to do with me. Eventually, they decided I'd make appearances across the country and capitalize on the publicity. I signed with the William Morris Agency and did a Seven-Up commercial with Magic Johnson (who, along with Larry Bird, comprised that year's most eagerly anticipated college draft picks). In between appearances and commercials, I sat in the booth with Bob Lamey as the Pacer's color analyst, a position my brother, Mark, had negotiated into the personal service agreement should I not make the cut. Seems I was still carving new territory, since no woman had ever broadcast an NBA game before.

"So you're my new sidekick, huh?" Bob said the next time I saw him. He'd never worked with a color analyst before, not during his announcing the Pacers games, or those of the two Indiana hockey teams. Now he would have to share the microphone, and with a woman no less. It was clear from the start that Bob liked sitting next to some dame delivering her bent on the finesse of the game about as much as Slick had liked the idea of my playing with the Pacers. They'd both have preferred to see a proctologist.

It didn't take long for the letters to flow: *"What's a woman doing broadcasting a man's game?"* I had taken a broadcasting course at UCLA with Professor Art Friedman and had broadcast two UCLA Men's Basketball games, but I still had plenty to learn.

"Did you see that?" I'd yell into the radio microphone and Bob would turn to me with this distressed look, mouthing *"Huh?"*

And the letters kept coming. *"You don't know what you're talking about, lady."*

The Midwestern mores that had bred men like Slick and Bob, and which permeated the region, weren't much different from the values my siblings and I were raised with, except with one big exception: Men and women were equal. We grew up with gender-blind parents, who believed their six daughters could do anything that their five sons could do. In return, we didn't balk when the full force of an older brother's tackle was felt. There was no complaining, no "fairer-sex" allowances. We learned to hold our own. Now I hoped to hold my own with Bob Lamey in the broadcasting booth, but it wouldn't be easy. Bob didn't like it, and neither did the fans. *"Whose lame idea was this?"* one of the letters asked. It could have been worse. It could have been a radio call-in show. The talk around the water cooler wasn't much better.

Sandy Knapp, the head of public relations for the Pacers and the first woman in the NBA on the corporate side, put it succinctly. "I'm going to be straight with you, I didn't like the idea of you going out for the Pacers any more than anyone else." The tone of her voice set my hair on end. Sandy had been the one assigned to fly back and forth with me to do the New York City morning shows when the news of the bid first surfaced; and at 6'1", everybody thought *she* was the basketball player.

"What if you get hurt out there?" she asked during one of our flights.

"Well, I don't expect to get hurt. I've learned not to think that way."

"What about all this publicity? Is that why you're doing it?"

"Gosh no! I wish I didn't have to fly to N.Y. for these interviews because it's taking away from my workout time." I didn't know what she expected me to say.

Once Sandy realized I wasn't hunting for the limelight, and that I had no intention of capitalizing on the publicity or trying to turn it into some sort of money-machine, she warmed up, and we became close friends.

I think the fact that I was doing the color commentary kind of tickled her and her husband, who both decided to let me live with them while I looked for an apartment in Indiana. Broadcasting the NBA games may have invited the same kind of backlash that the tryouts had, but at least this time it wasn't from the press, and now I had Sandy in my corner.

The Knapps were very kind about helping ease the transition to living out-of-state and away from my family. Best of all, they insulated me from the fanged barbs of those few in the Pacers organization who were still vexed at the thought of having me around for the next three years.

In late September, with the Pacers' blessing, I accepted a three–day invitation to compete in ABC's *Superstars* competition, a televised decathlon-type event held in the Bahamas in December. I'd seen the show before. There were the men's *Superstars* and the women's *Superstars*. Both popular shows created all-around sports competitions and showcased elite athletes like Mark Spitz, Joe Frazier, O.J. Simpson, and Mark Gastineau in the men's competitions; and the likes of Mary Jo Peppler, Anne Henning, and Linda Fernandez for the women's competitions. It looked like something I'd be good at. The broadcasting booth wasn't getting any cozier with Bob, and my body and soul were aching for athletic competition. It had been my lifeblood for as far back as I could remember. Without it, I was still me, but an anemic version.

The weeks passed as I waited for December and the *Superstars*. But by November, I couldn't stand it anymore. I was itchy to play basketball, and the only way that was going to happen was if I played with the WBL, which meant breaking my NBA contract. I asked my agent at William Morris to quietly contact the WBL to discuss the possibility of reconsidering their offer. That's when we learned that the New Jersey Gems had gained me in a swap with the Houston Angels.

My agent asked me if I'd like to play for the Gems. It was a tough decision. On one hand, I sorely missed playing basketball. On the other, I had entered into an agreement with the Pacers, and I considered myself a woman of my word. I wouldn't break the contract lightly. Besides, the WBL had attacked me in the press after I'd declined to join their league, and now I was finding out that, for whatever reason, I'd been traded. I suppose in their eyes, I'd rebuffed the WBL only to turn around and go out for the NBA, and that was a slap in the face.

Would I like to play for them? Enough to break my contract with the Pacers?

I wanted to play basketball, that much I knew; but at what cost? The WBL commissioner, Bill Byrne, had publicly skewered me after I'd spurned his league to try out for the Pacers. One paper quoted him as saying, "There are ten people better than she is. Her time has come and gone."

At twenty-four? I was at the top of my game, and I knew I had another ten years, easy, before I'd peak. He also said that I was embarrassing myself in the bid to play with the big boys. Little did I realize this was his way of using the press to get exposure for the upstart WBL.

I, however, took it very personally. My whole life, I'd been raised never to speak ill of anyone, even in response to something nasty they'd said about me. It was difficult to think this man, whom I'd never met would lie about me. To my way of thinking, Sam Nassi had given me a once-in-a-lifetime opportunity to pursue my dream, and it was fundamentally, almost morally, wrong to pass that up.

Commissioner Byrne and I both knew there was no WBL player alive who, given the same opportunity, wouldn't leap out of her league to get a stab at the NBA if she really thought she was good enough. Furthermore, she'd do it so fast, she'd leave a whirlwind in her wake.

Now, after all the things Byrne had said about me in the past, suddenly, he was saying, "Annie, we're so glad you're going to come on board."

Well, I wasn't buying it. It was the WBL who was doing an about face. They still wanted me in their league, even though there was lingering resentment about my bid for the Pacers rather than signing with the Houston Angels. The praise continued. Lynette Sjoquist was the PR director for the Philadelphia Fillies after being waived as player during the '78-'79 season, told the press, "We were anxious for a player of Meyers's caliber to join the WBL."

It was odd how quickly things could change. She responded to a press clip that stated the WBL might actually have a bona-fide star now that I was considering joining by saying, "That's what the league certainly needed, was talent—all the talent we could find for us to cultivate a following." Only months earlier, her boss had publically said that I'd given up my integrity for $50,000 (the press wasn't aware that my brother had negotiated a three year contract for $150,000) by insinuating, as much of the media had, that my NBA bid was an attempt to remain in the limelight after what was considered a spectacular college career. It was hard to keep up.

In all honesty, had I been truly seeking the limelight, I definitely would have capitalized on the publicity after the trials. It wasn't like there was a booming job market for a Sociology major that would pay $50,000 a year. I knew that if any woman could play in the NBA, I could.

So while I wasn't playing in the NBA, I was broadcasting for them, and getting more comfortable doing the Pacers' games. But I was still only twenty-four years old, and I realized there would be plenty of time to further my broadcasting aspirations. Instead, I was eager to make a living playing basketball, and the WBL was the only game in town. Yes, the WBL commissioner and some of the franchise owners had badmouthed me, and the Angels had traded my rights, but I decided to play for the Gems anyway. Bottom line: I had to play while I still could, or I'd go crazy.

I got out of my contract with the Pacers and in doing so, forfeited the greater amount of the $150,000. They only paid me for the time I was there, and that amounted to about $8,300. In fact their association with me was a net gain for them because each time I made an appearance, I was paid a gratuity. However, that money would end up going back to the Pacers, since I was being hired out as "an employee." The lesson: Read the fine print.

In the end, none of it mattered. I wasn't in it for the money. I just wanted to do what I loved. I just wanted to play basketball.

3

The Man Who Was Not Intimidated

*"Some of these guys wear beards to make them look intimidating,
but they don't look so tough when they have to deliver the ball.
Their abilities and their attitudes don't back up their beards."*
~ Don Drysdale

In mid-November, the WBL scheduled a press conference to announce my joining, but didn't think to clear the date with me or my agent at William Morris, who had previously scheduled me to appear in Seattle with the Pacers a couple of days before the press conference. Since my brother, David, and the Bucks were playing in Portland and were about to play in Seattle at that same time, I thought I'd stay an extra day so I could see my brother before flying from Seattle to New Jersey.

On the day I was supposed to fly back for the press conference, the Seattle airport was fogged in, so nothing was flying in or out. In fact, Dave and his team had to take a five-hour bus ride from Portland to Seattle after having played the night before. I was able to stay to watch Dave's game, but I knew the WBL Commissioner and the Gems would be angry. Things were getting off to a bad start before I'd even hit the hard court.

When I finally got to New Jersey, the first order of business was to get my uniform. I was polite when requesting my jersey number. "But 15 was my number at UCLA. I'd really like 15."

They told me they didn't have it. I was dumbfounded. *Can't you make it?* My dad had been #15 when he played at Marquette, which is why I had chosen it.

"Okay, then I'll take number 6," I said, which was my Olympic number. It was also the same number of my idol growing up, Bill Russell, and my friend, Julius Erving.

"Somebody else has it," was the reply.

Now I was beginning to get frustrated. *I'm supposed to be your star player, and you treat me like this?* The owner of the Gems, Robert Milo, had boasted to the press only days before that I was the superstar the league needed to fill seats and bring excitement. *But he wasn't willing to make #15, or ask for #6?* The whole thing was starting to feel bizarre, like maybe there was more unfinished business than I realized. I ended up with number #14 and consoled myself with the knowledge that Oscar Robertson and Gil Hodges wore it as well.

Players may tell you that numbers don't matter, but it did to me. David wore different numbers and said it didn't matter. As a rookie, he gave up #21 and ended up wearing #8 because another kid came into the league who really wanted it. Then his second year, another kid from college came in and wanted to wear #8, so David gave it up. That's how we were raised, to think about the team above ourselves. But I never got comfortable with #14, just like I never got comfortable with the Gems, or New Jersey.

I didn't like the East Coast, which was so far away from home and filled with people who often seemed to be in a bad mood for no particular reason. Worst of all, unlike UCLA or Indiana, there was no one to take me in. I could talk to Mom or Sandy by phone, but it wasn't the same thing as being there with them. I was lonely, and it didn't help that I got the feeling the other players thought I'd big-timed them by not showing up for the press conference—like I thought I was too good for them.

Those first few nights, I lay in bed and looked around my small room at the Howard Johnsons near the Newark Airport, my home for the season. In the morning, I'd awaken and notice the wallpaper had inched itself free of the upper most corner of one of the walls. Each morning a little more would pull away, like a prisoner hoping to chisel his way out of prison, bit by bit, during the dark of night. It was understandable. The place was dreary, and it was nice that the autumn rain was just hard enough to obscure the sound of the noisy ice-machine outside my door. But it could have been the Taj Mahal, and I still would have felt lonely and frustrated without friends and family. Only the thought of playing again cheered me.

My first game was on November 24th, and I was pleased with my performance. Rather than smooth things over though, there still seemed to be a disconnect between the other Gems players, management, and me. And it only got worse when they found out about my prior commitment to appear on *Superstars* with ABC. Soon I was leaving the team I'd just joined and heading for the Bahamas for the *Superstars* competition. I knew there'd be bristled sensibilities, along with a hefty price to pay when I returned. By now, I didn't care. I was just glad to get away for awhile.

On the plane ride out, I was surprised by how many people recognized me. I'd been David Meyers's little sister back in California, now, I was the girl who went out for the Pacers. Of course, back then, ESPN was in its very first year. Had it happened in 1999 instead of 1979, the image of my face would have been broken down into a thousand pixels, broadcast through the airwaves, and then reconfigured through a million tubes onto a million TV screens. Had it happened today, I'd be a household name. Yet, that was the furthest thing from my mind. The attention embarrassed me. Sure, I wanted to be praised for my accomplishments like anyone else, but it also made me uncomfortable.

I hadn't seen my mom in months, and I missed her, so I asked her to join me in the Bahamas for some R&R. She was always a wonderful traveling companion, and I knew the weather would be beautiful in December. A bigger plus was that my brother, Mark, and his wife, Frannie, were traveling in Florida, so they joined us and made it all the more fun.

Mom and I arrived a day before the event, but my luggage hadn't, so we were sent upstairs to the wardrobe room where I was offered some clothes to tide me over.

That's where I met Donnie.

It turned out the Dodgers baseball pitcher-turned-broadcaster was there for ABC covering the event along with Bob Uecker, who was well known as the Milwaukee Brewers announcer. They were both so friendly, especially to Mom, who was much closer in age to them than I was. Since Mom and Bob were both from Milwaukee, they had lots to talk about, and the three of them hit it off instantly.

When Don introduced himself to me, I couldn't think of much to say other than, "Hi, I'm Annie."

"Yes, I know," he said, with a small grin.

He took me aback. *How could he know? Oh, right, everybody knows.*

I had heard that a broadcaster named Don would be there with ABC, but I had assumed it would be Don Meredith. That was the only broadcaster I knew of named Don. This Don was very tall and I noticed that when he smiled, his blue eyes lit up his bright smile, just like the entire Meyers family.

I returned his smile and resumed looking through the clothing rack for something to see me through the series of competitions in case my luggage never turned up. It felt good to be welcomed after my experiences with the Gems.

After picking out some things, I considered my next priority: rest. I knew I had to take time to relax before the series of events the next day. I was there to compete. Nothing and no one was on my mind outside of that. "Come on, Mom," I said. "We better go."

The next morning, I was fully rested and raring to go. The only problem was that I hadn't researched how the competition worked, and didn't consider there was a definite strategy to which events you chose and in which order you competed. The ten events that year were basketball shooting, rowing, an 80-yard chip over water onto a green, the bike ride, the quarter mile run, the 60-yard dash, the obstacle course, tennis, swimming, and bowling. I chose the last seven, even though I'd never bowled before. I hadn't really golfed either, but I figured between the two, bowling would be easier.

The island sun was beating down hard on us, and I could feel drops of sweat make their way from my hairline clear down to my neck and chest, which soaked the top I'd borrowed from wardrobe. My events that required the most exertion took place back-to-back during the height of the day's heat, so by the time I got inside the bowling alley, it didn't matter that I'd never thrown a bowling ball before—I was exhausted. My total bowling score barely broke 100. When the results came in on the final day, I placed fourth. I was furious...at myself. I wasn't used to coming fourth, and I made sure it would never happen again. By the following year, I'd developed the proper strategy and ended up winning not just that year's *Superstars*, but three consecutive years' in women *Superstars* events, and ultimately becoming the only woman ever invited to compete in the men's *Superstars*. Placing fourth taught me a lot about how to play the game. I also learned a lot about the man I would marry, though that was the furthest thing from my mind at the time.

The last night of the competition, ABC took their staff out, and Mom and I were invited to attend. I looked around and wondered why none of the other contestants were joining us. I later found out that Don had specifically asked that we be invited. Mom, Bob Uecker, and Don had a blast, while I did a slow burn over my performance.

The next day, everyone left the Bahamas, including Mom, Mark, and Frannie. My flight wasn't until the following day, so Don invited me out to dinner. Alone.

"What would you say if I asked you to marry me?" he said casually at the end of dinner.

Naturally, I was stunned. We'd only met a few days earlier, he was nearly twenty years my senior, and on top of that, he was already married. He had three strikes against him before he'd even gotten up to bat. I had no idea how to respond. I'd barely said two words to the guy during the entire event. While it had been fun watching him, Mom, and "Ueckie" during the previous night's dinner, laughing over their Milwaukee stories, listening to them harmonizing around the piano-bar while they tossed back scotch and sodas like it was apple juice, I had no intention of becoming anything but friends with a married man.

"Well, I would be flattered...but," I stammered, then stopped. *That's odd. Here I am ready to be very definite and...what?* Looking at him, there was no denying that I felt something. Was it his looks? No doubt he was attractive, but there was also an easiness about him. He was the first man who didn't appear intimidated by me in any way. Up to this point, guys had always acted like they needed to prove themselves around me, as if they felt they needed to be as strong or athletic as I was. But not Don. This man acted like he'd never felt the need to prove a thing in his entire life. I looked around the restaurant before settling my eyes back on Don, and searched for something to say. He was so casual with his arm stretched over the side chair, while I sat with both palms clasped together in my lap.

The waiter came by and asked Don, with no small amount of awe in his voice, if we needed anything else. I'd seen that same kind of deference from everyone who came into contact with him. Don looked up at him with an easy smile. "Just the bill, when you get a chance."

I wondered how it was possible for a person to feel so at ease in any situation. I knew that feeling comfortable around others required being comfortable with yourself, with every part of yourself. But it was different with me. I was good at sports, I wasn't bad at school, and I had friends. Even though my friends had told me I was cute, I always figured any boy who liked me only felt that way because I was good at sports. It sure wasn't because of my natural grace.

My senior year in high school, I'd gone on a date with a good looking football player, who had dark hair and biceps the size of grapefruits. We saw *The Last Detail* with Jack Nicholson. Afterward we parked high above the city lights, where everyone went to make out. The stifling haze of cigarette smoke and cheap cologne enveloped the area like a toxic cloud, but we thought we were so cool (though I would never so much as try a cigarette). As my date proceeded to put his arm around me, I did likewise and accidentally knocked him in the head with my elbow.

He sat up and rubbed his head. "Everybody said you'd hit me, if I tried to kiss you."

I could feel the blood drain from my face. *What else are they saying behind my back?* Torrents of pubescent self-doubt flooded my hormone-addled mind. *Had he asked me out on a dare?*

There were a few other dates; a lifeguard I watched compete in the Life Guard Competition and a couple of guys in college. But nothing ever came of it. I suffered the same problem of many young women—the boys I had crushes on never asked me out.

Here, now, Don was sitting at this table with me, someone who apparently found me attractive and whom I found myself becoming attracted to in return. *Was it possible?* But the roadblocks came back into razor-sharp focus; the obstacles of age, and that other thing, oh yeah…marital status. I realized we'd make an odd pair with my wholesome, shy, glass-of-milk persona and Don, with enough charisma to fill an entire stadium. I felt both comfortable and uncomfortable; both a part of a very special circle and an awkward outsider all at the same time.

Men had never been my area of expertise, but it was clear this was a man unlike any other. His proposal that night was the first of many to come, causing me to stay on my toes in a way that had nothing to do with jump shots. But then, I would have to stay on my toes on all kinds of fronts, namely the WBL and its ability to compensate me. Looking out for myself while chasing what I wanted was nothing new. It seemed as far back as I could remember, life had been a challenge. Nothing had ever come my way without a whole lot of work and an equal amount of resistance.

4

Let the Race Begin

"You're braver than you believe, stronger than you seem,
and smarter than you think."
~ *Christopher Robins to Pooh*

I was born in San Diego in 1955 with two X chromosomes. Things might have been a lot easier had that not been the case. Then again, if I'd been born a boy, I suppose someone else would have become the first woman to do a lot of things. So, as with everything in my life, I thank God for all of it—exactly as it was.

I may have been born in San Diego, but the hospital room was where my tour of the seaside city began and ended. Other than a short stint in Philadelphia, I grew up in the Catholic school system outside of Chicago in Wheaton, Illinois before moving to Orange County, California, where I attended public school at Arbolita Elementary because all the Catholic Schools were full.

Gone was the camouflage of the Catholic school uniform. Suddenly, individuality was inescapable—not so great for girls like me who had little taste or interest in fashion. Skirts and dresses were still required for girls back then, but I made sure I wore shorts underneath so I could play the kind of basketball and football with the boys that I was used to playing with my brothers and their friends. I wanted all my bases—and everything else—covered, since I was always the new kid.

I hated change as a kid, and each time I started a new school it began with my being pried from my mother's leg like a vine from a tree. It was a natural course of events, since my dad worked as District Manager for Sears. We'd moved so much, that by the fourth grade I'd grown accustomed to the stares of my classmates. I'd played the fish-out-of-water character so many times at so many schools that it finally stopped hurting. It was like aversion therapy for the meek and shy.

Now if I wanted to play basketball, I didn't wait for someone's invitation. Instead, when the recess bell rang, I concentrated on being first to the ball bin where the basketballs were kept, which meant the boys *had* to share the courts with me. One recess, Jim, the class jock, came up and challenged me to a 100-yard race to the fence at the other end of the field.

"You think you can beat me?"

Yeah. Probably. Students nearby gathered around as Jim and I lined up on the edge of the grass. Someone yelled, "Ready, set, go!" and we took off for the fence with a dozen or so kids cheering. *This will make them like me* was my boneheaded, ten-year-old, thinking as I reached the chain-linked fence ahead of him and waited for him to catch up. But when Jim got to the fence, he turned around and started back, yelling, "We're going the other way, too!"

The little sneak had a jump on me, so I tore out, caught up, then passed him to reach our starting point with everyone screaming and cheering, while Jim pulled up behind me.

"We tied! Didn't we, Annie? It was a tie." He stood there panting, looking me square in the eyes, daring me to say otherwise.

We both knew I'd beat him, so why should I pretend I hadn't? I didn't lose to my brothers unless they beat me fair and square, and even then, I hated it. But here, I was the new kid and more than anything, I just wanted to be accepted. I looked at Jim, who was still huffing and puffing like he'd just finished a marathon instead of a 100-yard dash, and then looked down at the ground, weighing my options. I finally kicked the dirt and just walked away.

In that moment, I'd broken some unspoken Meyers code of ethics that said you *never* gave less than your all. You *never* gave up, and you *never* spoke anything but the truth. It felt rotten, like I was the one who'd cheated. But it was either that or break a much greater, universal rule—the cardinal rule of school playgrounds everywhere—the one that said girls don't beat boys.

It was a rule among my teachers, too. It wasn't uncommon to hear, "Annie, you know you're not supposed to be playing with the boys," whenever one caught me on the field during lunch with a football safely tucked between my left ribcage and arm, going in for a touchdown like my life depended on it. And then, in a pained way, as if I'd committed some unspeakable profanity, she'd add, "It's not ladylike."

I wanted to scream. *Who am I hurting? What's the point of being ladylike on a playground?* Having been raised to be respectful, I said nothing. But her rebuke elicited a powerful sensation of shame. *"Not ladylike" means she's thinks I'm acting like a boy. But why are jumping, running, competing, winning, and all of those fun things, strictly allowed for boys?* I wouldn't dare ask. Instead, I lowered the ball, along with my head, and simply walked away. It had become my custom.

That same year, I learned that not all teachers were alike and that maybe I wasn't so unusual after all, when one of them suggested I do my fourth grade book report on Babe Didrikson Zaharias. At last, here was a girl who could beat the boys just like I could and she didn't care whether it was lady-like or not. That pb&j- stained paper-back became as much a staple in my hands at night as a basketball was during the day, further solidifying my dreams. If she could become an Olympic athlete, so could I. I also learned from Babe's brashness. *Who cared if not everyone at school understood my love of sports? Everyone at home sure did.*

Athletic competition was a staple in our family, like one of the four food groups, or the 11th commandment: Thou Shalt Honor Thy Desire to Compete. My father had played basketball for Marquette, and my mother wasn't only athletic, but she was quite possibly the original soccer mom. "Hurry up, we're gonna be late," was her battle cry on the way to a game, which was no small feat with eleven children, all involved in sports. My guess is she put 100,000 miles on that brown-paneled station wagon every two or three years. It was simply the way our family worked.

Patricia Burke Meyers was patient to the point of saintliness, but make a bad call during a game, or block one of her kids' shots, and she'd scream loud and long enough to rattle the bleachers and frighten every bird out of every tree within a half-mile radius. And if you think the birds were freaked out, you should have seen the faces on those refs and other parents.

Mom was our greatest fan. Somehow she managed to be at Patty's softball games, Mark and Tom's football games, Cathy's swim meets, David's basketball games, Jeff's Little League games, Susie's singing recitals, Kelly's basketball games, Coleen's soccer games, Bobby's tennis matches, and my track-meets — all in the same week, and sometimes several in one day.

And at each event, every official knew who Mrs. Meyers was. "Mrs. Meyers, are we going to have a good game today?" the refs would ask gingerly.

"I don't know," she'd respond, arching one eyebrow. Then she'd look them straight in the face with her Irish-Catholic laser-beam focus that could pierce steel and say, "You tell *me*."

She never complained about having to drive a half-hour each way to get me to my West Covina AAU track team, where I was setting Southern California high jumping records. The team would enter me into every possible event just to rack up as many points as possible. I'd compete against girls three, four, even five years older, but I loved it. My parents knew I'd dreamed of competing in the Olympics as a track athlete, just like Babe. They allowed David and me to teach ourselves to high jump in the entry way and living room by pulling down pillows and mattresses, where we would jump over strategically placed chairs onto the stuffing below. Then I would run the stairs and jump rope with ankle weights, and do slides for lateral quickness — anything to make my legs stronger.

My parents were aware that I hoped to compete in other sports on other teams, but the problem was there were no organized after school sports programs for kids in the 60s and 70s. When one was finally developed for boys, my parents went through some elaborate measures to clear my playing with the school district. Coaxing, threatening, pleading, signing endless releases of liability, filling out endless reams of paperwork, whatever it took, Pat and Bob Meyers weren't above it. Yet as busy as they were, not only did they never complain, but they never even let me know that it took any bureaucratic arm-wrestling. In fifth and sixth grade I became the first girl to play on the all-boys after school sports team. And if anyone had a problem with a girl playing on a boys' team, well they knew better than to let any of the Meyers get wind of it.

Around this same time, it became clear that we were actually, finally, staying put, which allowed for some routine to seep its way into our lives. Every Sunday it was the same routine; first we'd attend Mass, then my mother would make a huge brunch of pancakes, eggs, bacon, sausage, muffins, the works—all of it, tirelessly homespun from scratch. Like so many other Sundays, I changed out of my dress and patent leathers into David's hand-me-down jeans so I could tag along with him and his friends, who were riding their bikes to the park to play basketball.

But this time, David said something I'd never forget. "Why do you always have to follow me?"

David realized how much I idolized him, even when he was making fun of me for shooting hoops with two hands. I knew he didn't mean anything by it. I wore my blond hair short because it made it easier to play sports, but it also sort of made me look like him, and he seemed to think that was cute. He never minded me tagging along before.

"You're a girl, Annie! Act like one!" He hopped back on his bike and raced to catch up to his friends. I watched and waited for him to turn around, but he never did. The dust stung my eyes as he tore off. At least that's what I told my mom when she asked if I'd been crying. With so many children and a husband who was often on the road, she didn't need anything extra to worry about. She didn't need to know that those seven words coming from David hit the bull's-eye, where thousands of similar words from others had only skirted along the target's border. I didn't want her fretting about my feelings, and maybe I was also a little embarrassed by what David had said. But I shouldn't have been. Not in front of my own mother. When it came to the larger issue of how a daughter should behave, it took more than a wardrobe choice to concern Pat Meyers.

A girl in jeans with short hair who preferred playing basketball with the boys may have worried other moms, but not mine. There was never any assumption in our family that a girl who wanted to play sports was anything other than athletic.

While some folks in our neighborhood may have thought my clothes and behavior odd, conversation in our family never stooped to speculation about what others thought. How could it when we were so busy talking about things that really mattered: sports, politics, or being busy doing homework and chores? While everyone knew how girls were *supposed* to behave, I knew that I wasn't the same as most girls. I was a tomboy, and that was just fine with me. What I couldn't stand was that all of the sudden it might *not* be okay with David.

But if I wasn't playing basketball with my older brother and his friends as much, I was playing even more of it with the sixth grade boys' team at school.

"Ann Meyers emerges the unlikely leader to bring home the championship in the La Habra City School District basketball tournament," read the headline in one of the local papers above a photo of me holding a trophy surrounded by my all-male teammates.

Less than three months later, national headlines would bring the country to its knees.

It was June of 1968, and Bobby Kennedy was at the Ambassador Hotel where he'd opened his speech by congratulating his friend, Don Drysdale, whose shut-out streak was capturing the attention of Angelinos everywhere. "I hope to have the same success with my campaign here in California." Hours later, he was dead.

Meanwhile, on the other side of town, earlier that same day, the 6'6", thirty-one-year-old, Don Drysdale was pitching his sixth straight shut-out game for the Los Angeles Dodgers, ultimately beating the Pirates 5-0. Radios across the southland were tuned in to the game.

No pitcher had ever gone fifty-eight innings without giving up a run. The closest anyone had come was Walter Johnson, who pitched fifty-five shutout innings back in 1913. Certainly, I had an idea who Drysdale and Koufax were, since we'd been living in Southern California for a few years now and the Brooklyn Dodgers had become the Los Angeles Dodgers nearly a decade earlier. But I was more of a Giants fan because that's who my brothers followed. I especially liked Willie Mays and Willie McCovey. We collected baseball cards for the bubble gum. But even with that, the players' stats were a lot less exciting to us than the sound the cards made against the spokes on our bikes. Baseball just wasn't as important to me as some of the other sports I played.

Now the game was over and it was another Dodger triumph. Southern Californians celebrated with no inkling of the tragedy that would take place later that evening, just as at 13, I couldn't know that I would grow up to marry Donnie, or that he would carry around in his back pocket a tape recording of Robert Kennedy's address that evening for several years to come.

While I grasped the importance of a no-hitter on the one hand, and was saddened by the assassination of someone who appeared to be a great man on the other, I really couldn't think much beyond my own dreams of making the Olympics someday. Until then, I would simply continue navigating my way through puberty—tricky for a girl like me who could still beat the boys.

5
You Let Some GIRL Beat You?

*"To be nobody but yourself in a world which is doing its best,
night and day, to make you everybody else means to fight the hardest
battle which any human being can fight; and never stop fighting."*
~ E.E. Cummings

Junior high was when everything started changing. I continued to compete at sports, but now I did it wearing blue eye shadow. I also let my hair grow. I wanted to look pretty like my older sister, Cathy, but it was David's comment that set the transformation in motion. I wanted to be like others girls and have boys start noticing me for more than just the way I hit my jumper, went long for a pass, or because I had set a High Jump record at the Junior Olympics.

While making the Olympics in the High Jump event was still my dream, I liked the idea of playing just one sport as much as Liz Taylor liked the idea of marrying just one man. So once I turned thirteen and became old enough, I joined the same AAU Basketball team that my oldest sister, Patty, was on. By my freshman year in high school I was also playing volleyball, softball, field hockey, tennis, and badminton.

Whenever I couldn't find anyone to practice with, I practiced alone. Because I was so shy growing up, my imagination helped me a lot. When I was by myself shooting hoops, in my head I was always taking the last shot with the clock winding down. I was playing against the NBA greats of the day, and swish! *Meyers makes the winning shot.* Or I would step up to the free-throw line, down one, and I had to make two free-throws to win the game.

When I ran around a track, I pretended to be racing against someone like Wilma Rudolph. If I was hitting the tennis ball against the garage door, my imagination had me volleying against Billie Jean

King before a crowd of thousands.

There simply weren't enough hours in the day to compete at all the sports I loved, and there was no way to devote the necessary time to tennis when the demands from the various teams I belonged to were becoming even more intense. My coaches allowed me to miss practice in one sport, knowing I had a match in another, but missing practices in tennis will only take you so far. I never got better than becoming the #2 player, and by now I was used to being #1. It was a painful lesson in focus and the necessary reduction that comes at a certain point in almost every athlete's life. I loved tennis, but not enough to give up the other sports I loved, especially since my high school was known for its basketball program.

While I was freshman at Sonora High, David was a senior—but not just any senior. He was the star 6'6" starting forward. Since I played just about every sport the school offered, I was in the paper a lot. But each article about me would start, "Ann Meyers, sister of David Meyers..."It was great that my oldest sister, Patty, had been a star basketball player and championship winner at Cal State Fullerton, and my older brother, Mark, had been a star football player at UC Berkeley, but David was there at Sonora *with me*, so there was no degree of separation. The idea of being in high school with the brother I still idolized had sounded great, but the reality was something different.

The high school star, the MVP, the team captain, the CIF Champion was my brother. It was like having to stand next to a giant, and I felt small and inconsequential, certain that the only reason anyone bothered to speak to me at Sonora was because I was David Meyers's little sister. So when Darlene May, the PE coach at Cornelia Connelly, an all-girl Catholic High School in Anaheim, asked me to transfer my sophomore year, I gave it some serious thought.

Darlene had played sports with my sister, Patty, and was the first woman to officiate a men's international game. She didn't stop there; she also became the first female to officiate an Olympic women's basketball game when she refereed at the '84 Olympics in

Los Angeles. Dar not only extended the invitation to me, but convinced another girl, Nancy Dunkle, to transfer along with me. Nancy and I had known each other from junior high where we'd both played on the same sports teams. She had the prettiest skyhook you've ever seen, very akin to Kareem Abdul-Jabbar's hook shot, and eventually made a name for herself in the world of women's basketball. Nancy and I were like two peas in a pod in that we both played every sport available, though Nancy towered over me at about 6'1".

"Now we've got the makings for a basketball dynasty," Dar said once we both transferred. Sure enough, the Connelly Cadettes quickly dominated the high school girls' basketball landscape, raking up the honors. Suddenly female cagers weren't unusual at all.

Suddenly we were cool.

"Women's lib being what it is, it should be noted that the most successful high school basketball team in CIF was an all-girl school from Orange County," the *Los Angeles Times* wrote about us in April of '72. Of course, Nancy and I didn't even know what women's lib meant, we were just happy every time our names were mentioned in the newspapers. We were the two star players and thick as thieves — thieves who could steal the ball as well as any guy we knew, and *better* than some.

I should have been over the moon. Yet every day, after carpooling to and from Connelly in my twice handed-down '66 VW Bug that sputtered like a cranky mule, I'd cry once I got home. But it wasn't because of basketball, or Nancy, or my car. I loved that car. It was because I was also on the Volleyball team at Connelly where the coach just happened to be my sister, Patty.

"Don't feel well? Too bad. Sprained ankle? Go tell someone who cares." Patty was like Vince Lombardi; she only knew one way to get things done, and that was to play all-out, or go home. She seemed especially tough where I was concerned, maybe so no one could accuse her of favoritism. I'd end up crying to my mom daily (something I rarely did when my brothers were rough on me), and then she would come down hard on Patty, calling her up on the phone, yelling, "Why are you picking on Annie?"

Eight years older than I, Patty was the firstborn, and she'd always been stubborn and strong as a bull. But that was because she had to be tough. It was women like Patty who laid the groundwork for me and others like me. Patty knew what she wanted and went after it from the get-go, and made things happen through sheer will. If Patty said she was going to play pro softball some day, you knew she'd do it. Patty could do everything.

Later, in college and AAU ball, she'd come home after playing twenty-inning games in shorts, sporting huge raw raspberries on her thighs and calves from sliding into bases. She'd crawl into bed, exhausted. The next morning, the sheets and mattress were covered with blood and puss, but she never complained. She saw how quickly labels were affixed to women who complained: moody, cry-baby, can't handle the heat, just not *cut out* for the task. Not Patty. There were no excuses with her. One time she came home from a game with one of her eyes popped out of its socket and my mom had to pop it back in. All Patty could say was "Hurry up, I gotta go play."

I admired her—how could I not? She was the kind of woman who could change her own tire and believed that other women should be able to do the same in case something happened. In fact, while Patty was coaching volleyball at Connelly, she was also teaching Driver's Ed, so she would have her students go out to the parking lot and change the tires of her car. Darlene, my basketball coach and Patty's good friend, thought it was kind of silly, but Patty wanted them to be self-sufficient.

As luck would have it, some of Patty's students were driving on the freeway and who did they spy on the side of the road with a flat tire? Dar. The girls pulled over. To Patty's credit, there was no gloating, no smug smile, just happy to help.

"See girls," Patty told her Driver's Ed students, "this is exactly the type of situation I'm trying to spare you."

That was in 1972 when the word "feminist" was wielded around by everyone from stars to athletes to show they were current with the changing times. President Nixon had signed the bill enacting

Title IX into law, which gave female students equal public funding. And presto! A full-fledged women's movement was under way. But Patty Meyers couldn't have cared less. She wouldn't have called herself a feminist or a groundbreaker. She wouldn't have called herself anything. She was just who she was; the oldest, toughest, brashest, most passionate, and most athletically talented of all the Meyers.

Unfortunately, Patty had been born too early. Doors that had been closed to her were suddenly opening for me, and I wanted to walk through every one. But to brave any new world, first you have to leave the comfort of the one you've grown accustomed to. I didn't know it then, but that's why Patty was so hard on me. Connelly had been great, but Patty knew it was time for me to spread my wings.

The Connelly Cagers had won twenty-five straight games, many by over forty points, to become the only undefeated team in the Southland, and we'd claimed five titles to become the most successful high school team in CIF. In addition to taking the top honors, Nancy and I were singled out in every bit of news coverage.

"Ann Meyers can handle the ball as well as any boy," Dar told the press. "And she can jump right out of the gym."

Her words were prophetic. I jumped right out of Connelly's gym and straight back into the one at Sonora. Who wanted to make the long trek to high school when Sonora was right around the corner? That was the reason I gave, but David's graduating from Sonora was closer to the truth because I finally felt I could be my own person. And there was something else. I wanted that quality competition that any athlete wants. I wanted to push myself to become better, and for me that meant playing against the guys. It had become the yardstick by which I measured my ability. I still wanted to see if I could beat the boys. Even the ones I thought were cute.

Luckily, my high school education didn't resemble the rotating membership program that had defined my elementary school career (it was more like the revolving door program), but it was still tough on a social scale. I'd been very popular at Connelly, even being named Christmas Sophomore Princess. But I sensed the girls at

Sonora didn't like me because I was liked by the guys. What they didn't realize is the guys liked me solely because I was an athlete. Once I liked a guy back, he got scared. At night, I'd lie in bed and think about how to balance my desire to compete (both for certain boys' attention, and at sports) with my desire to be liked (both by the guys and the girls).

While I competed on a top level against the guys, I'd look in the mirror and like what I saw. My first love was to up the ante where athletic competition was involved, but I still wanted to be attractive, which was no different than any other girl my age when our hormones were ratcheting themselves up and ricocheting around inside us. In that, I stood pretty resolute, even if I wanted the boys' attention in a very different way lately. Just because my heart melted over a guy, it didn't mean I'd give up my sports. Softball, field hockey, badminton, track, volleyball, basketball, and tennis—I played them all.

Ultimately, I would win thirteen MVP awards and lead the girls' basketball team to an 80-5 record. Being on all these teams was like slack-lining before a partially hostile audience. It's great to be liked by your teachers, but everybody wants to be part of the "in" crowd. Looking back, it's still easy to remember how I'd hoped to fit in. That goal became harder to balance when I made up my mind to go out for the Sonora High Boys' Summer League basketball team.

"Coach, I'd like to talk to you."

"Annie, I'm late," Coach Kahn said, stepping up his pace, probably hoping I'd leave him alone.

"I want to try out for the summer team."

"They won't like it."

"But the girls don't play during the summer."

"And that's my fault?"

"No, of course not. It's just that I want to play, and I think I could help the team."

When he heard that he stopped and looked straight at me,

squinting slightly, like he was trying to read me. I waited, watching the wheels turning in his head, no doubt screaming, *Is she nuts?* Or hopefully concluding, *What the heck, she's a great athlete.*

Finally, he broke the silence. "Okay. But only if you cut your hair."

The day of the try-outs, the Sonora High gym was filled with the parents of junior and senior boys hoping to make the team. During the scrimmage, I went for an easy lay-up, then stole the ball in the inbounds and scored again.

One of the moms jumped up and yelled out from the stands, "You gonna just let some *GIRL* do that?"

I brushed it off. I had always played hard. You bet I was intense, and I wasn't going to apologize for that, even if there were people who resented it. But it was hard not to feel like it was me against the world. When you grow up in a big family, it's easy to get lost in the shuffle, especially if you're the middle kid. Sports was the one place where I wouldn't allow myself to be invisible, where I could make myself stand out. I didn't have time to worry about other people for fear of losing my focus. But each time I got aggressive, there was another comment from another parent.

"You're letting some GIRL beat you?"

Their jeers might have inspired me a few years earlier, but not now. I was just as attuned to what others thought and said about me as every other teenager on the planet. There were questions from the parents about where I'd shower, which bathrooms I'd use, where I'd change.

But the questions were smoke screens. I'd use the girls' bathroom and wait until I got home to shower. It didn't take a rocket scientist to figure that out. The truth was that they simply didn't want a girl on the boys' team, and Coach Kahn didn't do much to help. How could he? "It was a new situation for all of us," he'd later admit.

The week of tryouts continued, and so did the sideshow.

"If you get hit in the chest you'll get breast cancer you know." This came from a girl at Sonora.

"I've never heard that." *A bruise, yes. Cancer? I doubt it.*

"Well, you know what they say about you, don't you?"

"No." I was curious. She was like a human switchboard, connecting all lines of gossip from one end of the campus to the other.

"They say if you want to be on the boys' team so bad that you must be gay." She looked at me with a strange smile then walked away.

Gay? The term was never used in our house. I wasn't completely sure of its meaning, but I had an idea. *Why would they say that?* I didn't worry about what my parents would think. They would be fine. They never judged or criticized us for some innocuous infraction that might have reflected poorly on them the way so many other parents did. Those were invariably the parents who saw their children as nothing more than extensions of themselves. As long as we did what we knew was right, worked hard, and did nothing to hurt others, we were just fine in their eyes. But still, I wondered. *Was I gay because I wanted to play competitive basketball with the guys? But how could I be gay when I was attracted to boys?* I didn't know what the right thing to do was anymore. I wasn't trying to prove a point, I just wanted to play the game.

I had always just wanted to play the game.

When the names were announced for the summer team, mine was among them. The other players eventually welcomed me, though not exactly with open arms. The press had no easier time wrapping its pens around stories about a girl besting the boys. "Sonora High Boys Summer League apparently has the best prospect in attractive 5'8" Meyers," the paper wrote.

"She went in during the second quarter and led the fast break, and she is quick, fakes, and has good footwork," a college scout was quoted saying. "She is also cute and has a good figure."

This last part struck me as funny. Male athletes were never described physically in the newspapers unless it had something to do with their ability to play, their height, their weight, etc. While it was flattering to be called attractive, it also felt odd. It was almost as if no matter how well I might have played before this coach, he would never think of me as a real basketball player, but rather as a *cute* basketball player.

When my senior year started there were the inevitable questions about whether or not I would go out for the boys' varsity basketball team. After all that had happened, all of the comments from the parents about letting a girl play on the team, about allowing me to take their son's place, and the idea that my classmates would question my sexuality, I ultimately declined.

It would be the last time I would let anyone's opinion dictate my decisions.

6

Learning to Harness the Fire Within

"Control your passion or it will control you."
~ G.M. Trevelya

Not going out for the boys' varsity team turned out to be a blessing in disguise. Had I joined, I wouldn't have been available weeks later to try out for the Women's U.S. National Team.

It was a three-day invitation-only competition in Albuquerque, New Mexico, where the other contenders were seasoned USA players and three to five years older. I had some stiff competition, and the thin air didn't work to my advantage because it was hard to catch my breath. Still, in 1974, I became the first high school player to make it onto a U.S. Women's National Team.

Our first game was in New York City. I was so excited I could hardly stand it. I'd never flown without my mother and siblings before. Now I was in what felt like the capital of the world and staying at a small hotel across from the famous Waldorf Astoria. And if the hotel lacked the gold leaf trim and satin sheets I'd heard were commonplace at the Waldorf, I didn't care. I still felt like I'd made it to the big time. After all, we were about to play at the Felt Forum in Madison Square Garden! The whole thing seemed surreal. The night before that first game, I had one thought continuously pounding in my brain: *If I'm dreaming, don't anybody pinch me.*

The next morning the alarm went off at 7:30 but it felt more like 4:30 because of the time difference. Standing in front of the mirror, I ran a comb through what was left of my blond locks. *At least I don't have to worry about my hair.* The up side was that, apparently, I no longer looked like David. Now I looked like Doris Day. *Right, Doris Day versus the Soviets.*

Our rivals were the Soviet Union Women's Team, who'd dominated women's basketball for nearly two decades. Some were in their late twenties and thirties, and were mothers. A friend told me he'd heard that communist countries would inject the pregnancy hormone, HCG, into their female athletes because studies had shown that HCG helped the athletes perform better. It was whispered that many of these Soviet basketball players had become mothers for the same reason.

Whether that was true or not, there was no doubt these ladies had something extra. Their front line averaged 6'6", and their Latvian player, Uljana Semjonova, was 7'2". Semjonova's upper thigh was the size of my waist. Our tallest player was 6'3". Even so, I'd never entered any competition expecting to lose, and I wasn't about to. I reminded myself that David was 6'8", and I'd played against him thousands of times. *Semjonova doesn't scare me.*

The game had a good crowd, and it was televised. I received some attention right off the bat because John Wooden's UCLA team had recently won the NCAA tournament, with David helping lead the way. Many speculated he would be a future NBA top pick, so the Meyers name was already out there.

Being the only player still in high school and the youngest on the team, I was a substitute guard and didn't start. But I did play, and well enough to be named Player of the Game. I brought the same energy and passion to the court that David did and played every point like it was our last. As hard as we played, we lost by three points. But in coming so close, we caused the Soviet Union's national pride to suffer a terrible beating. After the game, Brent Musburger interviewed me, and all I remember saying was, "Yep."

All I remember *thinking* was, *The Russians aren't all that great.*

The following games in California, Iowa, and New Mexico would prove otherwise. We were in California, about to play a game at Cal State Fullerton and sharing a pre-game meal with the Soviet Ladies at a small restaurant on campus. I was seated across from the towering Semjonova. To my right was my roommate and team captain, Juliene Brazinski Simpson. Jules was from Jersey and an outgoing point guard in her early twenties, with a big personality who was as quick with a clever reply as she was with a bounce pass. Across from Jules, was Tatyana Ovechkin, the captain of the Russian team (her son, Alexander Ovechkin, is #8 on the NHL's Washington Capitals).

Semjonova was so tall that her knees wouldn't fit under the table, and her hands were so large and her arms so long that I imagined she could easily wrap them around a thick oak. With mitts larger than any man's I'd ever seen, I figured a basketball must have felt to her like a soccer ball felt to me. It was our understanding they spoke no English, so I exposed the palm of my hand and motioned for her to do the same.

"Your hands are very large," I said slowly, to which Semjonova just nodded. I may have been the youngest one there by several years, but I sensed right away that our Russian dinner partners knew more English than they let on.

"You're married?" Jules asked the team captain, pointing to her wedding band. Ovechkin looked at her hand and nodded. Semjonova was also wearing a ring.

"I'm married too." Jules held up her ring finger, then took off her band and motioned for the other two women to do the same so they could compare sizes. Semjonova's ring was large enough to fit a fifty cent piece inside and still have room around the edges.

The captain said something in Russian and both women laughed.

"That's what I'm saying!" Juliene joked loudly. "You've got really huge hands! I'll bet you have big Bozo feet too." Juliene snickered at the thought that she could be so rude and get away with it. I wasn't so sure.

Juliene had played on several USA Teams and was more often than not the captain. At 5'6 she was one of our shorter players, and we called her The Tank for her impenetrable blocking. Her commanding presence and confident strut were partly because she'd grown up in Jersey. She was the perfect counterbalance to my introversion and loved nothing more than letting off a little steam to get us relaxed. So in typical Jules fashion, she continued making outrageous comments, forcing giggles between us two, until it was time to leave.

"Well adios, ladies," Jules finally said in her unmistakable Jersey accent. "See you tomorrow."

"See you tomorrow," Semjonova replied quite clearly.

Juliene's face blanched as she spoke to the interpreter while shuffling out of the restaurant. "I thought they didn't speak any English."

"Not much. But they *understand* everything."

That evening the Soviets defeated us in a crushing 30+ point loss. With such a tight finish in the first game, we'd shamed them. Then Jules and I added fuel to the fire by insulting their team's best players, thus igniting their desire to pulverize us.

For me it was another life lesson, courtesy of basketball. Though we'd nearly tied them in the first game, it was no indication of what might follow. And so it always was: You could win a game, but you still had to start all over with the next one. Every day you had to get up and try your best. When you failed, it didn't kill you. It hurt, and you hated it, but it also drove you to be better next time. That first game had motivated the Soviet players to bury us, and Jules and my behavior during the pre-game meal put the nail in the coffin.

When the games against the Soviets were finished, I returned to high school and continued to play AAU basketball with my sister Patty.

Today when you think of AAU, you think of kids trying to earn college scholarships. Back then it was another outlet for women who played in and out of college to compete long before there was a woman's league. The team was called Anamill after the sponsoring company. We'd travel to Gallup, New Mexico for tournaments, but the team ended up disbanding when the sponsor went belly up. Rather than throw in the towel, Patty found a new sponsor in National General West, who paid for the girls to travel and compete. So I was back to high school and back to playing on the National General West team with the sister I looked up to.

Patty had played as starting center, captain, and leading scorer and rebounder on Billie Moore's 1970 AIAW championship women's basketball team at Cal State Fullerton. Together, they put the Titans on the map before Immaculata and Delta State became known for their women's basketball programs. Wayland Baptist was another college that won a lot of AAU Championships. They had invited me to play for them, but I hadn't given much thought to college yet. Heck, I wasn't even sure I wanted to continue playing basketball in college, since I still dreamed of making the Olympics as a high jumper. I figured when the time came, I'd probably attend the same college Patty had. But fate stepped in when I was offered a full athletic scholarship to play basketball at UCLA.

No woman had ever been offered a full ride to a Division One school before, so this was huge. UCLA was also close to home, which meant I would have David and my sister, Cathy, who'd just graduated from UCLA, in Westwood with me. I would also be in the presence of the greatest mentor that basketball has ever known.

John Wooden had already won nine national titles and been named college basketball's Coach of the Year seven times when I started UCLA. My freshman year, David was a senior, so I arranged to be out of class every day early enough to watch him during his practices with Coach Wooden. I loved sitting in Pauley Pavilion watching David, listening to Coach Wooden, absorbing the smells and sounds of Men's Division I basketball. Coach kept practice closed, but since he knew the Meyers, he'd let me hang out in the rafters.

It may as well have been Heaven.

In the late 60s and early 70s, UCLA owned men's basketball and Pauley Pavilion was one of the most exciting places to be in all of Southern California. John Wooden had created a dynasty unrivaled in the world of men's basketball. The Jackson Five, Lee Majors, Farah Fawcett, you name it, all the coolest celebrities and sports stars of the day came to those games. My family and I had been coming for the last several years to watch David play, and afterward Coach Wooden would come out to say hi to everyone. By the time I got to UCLA, his family and mine had become particularly close.

I also got to know plenty of the other coaches. While it was certain I would play four years of basketball at UCLA, I had no intention of competing in just one sport in college any more than I had in high school. I played volleyball, I ran track, and I also played intramural rugby my freshman year until some of the coaches got wind of it.

Someone in administration called me in to let me know that there would be no more rugby. "You realize you're here on a basketball scholarship, Miss Meyers? That means you're here to play *basketball.*"

I understood. Few cared if I scuffed my knees in the high jump pit or bruised my hand playing volleyball. With rugby, I could really get hurt and nobody wanted that—especially the women's basketball coach, Kenny Washington.

Coach Washington was a tall black man from Buford, South Carolina, with a deep, elegant voice and a passion for the game. He taught us the fundamentals of basketball, which he felt mirrored the fundamentals of life. It was exactly what he'd learned from Coach Wooden. In Coach Wooden's eyes, the basketball player had thirty lives a year, one for each game. Every game had its ups and downs, thrills, joys, pain, and challenges, and each ultimately ended in victory or defeat. But it was always *how* you played the game, the character you showed, that mattered to both men.

Kenny had played for Coach Wooden as a sixth player on his first two championship teams in '64 and '65, so he knew how to come off the bench and still play with heart. He learned that you could want something with every fiber of your being without allowing that desire to consume you and affect your better judgment.

But just as Kenny Washington wasn't a starter for Papa Wooden, he wasn't about to let me, a freshman, start for him now.

"I'm thinking of bringing you off the bench as a sixth player, Annie," Coach Kenny said at the start of the season.

"What? Why?" I was shocked. He knew I'd played on the USA Team, that I was the first woman to ever get a full ride to UCLA, and that I was his best player by a mile. But that didn't matter to Coach Kenny. As frustrated as he knew I was, there was no way I'd get special treatment. I'd have to earn it.

The first big game was at Long Beach. I was #15. I hated coming off the bench, but I was still playing my heart out. I was pretty fast and an aggressive defender, good at positioning. I saw myself as a smaller version of David, capable of playing with great intensity on both ends of the floor. That night, however, the official kept calling fouls on me for reaching. They were phantom calls, in my opinion, but it didn't matter. She was calling what she thought she saw.

The official's name was Rosie Adams, and I knew her very well. In fact, my whole family knew Rosie, and loved her. She'd played AAU with Patty and me, and she hadn't been long out of Cal State Fullerton herself where she had played college ball with Patty. But none of that mattered to me now.

At a pivotal point towards the end of the game, I'd collected four fouls. I was playing defense, and the offensive player with the ball beat me getting to the basket. I reached around to knock the ball away and was called for my fifth foul. Angry and frustrated, I was a pressure-cooker about to blow now that the chef had cranked the setting too high. The ball happened to come back to me. As Rosie lifted her hands to call a foul on #15, I rifled the ball at her gut, knocking the wind straight out of her. She couldn't have been more than five feet away. I was like a bull seeing red, and all I could see were black and white pinstripes, not our friend Rosie.

She doubled over and tried to say something, but couldn't.

From the stands I heard my mom's voice echoing against the one already yelling inside my head. "Annie, what did you do?"

Even though I was still incredibly angry, I looked up, searching for my mom's face, hoping I could telegraph my regret, hoping she'd let me know, instantly, that she understood, as she had so many times before when I'd broken something expensive horsing around at home or accidentally kicked someone while going for a punt. Instead what I saw was a combination of confusion and embarrassment.

With my fifth foul and a technical, I sat out the rest of the game and watched as we lost. At least I was down on the courts and not up in the stands. Many knew the Meyers name, and there was little doubt Mom, Patty, and the rest of my family were fielding more than a few sneers.

When the game finally ended, Coach Kenny came over to the bench and sat down next to me. "As great as you are, Annie, you can be better."

"But she kept calling me for fouls. For reaching, when I wasn't."

"You're gifted. But you lack discipline."

Discipline? Was I really hearing this? Was he really accusing me—one of eleven siblings who shared a bathroom with five sisters and always waited her turn without complaining *undisciplined?* "They were reaching all night and she never called a foul on them once. We should have won."

"First you have to learn to control your competitive nature, learn to harness the power that comes from that fire rather than dilute it through tantrums. *Then* we'll win." And with that, he got up from the bench, leaving me there to stew alone.

So that was it. There was no doubt I was competitive. I was fiercely and passionately competitive. A desire to win coursed through my veins, and I was glad for it. It was my life's blood. I had never considered that drive might need to be bridled, that a vein might burst. Coach Washington had begun his lessons. Today's was teaching me the first thing that every great athlete must learn; to control the mind and emotions, as well as the body. Papa's way of putting it was simple: "Don't whine, don't complain, don't make excuses."

Coach Kenny understood me because he'd been an explosive player himself, and he'd learned from the best how to control it. Now he'd make sure that I, too, would learn to manage my temper and still play with the same passion that I had from as far back as I could remember. I continued to get in the faces of teammates who slacked off. I still yelled at them on the courts and tried to fire them up, "Come On!" I'd scream. And while I can't say I never threw a ball again, that was the last time I ever threw one at a ref.

At San Diego State I kicked the ball into the bleachers after I got called for a foul, and Kenny put me on the bench next to him. At a game in San Louis Obispo, we were up by a lot when, after a fast break, I threw a behind-the-back pass and we scored. Kenny pulled me out of the game to sit on the bench. "The bench is a coach's best friend," Papa liked to say.

Coach Kenny and I butted heads all the time. I still had it in my thick skull that nobody could really teach me the game. Nobody could really know it or love it more than I did—well, no one except Coach Wooden. But the guys got Papa. I got one of Papa's protégé's. Though I cried plenty that year, Coach Kenny ended up teaching me a lot about basketball, and even more about myself. There would be no passing from behind, no tricky moves that dazzled the kids, and none of the fancy footwork that put the Harlem Globetrotters on the map. Mastering the fundamentals had been Papa's approach, and Coach Kenny would make sure that we mastered them, too. Everything we did was going to be by the rules.

Though I didn't start in the beginning of the season, I was moved up to start with Venita Griffey, Judy LeWinter, Leslie Trapnell, and Karen Nash. Karen's nickname was Mama Nash, and she was a brilliant young woman who would go on to become an oral surgeon. There were several seniors on the team during my freshman year who didn't start, but if they weren't as clever with a basketball, they were far cleverer when it came to books. They were the likes of Kathy Fitzgerald, Jane Wortman, and Jane Cohen, who graduated Phi Beta Kappa.

Fitz, Wart, and Coke, as we called them, were as tight as a well-woven rug. Nothing and no one could penetrate those bonds. Normally, we'd drive back from the games in two vans, but during a tournament in Santa Barbara we stayed in a hotel, four-to-a-room.

I was put in with the three best friends. No problem, I thought...until I woke up the next morning strapped into my bed with the sheets tucked in around me, and the mattress standing vertically against the wall. It was a good-natured hazing.

"You might be starting on the varsity team, but you're still just a freshman," one of them told me. I didn't care. I was happy to be in the same van with them. And based on how many times they passed me the ball, they seemed happy to be on the same court with me— even when they got hit in their exceptionally bright heads by one of my bullet passes.

By the end of the season the three seniors had been accidentally hit in the back of the head enough times that they had to step up their game. The drive to excel, so intrinsic to the Wooden Era at UCLA, was finally starting to permeate its women's basketball program. But I had no high cause. I simply wanted to win a championship for the school like David had.

It wouldn't happen in basketball, not that year anyway. But there were other sports. Toward the end of my freshman season, I made it onto the track team as a walk-on.

I loved competing in track and field, especially running the Mt. SAC relays. Mt. SAC was located in Walnut, about an hour southeast of UCLA, and I'd competed there as a child on the club team. With its history, Mt. SAC was sacred ground as far as I was concerned. And yet, so many world records were still to be set by people like Carl Lewis and fellow Bruin Jackie Joyner Kersee.

It was at Mt. SAC that I first met Wilt.

"Annie?" His voice was deep. Everyone knew Wilt from his days with the L.A. Lakers, from which he'd just recently retired. *But how could Wilt Chamberlain know me?* I had noticed him watching me for quite a while. When he finally came over to the high-jump pit and introduced himself, I was thrilled, nervous, honored and, as usual, tongue-tied. Wilt was a great high jumper himself and quickly put me at ease talking about the girls track team he sponsored. "It's called Wilt's Wonder Women," he said, "I'd like you to see them."

Wilt Chamberlain had grown up with many sisters, so he was always very supportive of women's sports. He loved volleyball but, like me, his first true love was track and field. In fact, as a younger man he thought basketball was a sissie sport. But at 7'1", The Big Dipper—so named by the way he'd dip his head before passing through a doorway—realized his height sealed his fate. He played for the Globetrotters his first year out of Kansas and, in time, developed a deep love of the game.

Wilt was born to play basketball. One of the greatest players of all time, he is still the only person to score 100 points in one game—a record neither Michael Jordan nor Kobe Bryant came close to busting. He was gifted, tall, and always smiling and talking.

Since he lived so close to UCLA, the two of us played a few pick-up games at Pauley Pavilion. But it was at the campus handball courts, near the men's athletic department, where we spent most of our time together. We played racquetball at least once or twice a week and if anything got my fire going, it was that. Wilt would hit corner shots that were impossible to return, which would make me terribly angry. Every time I missed one of those shots he would just toss his big head back and laugh, causing me to become all the more furious and to want to beat him even more.

Like Coach Kenny, Wilt helped me to understand and control my competitive nature. He also worked with me on my high jump technique. Track and field was one place my temper couldn't get me into foul trouble. I would become part of a championship team after all during my freshman year, as the women's track team ended up winning. But I still desperately wanted to win a basketball championship for the Bruin women just as David had for the men. If he could do it, so would I.

7

UCLA & That Old Nemesis: Change

"Talent is God-given. Be humble. Fame is man-given. Be grateful.
Conceit is self-given. Be careful."
~ *Coach John Wooden*

The December, 1975 issue of *People* magazine featured a photo spread and story on David and me. There was a full-page photo of me trying to block one of David's shots on a court near our home in La Habra—all four feet, knee-high in the air.

"I'm working for women, I guess," I told them in response to a question about the women's movement. "But I'm working for myself just as much—I'm doing it for me."

My freshman season I was the leading scorer and rebounder, shooting .528 from the field and .767 from the foul line, with 125 assists, 119 steals (#1 in freshman history), and twenty-five blocked shots, earning All American honors. I was part of a Bruin team that led with an 18-4 overall record and a first-place finish (9-1) out of six teams in the Southern California Women's Intercollegiate Athletic Conference. But in the conference championship game at Riverside, we lost to the Cal State Fullerton Titans by one point. I was not a happy camper. Still, I figured we had three more shots.

During my free time, I continued to watch David's practices and was consumed by David and the men's team during my freshman year. I was like a kid in a candy shop watching the guys practice under Coach Wooden. They'd lost the previous year with players Jamaal Wilkes and Bill Walton, to David Thompsons' NC State team.

"Goodness Gracious Sake's alive!" was all Coach Wooden said, showing his displeasure. That was the extent of his cursing, but I can attest to the fact that whenever the guys heard, "Goodness Gracious

Sake's alive," they knew they were in trouble. Wooden's UCLA team had won the championships in '64 and '65, and again from '67 to '73. They were expected to win in '74, but they only made it as far as the Final Four. In '75, Wilkes and Walton were gone, and no one expected them to do well. They had Marques Johnson as a freshman, and David was the captain. David was one of their top scorers, rebounders, and defensive players, and his determination and passion on the courts was always so intense that later, in the NBA, he would be called for a technical just because of the look he'd given a ref.

Now David and the team were playing in the Final Four, and the whole family had traveled to San Diego to watch. Even though David was hurt, he played solid. The first game was against Louisville, whose coach, Denny Crum, had not only played for Papa, but also became his assistant coach. It was a close game between rivals who were mirror images of each other. The crowd went wild when UCLA won by two on a last-second shot in overtime.

Coach Wooden seldom went into the locker room after a game, but he went in that night. When he told the guys it had been a great game and a shame that someone had to lose, they immediately sensed something was up. "I want you boys to know I'm bowing out. You'll be the last team I'll ever coach, and I've never been prouder."

They were flabbergasted. No one had any idea that the greatest coach to have ever lived had decided to hang up his whistle—not the press, not the players, not even UCLA's administration. I don't even know if he'd told his wife, Nellie. He let the players know before anyone. It was the night before the championship.

The game was against Kentucky who'd beat out Syracuse in the other semi-final. The Bruin men went onto that court and fought hard. None of them wanted the man they all loved and respected to go. But if he had to go, it would be on a high note. On March 31, 1975, Coach Wooden's team took him to his 10th championship in twelve years, and David helped lead the way with 24 points and 11 rebounds.

Afterward, the Meyers's celebrated at the home of Fon and Audrie Johnson in San Diego. Fon had played basketball with my father, and the Johnsons had been like second parents to me. We loved them and they loved us. But at the party, I noticed my father was standoffish. He kept to himself in a corner. My parents had come to every game of David's that last year, along with the rest of the Meyers because we were all so proud of our brother's remarkable college career. But in San Diego, the cracks in my parents' marriage were starting to show.

"He's angry that I won't let him rep me. He never wants to speak to me again." The Lakers had chosen David as NBA first round, second draft pick (behind David Thompson) after coming off his senior year playing in Coach Wooden's 10th and final championship. My brother's professional career was about to begin, and my dad was unhappy David hadn't asked him to be his agent. The party in San Diego had been just the tip of the iceberg.

"Well, what does Mark think?" I asked. Our older brother, Mark, who helped negotiate my Pacers contract, had been out of the house for several years and was a father himself. Mark had experienced his own run-in with Dad several years earlier when he and Frannie decided to get married and leave for Berkeley on a football scholarship.

I still remember my father's words. "I'm telling you now, Mark, you're too young. I won't let you throw your life away."

He felt Mark had what it took to go pro. Now, eight years later and graduated from both Berkeley and law school, Mark was proving to be every bit the businessman my father was. And every bit his own man.

David had already spoken to Mark about the problem. "Mark agrees with me. Says it's beyond his own scope, let alone Dad's."

David had asked Mark to rep him, but Mark knew he'd be a disservice now that David was about to play with the big boys. It wasn't Mark's expertise. Instead, Mark helped David find the best agent possible. David was picked by the Lakers and then ultimately traded with four other players to the Milwaukee Bucks for Kareem Abdul Jabbar.

My parents had both grown up in Milwaukee, where my dad was eventually drafted by their pro team, The Shooting Stars, after playing as starting point guard and captain for Marquette. He'd also been offered the coaching job at Marquette, but my mom's father talked him out of it because coaching didn't pay well in those days, and he had a growing family to support.

Dad had always prided himself on his business sense and had studied business law for a while in college. In his mind, he was as groomed as anyone to handle David's career, more so since he was family. Additionally, given the Meyers's history of lousy luck when it came to the big leagues, Dad felt he was entitled. After all, "shoulda, coulda, woulda" was in his blood.

My father's father had been named Majorowski, but he changed it to Meyers after being offered a contract to try out for the Chicago White Sox back in the 30s. But fate stuck out its foot and tripped things up when the war broke out. If my dad felt circumstances had put the kibosh on his own father's chance at success, he may have also believed that marrying young had prevented him from achieving greatness as well. In his mind, he'd tried to prevent Mark from making the same mistake. Now David was breaking the streak, and I suppose it was natural that Dad wanted to play some part in helping David grab the brass ring, which had proved so elusive to the Meyers men up to that point.

Around this same period, my parents' verbal sparring escalated, and while I couldn't have realized it, apparently my five younger siblings had ring-side seats. Their relationship had been strained for some time. And whether it was my father's annoyance at David's decision that set him off, or something else, he wasn't treating my mother kindly.

Anything he would do to upset her, upset me because she had always been so good to all of us. She used to stay up until midnight, sometimes lugging huge baskets of laundry downstairs, which was no small feat in a family as large as ours. I can't remember not hearing the washing machine or the dryer run. And when she wasn't folding, she was standing over the ironing board. Yet when friends wanted to come over to swim, she never said no, even though it meant more towels to clean. The Meyers's house was open to everyone, and she treated the neighborhood like family.

I thought about how my father told David he never wanted to speak to him or see him again if he couldn't get his way. It reminded me of how complicated our relationship with our father had been. As kids, we used sports to win his attention when he was home, though I'm sure we didn't know that's what we were doing at the time. He enjoyed athletics, we enjoyed athletics, and the moments we spent together usually revolved around some sporting event. Mom was amazing, but she was always there for us. Dad was the big fish, and athletic achievement was what lured him. Now David had the ultimate bait, but he was long past fishing for our father's attention.

It tore me up inside, yet as bad as I felt, I couldn't allow what was happening back home to derail my college career. There were too many classes and tests I had to make up after having been on the road with the team—along with other sports to pursue. I tried comforting myself knowing that Mom was tough. She'd survive. At least, that's what I kept telling myself. Fixing their marriage wasn't my job. My job was clinching a championship for Coach Kenny and somehow making it to the Olympics as a high jumper. And UCLA had the most famous track coach to have ever lived.

Ducky Drake had coached both Rafer Johnson and CK Yang at UCLA and at the '60 Olympic decathlon in Rome, where Rafer won the gold. Now Duckie was the trainer for Coach Wooden's men's team.

He and I had a special relationship. I could open up to Duckie. He never brought up the Olympics in Rome when we talked, even though everybody knew about it. It was just in the air, part of the fabric of UCLA sports. But for me, the story of Rafer and CK under Duckie's coaching was uniquely inspirational.

Both men had grown up on opposite sides of the world to become good friends and teammates under Duckie at UCLA. But when both then made it to the 1960 Olympics in Rome—Rafer representing the U.S. and CK representing Taiwan—athletes the world over held their breath. The two men were virtually neck and neck throughout, with Rafer ahead in one event and Yang the next. Each went into the final event thinking he would win the decathlon until they both discovered that they were paired in the same heat. Yang had always beaten Rafer in the 1,500 meters, but now he would have to beat him by ten seconds to win.

Each approached Duckie separately. Duckie told Rafer, "You have to stay with him no matter what. You can't let him get away." To CK Yang, he whispered, "He has never beaten you before. He cannot stay with you."

Yang crossed the tape in 4:48.5 with Johnson just behind him at 4:49.7. Ultimately, the score was Rafer - 8,392, Yang - 8,334. Rafer won the decathlon by 58 points to take the gold, but he would always say it was basically a tie. The two men remained great friends until Yang's death in 2007.

"Annie, you'd be a strong quarter miler," Duckie told me one day. "You should think about doing the pentathlon."

Duckie knew I held hopes to compete in the Olympics in track and field. He knew the high jump was my specialty, but my technique was more of the "Eastern Roll," where your body went over horizontal with the bar. I learned how to do the Fosbury Flop my freshman year at UCLA and kept my sights set on the Olympics with the most famous track coach encouraging me.

I took Duckie's advice and also competed in the Pentathlon at UCLA. Like Coach Kenny, Duckie was a great mentor. But then I had a lot of mentors during my years at UCLA.

And too many coaches.

During my sophomore year, UCLA women's basketball changed. I was upset to see Coach Kenny let go. In his place, they brought in Ellen Mosher. I had known Ellen Mosher since our days playing AAU ball. Ellen had been a shooter from Iowa where she played girls' six on six and AAU basketball for the Raytown Piperettes before she moved to California. Though she was good, my opinion was that she wasn't good enough to coach me. I'm not sure whether I struggled with authority or had a tough time with all the changes in my life, but I put up the same wall as I'd done when jumping from school to school when I was younger. Whatever the reason, I wasn't happy about switching to a different style of play. The result was that I was being extremely hard on her, which probably hurt the team's chemistry. All I knew was that I wanted to win a championship for UCLA, and I didn't see how that was possible playing musical coaches.

During my sophomore year, we were expected to win our conference. During UCLA's 90-48 victory over USC at Pauley Pavilion, I had nine steals that night (out of 82 for the year). Two nights later, we overpowered Fresno State, 96-47. In that game, I had fifteen assists bringing that stat up to 128 for the year. But the game at Cal Poly Pomona was a different story. We played against a team coached by Darlene May, and they had a game plan. I was still working on my emotions, and Darlene used that to her advantage by having her team get me in foul trouble. Meanwhile, Ellen Mosher was still walking on eggshells around me. She knew she needed to earn my respect, for my own good and that of the team. She put me on the bench in the first ten minutes of that game, and we saw our lead crumble, ultimately losing to Cal Poly by 28 points.

"So, did you guys beat them?" someone asked when we got back to campus.

I flinched my jaw. "It was a nearly 30-point loss."

"They lost by 30?"

"No," I said, a combination of anger and embarrassment streaking through my voice, "we did."

Nobody could believe it. The season continued with the Bruin Women 19-4 overall. In the end I was named All-American for a second time, however it was little consolation. Just as the previous year, we advanced only to the AIAW West Region in San Jose where we were again eliminated by Billie Moore's CSUF Titans. Then at the NWIT championship game, we once again lost to Wayland Baptist 90-77. This time, I attributed it to Mosher's coaching.

Looking back, I'm sure I was the worst kind of thorn in Coach Mosher's side. I could be stubborn beyond all rationale. I was born stubborn. As a kid, I could sit at the dinner table for three or four hours rather than eat my dinner if it was something I didn't like, like meatloaf.

"You'll finish that, Annie," my dad would say, frustrated that one of his children was every bit as defiant as he was.

No I won't. Instead, I'd look up at the framed Vince Lombardi quote that hung on the wall. "Winning Isn't Everything; It's The Only Thing." I'd fall asleep with my head on the kitchen table rather than give in.

Here again, what some might call a failing, others might call a strength. I'll bet Coach Mosher had her own choice words for it.

What I didn't realize then was the importance of one's attitude, especially in the face of adversity. When would I realize that I couldn't keep blaming others?

Don't Whine, Don't Complain, Don't Make Excuses. I needed to remember Papa's words now. "In order to be a good leader, you have to be a good follower," was another Woodenism, and I suppose it was true, regardless who you were following. But while my attitude may have stunk, my game did not. I was playing well and making a name for myself personally. The one hole in my heart was for our team to win one for the school.

Eventually I would help lead the Bruin women to their first and only AIAW Championship, however, it would seem like a long time coming. And it would be under a different coach, a woman who, like me, was rapidly becoming well-known in the world of women's basketball. But first, there would be a stopover for both of us in Montreal.

8

The Olympics - A Dream Comes True

"The future belongs to those who believe in the beauty of their dreams."
~ *Eleanor Roosevelt*

In the summer of 1976, the stars aligned. The dream I'd had for so long was finally about to come true, just not the way I'd planned it. Woman's basketball had never been an Olympic sport before, but our neighbors to the north were hosting what would become a historic first. There was only one problem. We took the Gold in the Pan American Games in Mexico, but we finished a disappointing eighth at the 1975 FIBA[1] World Championships in Columbia, and therefore didn't earn a berth to the 1976 Olympic Games.

As the host country, Canada was guaranteed a berth, as were the Soviet Union, Japan, and Czechoslovakia, the World Championship gold, silver, and bronze medal winners. There were only two more slots open, and I was determined that Team USA would nab one of them. Not only was I certain that we'd earn a berth, I was determined to help ensure we brought home a medal for our country, making us a part of history. But I never kidded myself that it was going to be easy.

The tryouts for the first-ever U.S. Women's Basketball Team to compete in the Olympics were held in four different regions of the country, and everyone and their mothers were invited. It was an open try-out, in keeping with the backbone of our national ethos in the year leading up to the United States Bicentennial.

In truth, the selection of players had largely been pre-ordained. It would be the same women who'd been the USA National Team

---

[1] The International Basketball Federation, originally the *French Federation Internationale de Basket-ball.*

star players at the World Cup, the Jones Cup, and the Pan Am Games. But the general public didn't realize that. Women from around the country hoped to make the team. They came from every social and economic class, and comprised nearly every ethnicity. Even those who knew they didn't stand a chance came. They wanted to be able to boast one day to their children and grandchildren that they had tried out for the 1976 Olympics.

The road to the Olympic tryouts for the western region was a long one. Nine hours to be exact. My oldest sister, Patty, drove me and Monica Havelka, an AAU teammate and competitor from Long Beach State, up the back route 395 through Lake Tahoe, where tall pines bordered a winding road that wrapped around a huge, crystal-blue natural lake. We stopped several times to settle our stomachs and then fill them. From there, we headed on the I-80 to a gym in Sacramento. It was the summer of 1975 and nearly hot enough to fry an egg on the asphalt. When the car conked out on us, we thought it had overheated. Come to find out, we'd simply run out of gas, thus solidifying the notion that if men refused to ask for directions, women (at least young women) refused to look at gauges.

It was late in the afternoon by the time we got the car filled up and over to the gym. There were nearly 1,000 players trying out across the country, and a quarter of them were here at the regional trials in Sacramento. I signed up, got my number, and rested.

On the second day I found myself playing on the courts with a mixture of women whose athletic abilities ranged from good to don't quit your day job. I was driving in for a lay-up when someone's foot came in underneath me. I went down, twisting my ankle. After bandaging it, I was still unable to play for the rest of the tryouts. The fact that I ended up making the cut anyway angered a lot of women who thought it was unfair that I should be chosen when I didn't complete the tryouts.

"Annie Meyers could beat any one of you hopping around on one foot," Juliene Simpson told a couple of women who complained to the officials.

By now, Juliene had competed with me in nine international competitions over the last three years, and who knows how many times we'd competed with or against each other in the AAU. She had taken me under her wing from the moment we'd met at the tryouts for the USA team up in Albuquerque, and we'd been roommates at every international event since. Whenever we had a scuffle on the court, we'd always leave it there. Juliene was a great friend, and now — like always — she was sticking up for me when the cat had my tongue.

"Of course Ann is going on to the master trials," Billie Moore told the Olympic Committee Members. "If I haven't seen enough by now, then we're doing something wrong."

Like Juliene, Billie knew my game inside and out, coaching against me both at the college and international level. Billie arrived at Cal State Fullerton from Kansas about six years earlier while Patty was in her senior year, and it took Billie no time to bring their women's team to a national championship. Both Patty and Billie had the same no-nonsense, take-no-prisoners style. I was glad that the ABAUSA[2] had picked her as coach of the first-ever Olympic US Women's Basketball Team, along with Sue Gunter as her assistant. We felt good about our leadership.

Twenty-four players emerged from the four regional trials to meet up in Warrensburg, Missouri for the final pre-Olympic tryout. If it had been hot in Sacramento, Warrensburg was a sauna straight from the underworld…hot and humid. Worse, there was no air-conditioning in the gym, so we'd arrive at the gym drenched from just walking from the dorms. And we'd stay that way. But we didn't mind. We were two dozen women literally dripping with hope. The Olympic Committee chose the twelve Olympic contenders — the athletes they thought could play well together and

---

[2] American Basketball Assoc. USA, the governing body for Women's Basketball before the IOC

get the job done.

Most of us expected the Olympic team would consist of the same players who'd made up the Pan Am team in '75. After all, the world of basketball was no different than any other. At a certain level, it became an exclusive group who knew each other, their strengths, their weaknesses, where they ranked, and whether or not they had what it took to deliver. The Susan Boyles of the world, those phenoms who burst onto the scene from out of nowhere, were very rare. But we were all surprised when three of the Pan Am team players didn't make the cut. Overjoyed as I was for myself, I felt terrible for the ones who hadn't made it.

Today, not only is it no secret that the Olympic rosters are filled long before the tryouts, but there are no tryouts. You go by invitation, and, of course, your professional status no longer renders you ineligible. In 1976 there were no professional female basketball players, and we were the best of the nation's college and amateur players.

Billie made it clear at the outset that we would have to learn to become chameleons. We may have all been superstars at our schools, but now we would be asked to play interchangeable roles for the good of the team. There would be no star point guard or center, only a well-greased unit with transposable parts, and that unit would have little time to practice functioning as a whole.

The twelve spots went to Juliene Simpson, Pat Head (Summit), Lusia Harris, Nancy Dunkle, Charlotte Lewis, Patricia Roberts, Sue Rojcewicz, Mary Anne O'Connor, Cindy Brogdon, Nancy Lieberman, and Gail Marquis. I was the starting 2 guard. We were women from every part of the country (although Dunkle and I were both from La Habra, which was extremely unusual). Even though women's basketball was still in its infancy, most of us were the emerging stars that world class women's basketball had come to know. Nine of us had played on the '75 Pan Am Team. At twenty-three, Pat Head and Juliene Simpson were the veterans of the team, and our co-captains.

I had played with or against most of these women and knew we had a strong group. Nancy Dunkle, who had been playing for Billie Moore's CSUF Titans, was now 6'2", and her skyhook was just as pretty as ever. Juliene was still the impenetrable tank as our starting point guard, and Lusia Harris, our starting center, who went on to win three national championships for Delta State, was our anchor.

Also starting was Pat Head. Pat had grown up on a farm in Tennessee, so what might have seemed like hard work to anyone else, was just part of daily chores to her. There's no doubt she was tough. She had hurt her knee when she was on the '75 Pan Am team, but that didn't stop her from playing any more than when she'd broken her jaw playing against the Russians on the '74 National team. There was a grit and determination in Pat that I related to and admired. Whatever challenge Pat was ever going to be faced with in life, she'd meet it head on. There was no losing with her, not to anything. I felt like she, Juliene, and I were cut from the same cloth.

As for my role on the team, Billie let me know that she expected me to lead through my actions on the court and my intensity. She knew I was quiet off the courts, but she'd watched me play long enough to know that I always gave it my all. She also knew she could count on me to do whatever it took to take home a medal, short of armed robbery. But first, we had to earn a berth.

Together with our coach, assistant coach, manager, and athletic trainer, we trained three times a day, seven days a week in Warrensburg, Missouri before heading to Hamilton, Ontario, where we would vie with nine other nations in the qualifiers.

Billie and assistant coach, Sue Gunter from Stephen F. Austin, worked us hard. We would have to do a three-man weave lay-up starting at eight and go down to two without missing under a certain time. There were twelve players, so we had four groups of three. If one group missed a lay-up anywhere in their sets, or it took them too long to finish, every group would have to start all over until we all had completed the drill. Talk about team bonding. We cheered for each other because none of us wanted to have to run again! But with three practices a day, run we did.

The morning and evening sessions ended with a half-hour of

what I called Blood and Guts, which were interval sprints from the baseline to the midcourt line, back to the baseline, then to the opposite baseline, and back again. Some call them suicides or lines. Once, a player collapsed head first onto the court, sobbing, and was told to get up, raise her arms above her head, and walk around. The worst thing you could do was not move your body afterward. Blood and Guts didn't just increase physical stamina, it proved you could get beyond the pain. You *had* to get beyond the pain.

Practice games were scheduled with NCAA men's college teams when they were available. Those games not only helped us physically, but they highlighted whatever kinks remained in our playing as a team. During a scrimmage against a Kansas City men's team, the opposing team got the ball on a fast break, and Juliene and I were the only ones back on defense against them, while Dunkle, Harris, and Trish Roberts stood at half court, just watching—a huge no-no, especially since Billie saw it. Pat Head, who had played under Billie at the World University games, warned us that the team would pay. "We'd all better get to bed early tonight 'cuz tomorrow she's gonna kill us."

Sure enough, the next day Billie had us spend the first half-hour of practice without a ball. We ran sprints, drills, and everything in between to the point where Blood and Guts was a walk in the park. Her point was to teach us a lesson. Players were running outside to throw up.

But Billie didn't let up. "There's no excuse for what happened yesterday. You're not going to walk down the floor or stand and watch. You'll either decide you want to play every minute, or you'll come sit on the bench near me. I'll go with only nine players if I have to. I'll go with six if there are only six who'll give a hundred percent."

To really drive the point home, *The Kansas City Times* had quoted her. They'd been covering the scrimmage and were shocked at how she spoke to us. But try as they might, they couldn't find one member of the team who would complain. "We deserved this," was all they got.

Billie understood the importance of playing defense with the same intensity as playing offense. It would be one of the hallmarks of her coaching style, and something we had very much in common.

With our short practice time in Warrensburg over, we headed to Hamilton and the qualifiers by way of Rochester, New York, which was just across the border from Hamilton, and where Team USA continued to train. It was June, 1976, a beautiful time to be in upstate New York. The dorms, however, were either condemned, or being renovated because not a soul was there. To say they were in poor condition would be like calling the Grand Canyon a ditch. But the price was right— free—and that's all that mattered.

There was no budget for a women's basketball team hoping to qualify for the '76 Olympics. We weren't officially an Olympic team yet, so all the money went to the men's team, which was assured a berth. Our venture was purely speculative in the eyes of the IOC, who probably weren't expecting a lot after our wildly aberrant performance in Columbia. Had it not been for Bill Wall's American Express card, Coach Billie Moore, and manager Jeanne Rowland's wiliness, we never would have made it through.

Bill Wall was the head of the American Basketball Association and he was responsible for both the men's and the women's basketball teams at all international events. Bill probably spent two-hundred nights a year away from home, and he liked to brag that he had racked up over two million air miles, long before United Airlines even started counting, and decades before frequent flier mile discounts ever existed. He'd been to Russia so many times that some people thought he was a secret agent. As manager, Jeanne Rowlands had the distinguished honor of figuring out where we were going to eat every day. There was no per diem…only Bill Wall's credit card with $500.00 left on it, and that would have to pay for everything.

In truth, it didn't matter to us where we stayed or what we ate. Even if we'd had to train in a shack using a hollowed out wastepaper basket as a hoop, it wouldn't have mattered, as long as we could make it to the qualifying tournament. Gail Weldon, our trainer kept us in shape, while assistant coach Sue Gunter was Billie Moore's right arm. We knew that Wall, Moore, Gunter, and Rowlands would see to it that, somehow, we got everything we needed. There was one day, however, when we got far more than we needed.

One day we were treated like queens.

Bill and Billie had arranged for our accommodations at the dorm by ringing up William "Hunter" Low, known as the "Father of the Kodak/All-America Team." Hunter was the manager of the US sports and events program for the Kodak Company. I'd already received two of the prestigious Kodak All American Awards, so I knew Hunter and liked him.

One day, Hunter invited us up to a Kodak executive's home on the lake in Rochester. I had never seen anything like it before. The large main house was surrounded by well-tended lawns and gardens commanded a sweeping view of the lake. Everyone snapped pictures of the view and of each other, completely oblivious to the historic significance those pictures might have. After all, we were going to be the first US Women's Basketball Team to the Olympics.

The press didn't seem to care much except when the Chinese women's basketball team scrimmaged with us. It was a first for the communist country and, at that, the press only took one group photo of both teams. I don't remember any photographers following us around, not even emissaries from Kodak! I took comfort in my own thoughts. *They'll wish they'd have snapped a few pictures of us once we medal at the Olympics.*

We finally got to Hamilton for the qualifiers on June 22 and knew it was do-or-die time. We were placed in a preliminary round pool along with France, Mexico, and Poland. We tore through the first contest for an 80-57 victory over Mexico, then went on to defeat France 71-59, and closed out the preliminaries with an 84-66 trouncing of Poland.

USA and Poland, with a 2-1 record, advanced from Group A to

the final round. In Group B, which included Bulgaria, Cuba, Great Britain, Italy, and South Korea, there was a three-way tie atop the standings, as Bulgaria, Cuba, and South Korea had identical 3-1 records. FIBA's tie-breaking formula dictated that Bulgaria and Cuba head to the final round to face the United States and Poland.

In the round robin play we clobbered Cuba 89-73. Now there was just Bulgaria remaining for the championship to determine who would be first or second to go to Montreal. We knew it would be a difficult and very physical game. The Bulgarians were a veteran team who knew how to play with each other. Their timing was nearly perfect because they'd had so much experience together, and that can make all the difference. Even so, basketball was still the United States' game. We had the same mentality as the guys: This is *our* game and only *we* know how to really play it.

But it was tough. Thanks to Billie and Sue's coaching, we just squeezed out a final win over Bulgaria 76-75 to take the first of the two remaining births.

Bill Wall's relief at our win was palpable because it meant he would be reimbursed by the IOC for the charges he'd accumulated. He didn't just wipe his brow and sigh. His mop of white hair got the once-through with his handkerchief, and he nearly cracked his face with his smile. We were no longer flying without a net. We were an official Olympic team. From the time I was ten, I'd expected to go to the Olympics as a high jumper. Now I was going as a basketball player. I'd had my plans, but it appeared as though Life had had its own plan. Meeting somewhere in the middle was just fine by me.

My dad came up to Hamilton for the qualifiers, along with David, his wife, Linda, and their new daughter, Crystal. It was good to see him and David, but I was a bound up ball of nerves. We were all still uneasy around Dad. I was excited he was there to see me play, but he'd left Mom by then, and it didn't sit well with me. There was also still some strain between my dad and David, and I just hoped everyone would get along. But it was hard. He was a complicated man, and our feelings about him, no less so.

Before Havlicek, or any of the other masters from whom we drew inspiration, our greatest idol had always been our father. He was a tenacious football player and a gifted basketball player who married and started a family at a time when pro ball didn't pay enough to support a family of four, let alone a family of thirteen.

Now his own marriage had unraveled like a rope under too big a strain of a load it wasn't meant to bare, so he left. Actually, he'd been moving out of the La Habra home for years, taking off for weeks at a time only to return out of the blue. I know it was an intensely difficult time for my mother, who was trying to comprehend where her life had taken her and how she could be left to raise so many young children alone. Outwardly she took her licks, complaining little, and always the stalwart. Inwardly, I know she was crumbling.

Dad told me he was proud that I'd played well against Bulgaria. However I may have felt about him for hurting Mom, his opinions on how well I played still mattered to me. There was a hidden part of me that was still a small child, wanting his approval. I told myself I wasn't being disloyal to Mom by being civil to Dad. *Allegiance.* The very word meant you had to pick sides. Fine for playing a game, horrible when you're talking about a family.

As for Mom, I knew that she, Mark, and Frannie would come later to Montreal to watch the Olympic Games, and I was looking forward to that. But for now, I was with Dad, and a nervous wreck. I needed to focus on what I had come here to do, and that meant playing well in Montreal and not letting anything distract me, not even the family baggage that had flung itself into the backseat during this crucial trip.

Being on the road and living with a bunch of women was an open invitation to all kinds of new things. For instance, Lucy Harris taught me how to pack a suitcase. I wasn't exactly new to the idea of packing, but Lucy had one up on me, as we packed for Montreal. "If you roll your clothes instead of fold 'em, you'll fit more into your suitcase and less of it will get wrinkled." Who was I to argue the logic?

Lucy Harris and I had played on several teams together and we just clicked. At 6'3", she was a specimen by nature and a seamstress by necessity. She had to make all her own clothes because she was such a big gal. And she managed to keep that wardrobe wrinkle-free.

I'd never met anyone so meticulous about her clothing, but I would be, too, if I had to create and cut patterns, then sew everything together. I, on the other hand, was like speedy Gonzales with respect to clothing, packing, eating, playing, and everything else. I wanted to get things done *now*. Not Lucy. She took her time both on and off the courts, which frustrated all of us because we liked to play fast.

Part of her style had to do with the specific type of game she'd played while at Delta State, where the coach, Margaret Wade, believed in a very deliberate post-up offense. Lucy was our center, and she could rebound like nobody else. Once she had the ball, however, she took her sweet time getting down the court. We liked to run the ball, but we'd have to wait for Lucy to set up in the post. When she got there, though, boy was she strong inside.

The qualifying games had given us a chance to practice together as a team, readying ourselves for the Olympics, which were now only days away. Since Hamilton, Ontario was just fifty minutes from Niagara Falls, Bill, Billie, and some of the others decided we had time to view the Falls from the Canadian border before heading to Montreal. The mist coated our faces as we all lined up against the rail to gaze upon the breathtaking view. The rumble of the falls made it hard to hear anything other than my own thoughts. I considered how many places I'd seen, courtesy of my basketball career, and here was another. It was a chance for all of us to relax and to gear up psychologically.

Wiping the moisture off my face, I contemplated our

chances. It was no secret that the Russians were considered the best in the world due to their undefeated record for nearly two decades. But basketball was still a U.S. game. The Americans simply played it better than anyone else. Likewise, I'd trained myself to go into every competition believing we would win, no matter what. I'd learned a long time ago that success begins with one's will. It's a state of mind. The moment you think you're outclassed, you are.

That day at the Falls was July 3rd, 1976, the day before the country's bicentennial. I was reminded that believing in oneself, having that winning attitude against all odds, wasn't just part of being a Meyers, or an athlete—it was part of the American spirit. And I decided that no Soviet team, no matter how great, could ever eclipse that.

As we turned to leave Niagara Falls, the sun peeked through mist, causing a full rainbow to appear above the crashing water below. I saw it as a prophetic sign that the pot of gold was within reach.

9

"Precious Medals"

Once we got to Montreal, the twelve of us stayed in one, two-bedroom apartment with two bunks in each room and four beds in the living area. Since there was only one bathroom, we'd use the kitchen sink to brush out teeth. I was from a big family so I knew how to share a bathroom, but I missed having some semblance of privacy. Privacy or not, the accommodations were a far cry from the ramshackle dorms we'd been living in. But aside from all that, we were living in Olympic Village, so there was a sense of reverence. We'd made it to the Olympics!

Security was everywhere, so we knew everyone would be well-guarded. After the '72 Olympics in Munich, where eleven Israeli athletes were taken hostage by Palestinian gunmen and killed, Olympic security was ramped up to the max.

If it wasn't security, it was politics. The Republic of China (Chinese Taipei) and the People's Republic of China had boycotted the games denouncing each other's legitimacy. When we first arrived, we were told not to unpack because there was still a chance that the U.S. might walk out if the issue regarding Taipei and China was not resolved to our country's liking. And Africa boycotted because of apartheid.

For an athlete, the opportunity to compete against the world's best on this most esteemed platform means everything. Olympic medals can only be attained through the intersection of three things: ability, desire, and opportunity, and that opportunity only comes every four years. Back in the 70s that was a narrow span in the life of a world-class American athlete because you had to be an amateur. Back then, the majority of U.S. athletes competed in one or two Olympics, if they were lucky. There were few Al Oreters or Wyllie Whites who competed in four or five Olympics.

A lot of the players on my team felt it unfair that the international teams were paid by their countries and were still considered amateurs. Not only were they making a livable wage, but they were also growing stronger as a team because they were able to stay together for a long time, whereas we'd only be together for a few weeks at a time. But when anyone started to grumble about it, the coaches told us to knock it off. Focusing on our resentments would only destroy the team from the inside, like a cancer. We needed to focus on our strengths. Besides, it still wasn't certain that we were even staying.

Once it was finally determined that the U.S. would not be pulling out, we relaxed and got to know our surroundings. The Olympic Village had the most enormous cafeteria I'd ever seen, and during the midday meal, everyone from Nadia Comaneci to Edwin Moses, Bruce Jenner, and Sugar Ray Leonard were there.

The games were opened by Queen Elizabeth II, as head of state of Canada. The queen's daughter, Princess Anne, was there to compete with the British riding team. She was the only female athlete not made to undergo a sex test. It was a first at an Olympics that saw many firsts. The only one we cared about, though, was that the Games of the XXI Olympiad would be the first to include women's basketball.

The opening ceremonies were amazing. I'd marched into a stadium and represented my country before hundreds of thousands of spectators at the Pan Am Games in Mexico. But this was different. Chills goosed up my spine, knowing the whole word was watching. There is nothing more prestigious than the Olympics. Every other competition, from the World Championships to the Jones Cup, was preparation for this.

There I stood along with other U.S. athletes from every sport on the world stage. It was my childhood dream come true. Soaking it all in and hoping to capture a mental image of the moment forever, I beamed with pride as they released the doves and— *splat*—I got nailed. We all knew to take cover when the birds were let out but, uncharacteristically, I wasn't fast enough.

There were six women's basketball teams competing in round robin, meaning every team would play each other. Today there are sixteen teams with four pools, so you could lose in your pool, come in second, and still have a chance at the Gold. In '76 we had to win as many as we could of those five games.

Under Sue Gunter, we had always beat Japan in other competitions except for the one time we played them in Osaka. They played a different style from us. They were quick, good outside shooters, and they passed the ball well. On every play they yelled, "Aye, Aye." Whether they were cutting cross baseline or to the basket, they were yelling. It was a pattern that worked for them. But hearing their shrieks throughout the game was distracting. We knew it would be tough because now we were without Sue, who was familiar with their unusual style. Sadly, her father had died and she had flown home the previous day.

The game was scheduled for 9:00 a.m., so we got up at 5:00 a.m. each morning to practice. It was the '76 Olympics' first team-sport competition, and Lusia Harris was the first to score that historic basket. She'd end up with seventeen points and seven rebounds; but the Japanese were ultimately the ones to dictate the tempo of the game. We struggled with Sue not sitting on the bench with us and were seriously jarred when they beat us 84-71. Once I got over the shock, I got mad. With all of the training in Warrensburg and Hamilton, had we peaked too soon? I immediately banished the thought. There was no way I'd come this far to jeopardize my dream, not by this loss, not by anything.

"There will be a lot of other women's Olympic basketball teams," Billie Moore told us that day. "But there will never be another first. You will *always* be the first." That did it. Everybody toughened up. The second game, we had an easy gain over Bulgaria 95 -79, with Dunkle scoring seventeen points, Trish Roberts scoring sixteen, and I scored fifteen. We'd refocused after the loss to Japan. Best of all, we now had Sue back, which helped Billie.

Two days later we played the host country, Canada, and won 89-75. Many years later, when asked about these Olympics, and me in particular, Billie would say I had the ability to dictate the course of a game all by myself. There was no doubt I wanted to win so badly that I could taste it, but basketball is a team sport. No one person can dictate the course of a game. Billie had put together a winning team and she knew that, more than anything else, I simply wanted to be part of a winning team.

We knew our next game would prove our most daunting. The Russians stood tall when they saw us coming. We were their rivals in all things, so we always commanded their attention. But the U.S. would never come as close to beating the Russians as we did in that game at Felt Forum in 1974. Since then, that three-point loss had been squared, and even cubed, by them. And Semjonova always made sure we felt the full force of her girth and height.

Juliene was one of our strongest defenders, but she'd injured her ankle in the first half.

"Are we ever going to score?" Billie asked Sue when the Russians were up 15-0. By the end of the first quarter, Semjonova had already connected on fifteen straight lay-ups without her size-18-foot ever leaving the ground.

I wondered the same thing. I had a pretty good jump shot, and I was able to get pretty far off the ground. In fact, Dr. Gideon Ariel, director of biomechanics and computer sciences for the US Olympic Committee, would conduct a computer analysis using electrodes—very high tech at the time—and reported in the medical journal that my leaping ability was equivalent to the 1977 world high jump record. Problem was, Semjonova didn't need to jump.

Even though the odds appeared to be against us, I never let myself think for a moment that we might lose. I knew it would be a tough battle, but I never allowed myself to envision any outcome but one: winning. If I was stubborn about most things, I was dead-stubborn about that. The worst thing that can befall athletes is letting their thoughts defeat them, so I stationed a guard-dog inside my head, ready to attack negativity. I played every minute as though it were a one-point game. When we ended up losing to the Russians 112-77 points, I was just as devastated as when we had lost to the Japanese in the first game. The mood was somber at the apartment that night. Losing hurts. Losing to your biggest rival by thirty-five points hurts worse. Semjonova ended up with thirty-two points and nineteen rebounds. We were 2-2, now playing for the Silver.

A photo of me trying to hold Semjonova off after she'd been passed the ball appeared in the papers the next day. "Maybe Ann Meyers (6) should have used an ax..." the caption read. I crumpled it up and threw it away. There was still the Silver. It wasn't over until the fat lady sang.

After the Russians, our last game was against Czechoslovakia. We *had* to win that game. The score was tied at half time 37-37. We went into the second half playing pressure defense, and ultimately beat the Czechs 83-67 to take the Silver Medal.

U.S. beat Bulgaria, Canada, and Czechoslovakia.

Bulgaria beat Japan, Canada, and Czechoslovakia

Russia beat everybody.

Of course, they weren't called Russia back then, they were the Soviet Union, and by the end of the Olympic Games, they'd totaled up 125 medals, 49 of which were Gold, including the Gold for Women's Basketball. The United States ranked second in total medals (94) and third in Gold Medals (34), after East Germany, which garnered 40 Gold Medals, for a grand total of 90 Medals.

There's nothing quite like that sense of patriotism you get from hearing your national anthem play as the Gold Medal is placed over your head, as I had at the Pan American Games and other competitions. But this was the Olympics, and I was happy to have done as well as we had.

The third place team went up and received the Bronze, and now it was our turn. Once we each had our Silver Medal, we all raised them toward our two coaches, Billie and Sue, as a sign of our respect and love, and then bowed. My heart swelled with pride as our flag was raised. For now, Silver was very sweet.

The U.S. Women's Basketball team would eventually take Olympic Gold, but that would be in large part because the long-standing rivalry between the Soviet Union and the USA would not play out again in this most esteemed international platform for many years to come.

When the Olympics ended, I flew back home with Mom. When the flight attendants announced my name as an Olympian, the whole plane cheered. As usual, I was both proud and embarrassed to be singled out. There were so many small gestures of acknowledgment that followed the Olympics, and each was moving. But when all of the U.S. Olympians were invited to the White House to meet President Ford (introduction compliments of none other than famed Olympian, Jesse Owens), I was overwhelmed. I had no idea it would be the first of four such visits with four different presidents, or that years later when Donnie and I were married and living in the desert, President Ford would come over to play golf at Morningside and invite me to play nine holes with him.

It was still July when I got back to California, and with all the notoriety from the Olympics, I was invited to compete in the annual Dewer's Sports Celebrity Tennis Tournament in Las Vegas with players from the NBA and the NFL. There were a handful of women invited: skier Suzy Chaffee, Diana Nyad, swimmer Donna De Varona, and Wilma Rudolph. I had long admired Wilma for what she had to overcome to be a top athlete. As a young girl, Wilma had polio. She was put in leg braces and told she'd never walk. Wilma not only proved them wrong, but she became an Olympic Gold Medal sprinter. I had always been inspired by her story of courage as a young girl myself, and I was glad now for the chance to become friends.

I also became good friends with some of the guys, such as Joe Washington, Walter Payton, Calvin Murphy, John Havlicek, Franco Harris, Rick Barry, Paul Westphal, John Naber, Julius Erving, and

Hank "Hammerin' Hank" Greenberg. Hank was in his late sixties while the rest of us were in our twenties. In comparison, he seemed ancient at the time. But older or not, he was one terrific tennis player. His placement was superb, and he could return anything you shot over the net. We played hard, but there were some nice benefits. After the tennis, we'd lay out by the pool with the families and take in dinner and a show, while others would gamble.

Since I was still just a kid in college, I'd suck in my breath watching some of these guys throw away a fair amount of money in those casinos. Then again, as older, more established athletes who were men, they were also earning a whole lot more money than I was, so it was a matter of perspective, I guess.

"Here's a fifty, see if you can parlay it into a grand," Hank said to me more than once. I'd take the $50, then promptly lose it at the roulette table. But each time he gave me the money, he always made it clear that if I *did* win, I was to keep it. Hank was wonderful to me.

However, it was during the afternoons that I had the most fun. Following the tennis exhibitions, before the casinos and shows, a bunch of us would high-tail it to the local gym to play basketball. The football players stormed the hard court no differently than they did the football field, so you had to get out of their way on a drive or you could easily end up a mangled human doormat. But even if you couldn't stop Franco Harris, you *could* block his shots. I remember 5'9" Calvin blocking one of Harris's shot off the backboard. There must have been four feet between his soles and the ground, he got so high.

Julius Erving brought his family, and we all hit it off. It's funny, we can never know who we'll click with in life, but Julius and his wife, Turquoise, became like a brother and sister to me from the very start. Later, if I happened to be back East, sometimes I would stay at Turq and Julius's home in Philadelphia when Julius was playing for the 76'ers. I always missed family when I was on the road, but not when I was with Turq and Julius. They *were* family.

A couple of afternoons, Turq and Franco's wife, Dana, took me through the Las Vegas boutiques to try on clothes and pick out purses, which has its own irony since I seldom used a purse, and rarely do today. But they were great, and I loved them for that.

"Annie, I bet this lipstick would look great on you," or "You'd look so good in that dress, Annie."

They were very sweet. They loved to shop, and they wanted me to enjoy it, too. And I did enjoy it, but only because it was time spent with them. As for pastimes, I'd much have preferred being on the court competing. That's where my pulse quickened. I wasn't used to Saks. I was more of a Sears girl.

As wonderful as Turq and Dana were, I was afraid to say anything about where I'd rather be. It brought back too many memories of elementary school and being told that I wasn't behaving "lady-like." When I finally explained that as much as I enjoyed their company, shopping really wasn't my thing, they were terrific.

Nonetheless, I would be invited to several more Dewer's events in Vegas, and each time I'd end up bringing home another purse.

10

The Championship, At Last

"Women, like men, should try to do the impossible.
And when they fail, their failure should be a challenge to others."
~ Amelia Earhart

When the tennis tournament in Las Vegas ended, I returned to California and continued to play USA basketball (taking Silver at the World University Games after racking up Gold at the Jones Cup) through the rest of the summer until school started back up. As a junior at UCLA, I was now competing on the women's volleyball team (which would make it to the Final Four), as well as our basketball team where Mosher was still coaching.

As before, we were expected to win, probably more so now that I'd come off the Olympic team. In a 98-45 win at San Diego State, I had one of three triple-doubles in Bruin women's basketball history, with fourteen points, ten rebounds, and twelve steals (No. 2 in single-game history). Overall, we were 20-3 and West Coast Athletic conference champions. However, we again lost to Coach Moore's Fullerton Titans 91-87. At the end of the season, I had led the team in scoring (18.3) and rebounding (7.3), and for the third consecutive year, I earned All-Tournament honors and was again named Kodak All American. Ironically enough, the first-ever three-time All American basketball player had been John Wooden. I couldn't ask to be in better company, but it still wasn't enough.

As honored as I was to receive the prestigious awards for a third year in a row, we still hadn't taken the championship. Instead we were relegated to runner-up for a third time by losing to that other monkey on our back, Wayland Baptist, at the NWIT. The personal accolades felt like consolation prizes. What I needed was for the

Bruin women's team to win a national title. Under Coach Wooden, my brother had won two for the men's team—one his sophomore season and one his senior year. I wanted to be part of a championship team. Now, going into my senior year, I knew this would be our last chance. The thought of falling short was unacceptable, and I remained concerned as to whether we could do it under Coach Mosher. Apparently, the UCLA athletic department had the same concerns, and I started my senior season with my third coach. It would be the same woman who'd helped Team USA medal in Montreal.

With Billie Moore at the helm, I had no doubt we could win the AIAW National Championship for UCLA—just as she and my sister Patty had done for Cal State Fullerton in 1970. Billie would later say she liked coaching me a lot more than she liked coaching *against* me.

Our starting lineup for the '77-'78 season consisted of 6'1" freshman, Denise Curry (who went on to be a three-time All American and win Gold at the '84 Olympic games), 6'1" senior center Heidi Nestor, 5'6" sophomore guard, Dianne Frierson, and a 5'8" junior named Anita Ortega, who we nicknamed 'Juice' because she had as many moves as O.J. Simpson. She would both go on to play in the WBL with the San Francisco Pioneers and eventually become a police sergeant and the first Afro-Puerto Rican female to supervise an Area command after being assigned to the police station of L.A.'s crime-ridden Hollenbeck precinct in 2009.

Denise Corlett and Beth Moore were the sixth and seventh players on the team. Denise became a three-time champ at UCLA in volleyball, basketball, and badminton (beating me by a championship). Beth was a smart player and good friend, and our resident cheerleader before each game. "Annie will have your backs. Annie won't let the team lose."

What she failed to mention was that I wouldn't be diplomatic about it. "Come on! What were you thinking? Son of a biscuit-eater, get your head in the game!" were my standard lines. When I'd get all Mr. Hyde on my teammates on the courts, they'd scratch their heads, confused. "Was that *Annie?*"

That I was quiet and demure off the courts and loud and aggressive on them was nothing new. I'd always been that way. "An animal on the courts, and a perfect lady off," is how Coach Kenny described me. I wish I could say it was something deliberate, but I had as much control over it as Dr. Jekyll had over his transformation once he'd swallowed the potion. Once I hit the hardwood, some sort of chemical response in me kicked into high gear and I became another person.

My split-personality reputation had travelled throughout the national collegiate women's basketball circuit, but up until my senior season, our UCLA Women's team hadn't been further than San Louis Obispo. And we travelled by van because, back then, most colleges didn't have the money to travel out of state like they do today. (Thank you Title IX.)

Now, in my senior year, we were flying back to New York to play in a tournament at Madison Square Garden, which brought back memories of that first game against the Russians back in '74. Our first opponent was the defending three-time AIAW Champs, Delta State, who had just graduated Lucia Harris, their Player of the Year. We lost in the first game to Delta State, but beat Rutgers (who had lost to Carol 'Blaze' Blazejowski's Montclair State) in the consolation game.

From there, we flew to College Park, MD to play ahead of the men's game. There was a great rivalry between UCLA and Maryland men when my brother played. Now there were at least 14,000 people in the stands at Cole Field House, and we lost in front of every single one of them (88-92). Then we went to Greensboro to play North Carolina State, where David's team had lost in '74, so it was another great rivalry, and again we lost. So now we had lost three of our last five games, were 6-3 overall, and I was beside myself. *Are we not going to make it again!?*

After that game, I got in the locker-room shower and cried for a good fifteen minutes as the hot water rushed over me. I'm not sure whether I felt sorry for myself, the team, or the school, and what looked to be a repetition of the previous three strikes, but when I got dressed, Billie told me she wanted to talk back at the hotel.

We sat in the lobby after everyone had gone up to their rooms. "This team needs you, so you have to be a leader. You can't quit because they count on you. This means you have to pull yourself together and refocus."

She was right, but I didn't want to hear it. Billie wouldn't let up, though, because she knew how upset I could get, and she was concerned that my energy could spread throughout our team like a contagion. It could be deadly or euphoric, depending on how I felt, and Billie wasn't afraid to do whatever it took to snap me out of it. Even when she got mad at me, I may have pouted inside, but I still was able to play at the higher, more controlled level she was looking for. She knew when to praise me, and when to be hard on me.

After her talk, I felt a sense of urgency, and I did everything I could to convey that same sense of urgency to my teammates. Had any psych majors played on our team, I'm sure they would have tossed me on a couch and declared that my need to go all the way was some holdover from a childhood competition with David. And I'd have said, "Fine. Call it whatever you want. Just get out there and play to win."

I wasn't into psychobabble. I wasn't into the *why*'s of anything. All I cared about were the *how*'s. The paralysis of analysis wasn't for me. I was all about action. And I consider praying to be active.

In our next game against Long Beach State, I was in the zone, posting up, driving, getting all my free-throws, making my shots from outside, and all my teammates got me the ball. I scored a career-high thirty-nine points, tying my brother, David's, career high. I also had eleven rebounds, four assists, and six steals. The final score was Bruins: 107; Long Beach State: 94. Next came a 99-72 win over Cal Poly Pomona at Pauley Pavilion, where I scored thirty points. In a game against Stephen F. Austin's team, which was coached by Sue Gunter at Pauley, I remember being sick going into the game. I'd had chills and thought I might throw up, but my focus didn't waiver. I recorded the only quadruple-double in UCLA basketball history — twenty points, fourteen rebounds, ten assists, and ten steals. A season that started out so dismally was suddenly shaping up. And we wouldn't lose another game going into the regionals.

The first Regional game up in Palo Alto was critical. It was against Long Beach State, again. It was a close game that went back and forth. With seconds left, Beach up by two, Anita Ortega came in with the play of the game, stealing the ball to tie it up in regulation. Long Beach had a chance to win it at the buzzer, but missed a twelve foot baseline jumper. We scored five points in overtime to beat them by one point. Now we only had to beat Las Vegas to make the Final Four. We ended up beating them by 100-88, reaching 100 points for a thirteenth time that season.

At last we'd made it to the Promised Land: The Final Four to be played at Pauley Pavillion.

In the semi-final against Montclair State, we were going up against Carol Blazejowski, the nation's leading scorer, who was averaging over thirty-three points a game. We knew we couldn't stop her, but we would do our level best to contain her. Nobody else on her team scored in double digits, and we had the home court advantage. Still, we were lucky to hold Blaze to forty points, beating them 85-77. The *L.A. Times* described most of the action as "Meyers against Blazejowski." All I could think when I saw the article was, *Thank God the Bruins won.*

We'd wait to see whether we'd be up against Wayland Baptist or Maryland. Either way it would be a re-match; and no one in the bleachers would want their money back—not with all the history there. I was more invested than anyone. If the Olympics had been a dream come true, winning the championship was every bit one of my dreams.

March 25th, 1978 was the final game at UCLA before an AIAW record crowd of nearly 10,000 spectators, while five NBC cameras nationally televised to millions more. My teammates and I hunkered down for the game that would decide it all. We were up against Maryland, who had beaten Wayland Baptist College in the other semi-final, and to whom we'd lost earlier in the season in large part because I'd allowed myself to get into foul trouble yet again. It's not often in life you get a second chance. And this time we were on our turf with our family and fans in the stands. It was payback time.

I scanned their faces as the crowd shuffled in. Making their way to the same spot in the bleachers where they always sat were the Meyers clan, each wearing Colgate smiles and the Bruin blue and gold. Wilt Chamberlain was also there, along with Coach Kenny. Missing were Coach Wooden, who was at the Men's Final Four, and David, who was playing in the NBA with the Bucks. As for Mom, there was nothing that could have kept her away. She had yet to miss one single game my entire senior year. She'd come to see me in the Olympics and she'd come to the Pan Am Games. She was always there, up in the stands, cheering, just as she had been when I was younger, just as she had been for all my brothers and sisters. She knew we were playing on a very special night. It was March 25, 1978. The next day I was turning twenty-three years old.

This was going to be a difficult game. Billie put me on Maryland's starting point guard, Tara Heiss, an offensive All-American powerhouse who went on to become Maryland's first women's basketball player to score 1,000 points, and who was largely responsible for their win earlier in the year. Billie was sure that the game would come down to defense. It didn't matter, since I loved playing both ends of the court, and I knew defense was a fundamental, pivotal part of the game. And in this game, particularly, it would be crucial that whoever was holding Tara off needed to burn with the same intensity most players reserve for offense. Billie knew I could do that.

In our first meeting against Maryland, my fellow teammate, Diane Frierson, had matched up against Tara. I'll never forget the look in Tara's eyes when she had the ball on the first play of that final game and realized that I'd be guarding her. She'd played against the Bruins enough to know that I played every possession like it was my last. I was able to contain her during the entire first half, and she went scoreless. Meanwhile, I was posting up and getting shots inside and getting in the free throw line and hitting my jumper. At the half, the Tarrapins walked off the court like they heard bagpipes. Their coach rallied them for the second half, because Tara woke up. But by then, it was too late. The tone for the game had already been set.

We defeated Maryland 90-74 winning our 21st consecutive game. My stats were strong (20 points, 10 rebounds, 9 assists, 8 steals), but my Bruin teammates contributed every bit as much, especially Anita Ortega and Denise Curry. Now, at last, we had taken the AIAW National Crown.

My brother, Mark, came down onto the court, hugged me, and then hoisted me onto his shoulders to a chorus of "Happy Birthday." The band joined in followed by the crowd. Through the players and throngs of spectators, Mark carried me over to the hoop so I could take down the net to the beautiful sounds of UCLA fans cheering. It's one of those special times I think back on and find it impossible not to smile.

We'd finally done it. The Bruin women had won their first and only championship. Through my tears, I saw Billie Moore heading toward me. "I know you could have doubled the points you scored this year," she said "but then we wouldn't have won the championship."

It sounded a lot like what Coach Wooden told Kareem Abdul-Jabbar (Lew Alcindor) when he was at UCLA, "Lew, you can lead the nation in scoring, or you can win."

Lew won three titles for UCLA, and now the women's team had finally done it.

Four years later, the final chapter would close on the AIAW. The Association of Intercollegiate Athletics for Women had begun twelve years earlier and had represented one of the biggest advancements for female athletes on the collegiate level. The association had functioned in the equivalent role for college women's programs that the NCAA had done for men's programs at a time when the NCAA had no interest in women's sports.

"Women In Sports" was the heading on the June 26th, 1978 cover of *TIME Magazine*. Inside was an article along with a picture of me in the winning game at UCLA. It pointed out that the Bruin women's game had averaged crowds of 4,000 that final year, with gate receipts more than offsetting expenses. Not long after, the NCAA finally came to realize that women's athletic programs could actually be profitable.

By the end of my Bruin career, I held twelve of thirteen school records, and I remain number one on the charts for steals (403) and blocks (101). I won my fourth consecutive All-American honor along with the Broderick Award as the nation's top women's collegiate basketball player. The Bruin women's volleyball team I competed on my junior and senior year again made it to the Final Four, and at the end of the year, I received the Broderick Cup as the Collegiate Female Athlete of the Year. I was also named the first All-University Athlete of the Year.

1978 happened to also be the inaugural year of the Wade Trophy, presented to the best women's basketball player in Division I competition. Even though we'd won the championship, the Wade Trophy went to Montclair State's Carol Blazejowski. My name was known across the country, but in a strange twist, there was another player named Anne Meyers from Dayton University, and a lot of the coaches back East unknowingly voted for her even though she spelled her first name differently. Again, it came down to budget. There were no big travel allowances for women's basketball back then, so just because the women's coaches might have heard about a good player on the other coast, they didn't always get to see her play like they do now. Blaze was certainly deserving of the Wade Trophy, but to this day, I believe I should have received one with her.

11

A League Of Our Own

*"Maybe we weren't at the Last Supper,
but we're certainly going to be at the next one."*
~Bella Abzug

By the time I was wrapping up my senior year at UCLA, a group of suits on the East Coast had formulated a professional women's basketball league from a plan that had been percolating since the time I'd started college, and which drew strength after the women's team had done so well at the '76 Olympics. In the summer of 1978, with twelve teams participating, the league held a player's draft in Manhattan at the Essex House. The Women's Professional Basketball League, or WBL, planned to play a 34-game season with teams Chicago Hustle, Houston Angels, Iowa Cornets, Milwaukee Does, New Jersey Gems, New York City Stars, Washington Foxes, Philadelphia Fillies, and teams in New Orleans, San Francisco, Long Beach, and Dallas. The fact that not all the teams had made firm commitments to the league, or had even chosen names for themselves, didn't seem to matter.

I was flattered when I got a call stating that I was the WBL's overall first draft pick. But the timing wasn't right. I needed to finish up a few more courses at UCLA to earn my degree. With all the traveling I'd done playing USA basketball, I'd missed some classes, which I could make-up in my fifth year. I'd also been given a wonderful opportunity by my broadcasting professor, Art Friedman, to do the commentary for a couple of the men's UCLA basketball games with Ross Porter.

My hands were full, and they were bound to get fuller because I had my sights set on the 1980 Summer Olympics, which meant I had to retain my amateur status. I had little choice but to decline the Houston Angels' offer.

It ended up that I wasn't giving up a lot. Franchise owners estimated salaries at between $3,000 and $5,000. Eventually, the average salaries would be closer to $9,000. No one knew it at the time, but the problem was that many of those salaries would go unpaid. In my stead, twenty-year-old Molly Bolin, a blonde from Iowa, nicknamed Machine Gun for her ability to fire off shots, signed with the Iowa Cornets to become the first official member of what was already proving to be a beleaguered league before it even got off the ground.

No one had any idea the WBL might be cursed. Most of us were still hopeful that its existence was a sign of our viability as professional athletes. Men had been playing pro in the NBA since 1946. While we'd been made to wait forty years before we were allowed to get in on the Olympics action, it seemed our wait to get into the professional realm wouldn't be quite as long.

Women's basketball had come a long way in the last several years, advancing much further than it had in its entire eighty-three-year history. So much had changed in women's basketball since the days when snatching the ball was prohibited. But so much more had changed just in the time I'd been playing. And even though I wasn't ready to give up my amateur status, the formation of a professional women's basketball league was proof that the ladies' game had finally come of age. Little did I know that was still nearly two more decades away.

But for now, the immediate future looked bright.

1979 was shaping up to be almost as exciting as the previous year. I had been the captain of all the international teams I'd played on that summer and the first woman to carry her country's flag at the Pan Am Games, where the world's best athletes competed. I kept a journal. In it I wrote:

Saturday 6-30-79: *I was nominated to carry the flag, and I won the voting by "a lot"! I'm so excited and honored. It's really a great feeling, and I feel so proud and thankful. It's the first time a woman has ever been nominated!*

All of the different captains from the different sports had voted for their choice to carry the U.S. flag. As captain of the women's basketball team, they wanted me to have that honor. That feeling of fitting in, the one I'd searched for throughout elementary school and high school, the sense of acceptance I wanted playing basketball with my older brothers as a kid, the approval I sought from my parents, the perception of belonging we all long for from the moment we are conscious of being an individual—all of that was now filling me up in spades.

On July 1, I carried the American flag into the arena near the Pan Am Village in Puerto Rico with the United States congregation following behind me. I was careful not to dip the flag. It's well known among athletes that the United States doesn't bow to sovereign powers. Other countries may bow to the host country, but not the U.S. We never have, and it sure as heck wasn't going to happen on my watch.

Puerto Rico was hot and muggy. As a proud athlete representing her country, it could have been twice as hot and the ceremony twice as long, and I still wouldn't have minded. I looked up to see 100,000 spectators in the stands that day, and couldn't help but wonder what my parents would have thought had they been there. They'd both come to the Pan Am Games in Mexico a few years earlier, but their relationship had become so strained that I'd had to invite Juliene everywhere we went just to provide a buffer. This time, I was on my own.

The '79 Pan Am Games Opening Ceremony lasted almost six hours, and I held our flag high the whole time, the first woman to do so. If it was heavy, it was worth it. But with these games, there were new responsibilities...and pressures.

At these Pan Am Games, one of my former teammates from the '76 Olympic USA Team had also been given a new responsibility. She was now my coach. And the adjustment for both of us was difficult.

Pat Head (Summitt) had not coached a USA team before this summer, and she and I seemed to butt heads (obviously not unusual for me). She was a lot like Billie Moore in that she was a tough coach and I was a tough player, and we challenged each other. I had been relegated to coming off the bench, which was incredibly frustrating. Not only was I the captain of the team, but I'd been the captain of every USA Team to play in every international competition that summer. But as the coach in each of these events, she'd have me come off the bench—the same thing Kenny had done to me my freshman year. I'd been a starter with Pat on the Olympics team, I'd won a national championship, and been named Player of the Year since then. I was confused and hurt...and it didn't help that I kept my emotions to myself.

We were two strong-headed women, both equally determined in our beliefs. I believed I should be starting and playing more. I don't know whether Pat felt I wasn't playing up to her expectations or felt I wasn't leading. But having me come off the bench was like putting me in a straightjacket, and when I came out, I usually came out swinging.

More than anything, I wanted to prove I was worth my weight in gold, even if Pat didn't think so. As usual, when I was feeling frustrated, I looked to my family for guidance, so I called home.

Patty had answered the phone. "Looks like the first woman to carry the flag for our country is getting a lot of press. You're all over the front page of the *L.A. Times* carrying the flag!"

It all felt surreal. "I was also interviewed by this guy with *Sports Spectacular,*" I told her. It had been a young Dick Stockton, one of the many journalists I would work with later in my career who would tell me he was shocked to see that an athlete so timid when answering reporters' questions had opted for a broadcasting career.

"We're saving the newspaper for you, Annie. It's a great shot," Patty said. "Word around town is that you're joining the WBL."

That came from Ed Arnold, a newscaster for ABC TV, Channel 7. Before leaving for the Pan Am Games, Ed had asked me if it was true that I was going to join the new women's basketball league. Early on, the WBL was getting ink. *Sports Illustrated* said, "It was as if ABC was getting ready to replace *Charlie's Angels* with a woman's basketball league," and I was getting a lot of questions about my possible involvement. I'd kept my answer short and sweet with Ed. "Nope. I'm going to play in the Olympics." Now the piece was airing in L.A. while I was in Puerto Rico.

We ended up winning the Silver at those Pan Am games. And after I arrived back to the States, I received Sam Nassi's call about trying out for the Pacers. After Mark and I met with him and Slick, I confirmed my decision to go out for the Pacers and announced it to my entire family when we were all together on a family trip in San Diego.

While it turned out that playing for the Pacers had been a fantasy, signing with them was not. I'd become the first woman to broadcast an NBA game as a result of Mark's negotiations, but eventually I missed playing basketball too much to stay on in the booth.

Now a new decade was about to dawn literally and figuratively. I was playing with the Gems in New Jersey and when the off season would come, I'd train for another shot at the *Superstars*. There was just one problem. It was looking more and more like the WBL had bitten off more than it could chew and soon the bill would be coming due.

7-Up Commercial

1980 New Jersey Gems

Voted "Most Athletic"
in High School

1975 All American brother and
sister - me, a Freshman,
David a Senior

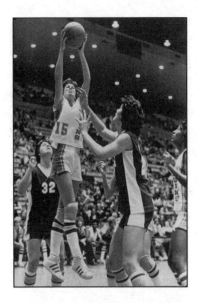

One of my favorite things to do:
Rebound

Me trying to box out 7'2" Uljana
Semjonova, on a rebound"

Battle of the Sexes, me being
interviewed by Vin Scully while
Cazzie Russell waits patiently

1979 Indiana Pacers
Press Conference

1979 World Championships
Receiving the Gold

Retired UCLA numbers
Ann Myers Drysdale,
Kareem Abdul-Jabbar,
John Wooden, Bill Walton

Sister Kelly, Freshman year
at Pepperdine

Revisiting the
Basketball Hall of Fame

Don with our
daughter, Drew, 1993

2007 named GM
Phoenix Mercury
and VP of Phoenix Suns

July 23, 2011 Dodgers Tribute to
Don's 75th Birthday

Two-time WNBA Champions
Phoenix Mercury

Christmas 2010
DJ, Drew, and Darren

Vero Beach Spring training
family under
Don Drysdale Drive

Celebrating 1975 UCLA championship with parents
on the eve of my 23rd birthday

Anna's Bananas 1977-1978 Champions

Hall of Famer, idol, friend, Bill Russell

Meyers Family, Back row: Ann, Cathy, Susie, Coleen, Patty
Front row: Jeff, Bobby, Tom, Mom, Mark, David

Olympics 1976 - First Women's Basketball Team Silver Medalists

My Big Hair days

Bringing up the rear with Gold Medalist, Edwin Moses, and
BB HoFamer Rick Barry in the *Men's Superstars*

Starting my next career: Broadcasting

Kicking back with Franco and Dana Harris, Turquoise and
Julius Erving, and me at the Vegas Dewar's Tennis Tournament

Don and Bob Uecker watching me play at a NJ Gems game –
Bob finally getting a front row seat

Olympians and Hall of Famers:
Lusia Harris, Carol Blazejowski, Anne Donovan,
me, and Cheryl Miller
Not a bad starting five

Hanging with the brightest minds of the game:
Mike "Coach K" Kryzewski, Pete Newell, Papa and Bill Shaman

Dinner with Papa, brother Dave, and Mom

Like a thorn between two roses,
Me with Sandy Koufax and Don

Duke Snider, Don, holding Darren,
Tommy Lasorda with DJ

LA Olympic Luncheon 1995: Al Joyner, Sammy Lee, Muhammed Ali,
Florence Griffith-Joyner, me and daughter, Drew

Elton John, me, and Women's Sports Foundation Founder, Billie Jean King
circa 2009

"Welcome to the White House" -- DJ, President Bush, and me

Special Olympics with
Maria Shriver and Rafer Johnson,

Our wedding day picture with Don's family
(L to R) Kelly, Nancy, Ed, and Scott Fieux, me, Don,
Don's daughter, Kelly, and parents, Verna & Scotty

High School – Freshman Year

12

The Right Strategy Equals Success

"If you don't have a plan for yourself, you'll be a part of someone else's."
~ *Anonymous*

My deal with the Gems was a three-year commitment for a total of $145,000—the equivalent of almost a half million dollars today. It was a considerable amount for a league that was paying salaries of on average $9,000 a year, and why, I later learned, the Houston Angels had given up my rights. It was simply too costly. But it was my agent at William Morris who was setting the price tag for me now. While nearly $50k a year was a good amount of money, especially for a female basketball player, it had been the price established by my brother, Mark, when he'd negotiated my contract with the Pacers, and what my new agent was using as the bottom line to get me *out* of the Pacers and *into* the WBL. His pitch was simple. "She's the greatest female basketball player in the world."

Ultimately, I would only see about $60,000 of that contract. Looking back, it's clear that the reason the Gems couldn't create the #15 jersey was because his team, like so many in the league, was hemorrhaging cash right from the beginning. The high profile Stars team, which had been considered well-heeled and was playing in New York City, was initially approached by Houston for my trade, but ultimately even they decided they couldn't afford to enter into a $145,000 agreement. Ironic, considering the owner of the team had accused the Pacers of trying to put the WBL out of business by signing me in the first place.

In the league's first year, the New York Stars had lost $350,000— well over a million dollar by today's standards—because they simply overspent. The Stars were to play eleven games at Madison Square

Garden, six of them WBL-NBA doubleheaders with the Knicks. They knew they couldn't make money with $300,000 rental costs. "But the Garden is the sports Mecca of New York and the world," the Stars owner, Ed Reisdorf, told the press. "We are no longer a secret."

The Stars' primary concern was no different than that of the other teams, which was to get the word about the WBL out there, and he felt he could do that best by working with the NBA.

In hoping to go big as quickly as possible, most of the teams were making the same over-reaching, overly enthusiastic mistakes by renting venues that were too expensive in the early formation of the league, trading players back and forth like baseball cards, and underestimating costs. Still, the league had high hopes for the second year. In addition to signing me, the prospects for the second season included a televised season opener All-Star game at the Superdome in New Orleans, which held 30,000 people. It was an ambitious goal considering the games were drawing an average of 3,000 spectators. The All-Star game was sold-out, but ended up being played in Chicago at DePaul. And while it was filmed, it was not broadcast. In spite of this, they booked other grand venues and continued to sign other players.

Meanwhile, President Carter had made good on his threat to boycott the upcoming Soviet-hosted Olympic Games because the Soviet Union hadn't retreated from Afghanistan. This brought other players on board with the WBL. Olympic teammates Nancy Dunkle, Gail Marquis, and Charlotte Lewis joined teams in California, New York, and Iowa, and played the first and second seasons. Eventually my friend, Carol Blazejowski, would sign on, but it would be too late.

While the WBL had the most talented players coming out of college, it didn't know how to market, and its attempts at getting the word out about the new professional women's league were misguided and ineffective. The WBL was simply too new and untested. And unfortunately, the league's rookie mistakes would continue throughout the '79-'80 season.

Team owners thought they could acquire dream teams overnight rather than trying to build great teams over time. With the talent they did acquire, the WBL didn't consider the importance of capitalizing on the player's existing fan base. Instead, they allowed franchises on the West Coast to sign players from East Coast schools, and permitted New Jersey to sign me, when I should have been playing in the West. A strong college player who might have developed a following in Florida had little chance of bringing those same fans to home games in California. As a result, ticket sales weren't near what they needed to be.

Now the League's hopes were riding on me to come in and build momentum. "Meyers is the woman that the Women's Professional Basketball League hopes will do for it what Joe Namath did for the American Football League," a reporter from the Philadelphia Inquirer wrote.

Others had more to say:

"Meyers is a Renaissance Lady of Basketball."

"If the Women's Basketball League is to survive its embryonic years, it is going to have to have more players like Ann Meyers."

While it was flattering, it was completely unrealistic to suggest that a league could be floated by one player. Even papers like the *Chicago Tribune*, which had sharply criticized my salary coming into the WBL wrote, "She's worth every dollar of her salary package with the Gems," after seeing me play an away game early in the season in Chicago where I'd scored thirty-four points, thirteen rebounds, and three assists. Good grief, even the organist for the home team played "Jesus Christ Superstar" upon my entering the arena, to which the entire crowd stood and cheered.

The adulation was amazing, but I was conflicted. It was embarrassing to be singled out when the hard work of other team players was every bit as crucial to a win. I hoped they understood that much of the hoopla was about publicity—not me. And to that end, I was happy to do what I could by doing appearances for the Gems and for the entire League, regardless what the commissioner and some of the team owners had said in the press. I was raised to be a team player, and that wouldn't change. Still, the Gems management and I never did seem to click.

Howie Landa was our coach in New Jersey. He's become a dear friend in the years since the Gems, but back then we didn't see eye to eye. I admit that I came into the league with a chip on my shoulder because of the trade from Houston and what the WBL had said about me. I was guarded. It was in my DNA to be careful when it came to opening up to others, and Lord knows I was never good at small talk. Now I was doubly guarded because of all that had happened in the last few months over the bid with the Pacers.

At UCLA, my brother, David, and I had only been celebrated in the press. The same was true for me at the Olympics and playing on the U.S. Team. I had no idea that sportswriters could be so fickle, or that the WBL would jump on the Ann-bashing bandwagon in order to tag along in the news with the Pacers story and, thereby, get some much-needed publicity. I felt blindsided, and I'm sure poor Howie got the brunt of my whiplash.

There's no doubt that another drawback was that I'd just come from the Pacers organization where I'd been playing with guys who performed at the very highest level, and now I was throwing the ball around with players who struggled to dribble, make lay-ups, and catch the ball. In my aggravation, I alienated people. I know there were more than a few days when I angered Howie.

"You're picking up your left foot, Meyers," he kept saying one day when he had us doing a drill where we'd catch the ball on the wing and then ball-fake the defense, put the ball on the floor, take two dribbles and do a pull-up jumper or go in for a lay-up. I was doing what I did all the time, what the NBA guys did all the time. I would use my left foot to pivot, fake with my right, and then pick up my left foot and put the ball on the ground, which was a travel. Today it's called the Michael Jordan move, but Michael wasn't around back then.

Howie kept taking me back and teaching me the fundamentals, which I already knew. He made me do the move his way six times in a row, and the more I did it, the more frustrated I became. When I got back to the hotel, there was no one to call. Even with the Pacers, I always felt like I could pick up the phone and reach out to people within the camp who were supportive of me. I knew I had Sandy and Bill Knapp on my side. In New Jersey, it was looking as though I would have no one.

I'd plopped myself down on the bed and turned on the TV, hoping to find something that would lighten my dark mood. Flipping through the channels, the phone rang. I figured it was housekeeping, wondering if I needed a change of sheets. "Hello," I said, not bothering to hide the fact that I was dead-tired and in no mood for idle chit chat.

"Hi Annie. It's Don. I just wanted to make sure you got back safe and sound."

Don? Don Drysdale? I couldn't believe he was calling me. It had only been a couple of days since I'd returned from the *Superstars*, but so much had happened it felt like years had passed since we'd had dinner together in the Bahamas and he'd casually asked me to marry him. Now, here he was again. All thoughts of Howie and my frustrations with the Gems vanished.

I smiled into the phone. "What a wonderful surprise."

My heavy heart suddenly felt as light as air, like it wanted to sing. We spent at least a half hour on the phone talking about how much fun we'd had together at dinner, about Mom, Ueckie, the Gems, about everything and anything. I heard that same warning clanging in my head. *Don't get ahead of yourself there, Annie. He's a married man.* Even though the thought kept popping up, I felt a wave of joy travel all the way from the top of my head to the tips of my toes. It was the same tingling sensation I'd had as a child trying to fall asleep on Christmas Eve, knowing that so many wonderful things lie in store for me.

But this wonderful thing could be at the cost of someone else. He's married. I really enjoy his friendship, though, especially now. We can be friends after all. Can't we? I wondered when the cheesy cartoon characters, one with wings, the other with horns and red cape, would sit on either shoulder. I must have been silently wrestling with the voices in my head just a little too long because Donnie spoke up as though sensing my internal struggle.

"Annie, my marriage was over a long, long time ago."

I didn't know what to think. I didn't know him well enough to know when he was teasing or when he was serious. All I knew was that I'd watched my mother's strong sense of herself, her confidence and wherewithal, dissolve little by little at the hands of a husband who would come and go. I would play no part in another's pain. I would never be the *other woman* any more than I would ever let any man do that to me. Still, he seemed so sincere, so nice. I wanted to believe what he was saying was true. I wanted to believe that this whatever-this-was could work out with everyone walking away unhurt.

That night I fell asleep thinking back on a Christmas morning when I was five or six and, as usual, I'd awaken to find a hundred presents magically appearing around our ten-foot tree. But this particular Christmas morning one of my little brothers told Dad that Santa left one less present for him than for the rest of us. About an hour later, another gift-wrapped box somehow showed up under the tree, making it an even count for everyone. I learned much later that Dad, who had spent hours on the road the previous night to be there with us on Christmas morning, had snuck out and searched all over Wheaton for a store opened on Christmas Day.

The memory made me wonder if we were we all just Jeckylls and Hydes...some of us quiet and shy off the court and angrily kicking balls into the stands on the court, while others were sensitive and unselfish in some ways and exactly the opposite when it came to their wives. My final thought as I finally drifted off to sleep was that maybe this was simply part of being human.

13
Burning Up the Courts Like Lava

"If you quell your own anger, your real enemy will be slain."
~ *Nagarjuna*

In January, 1980, we played a home game against the Iowa Cornets. Molly Bolin was one of the best shooters in the league, scoring an average 34 points per game, and this particular night she was on fire. It was going down to the wire with about a minute and thirty seconds left in the game when I went in for a lay-up and got knocked down hard. I'd been labeled the WBL's best, so many of the other players felt compelled to knock me clean off the floor and into the next zip code. I'd get double-teamed and fouled on nearly every single shot and end up with a 35% shooting rate for the season.

My nose started to bleed. Howie called a timeout, and helped me up. "Annie, I'm sorry but you got to come out."

"Get away from me."

"But Annie…"

"Get away from me, Howie. I get paid to *play!*"

I let our trainer, Ron Linfonte, clean me up and pack my nose with gauze to stem the blood flow before running back onto the court. I was painfully conscious of what it was costing the Gems to sign me, and I never wanted to let them down, especially after that first press conference debacle. The front of my jersey was stained pink, but I'd had my nose broken plenty of times, and I didn't think it was broken now. We won that game. Afterward, I apologized to Howie. I wasn't looking for absolution, I just needed him to know that he deserved better.

"Honey, you don't have to be sorry. You're one hell of a competitor." Even though we had our differences, Howie had this great Philly accent and kind face, which made him such a likeable guy. He was like a Jewish father calling us all "honey" and wanting to protect us. He never went by Howard, it was always Howie. He was also a terrific coach—he was the only coach to bring Trenton Community College to two men's championships before coaching the Gems. As a tough player himself, Howie broke every record in the small Philadelphia school he attended, and his jersey was the first to go up in the rafters of the gym.

Ultimately, Howie and I both just wanted the same thing—to win. Later, the N.J. Gems would fire him when he refused to let a player continue to play after suffering a concussion. Howie wanted to win, but not at the expense of his team's health. The WBL, which was often criticized for firing coaches at breakneck speed, saw things differently. They needed return visitors, happy spectators, paying customers, and if it meant allowing those customers to watch the aftermath of a deadly crash, so be it. Soon, the league and I would be on a collision course of our own.

But first the Gems were scheduled to play in California in February, and that was a ray of hope. I would finally see my family. The game was in San Francisco, and everyone drove up to see the game. We all went to dinner afterwards, and then my older sister, Cathy, walked me back to my hotel.

"You've really changed." The look on her face made it painfully clear this wasn't meant as a compliment.

I suddenly felt exposed. I'd been looking forward to seeing my family for weeks, but her observation made me fearful that my frustration with the Gems was seeping out through every pore and coming across…as what? A sense of entitlement? Was I suddenly acting too big for my britches? Cathy seemed to think so, and I worried that it was true. After all, we weren't raised to think that way. I tried explaining that I was just aggravated by the level of some of the talent in the league and it was affecting me because, almost overnight, I'd gone from anticipating a career in the NBA to playing in the WBL.

Cathy's comment made me think. Yes, the adjustment had been tough. I felt like I'd packed for Harvard and ended up at Podunk U, and now I was acting like a spoiled brat because of it. Maybe I resented the fact that I wasn't playing with the Pacers. I tried not to rehash it, but every now and then I thought about Slick and what I considered to be a raw deal. Whether I belonged with the Pacers or not, whether Slick was right or whether I was right, I had to face facts that it was what it was, and there was nothing to gain by dwelling on it—or acting like a little horror.

I was playing for the Gems now. And every time I went out there I felt I needed to demonstrate to the world exactly why I'd been asked to try out for the Pacers, to prove that I was capable of playing as well as some of the NBA players, to dispel any suspicions that my bid was just a publicity stunt.

I was upset with myself. Nothing had changed from that kid on the playground who spent her youth trying to prove that she could play with the big boys.

But just as with every other situation in my life, God had closed a door only to open a window. Don appeared at our next game.

We were playing at the convention center in Long Beach. I'm not sure if it was because Don was there, or Cathy's comment weighed heavily on my mind, or the fact that my family had followed us down from San Francisco, but I wasn't having a good game. I got a technical and picked up three quick fouls in the first two minutes.

Mt. Vesuvius was threatening to blow again, and I took my frustration out on the official. "Cripes! That was a clean play. What do you need glasses?" I kicked my chair, growing hotter and hotter by the second. Ironically enough, we had been in Long Beach when Coach Kenny had first warned me about my temper and the importance of controlling it. I tried to contain myself outwardly. Inside, I seethed.

When the game ended, everyone went to my brother, Mark, and sister-in-law, Frannie's, house for a party, including Don. The moment I stepped through the door, I felt the tension melt away, and I started to relax. Here I was among my clan, feeling right at home, as though New Jersey were some distant planet.

Some of the guests' behavior around Don surprised me. My family wasn't easily impressed, having been around their share of famous people, so I hadn't expected the guests' sense of awe. Many seemed stunned that Don would come to one of my games, let alone show up at the after-party. I wasn't sure what the big deal was. I still didn't comprehend the impact the Dodgers' legacy had on Southern Californians, and maybe Don found my naiveté refreshing. I was too young to appreciate what he'd accomplished in baseball. Had he been a basketball player, it would have been a whole different story.

I enjoyed his company and felt comfortable around him because he seemed so entirely comfortable around me. At UCLA, if a guy actually worked up the nerve to ask me out on date, I got the sense he was behaving a certain way because I was David Meyers's little sister. Later, when I asked Marques Johnson why he or any of the other guys never asked me out in college, he said, "Because Dave would have beat us up."

Don was so comfortable in his own skin and that put me at ease. He knew who he was as a person, and he didn't care what anybody else thought. I got the sense he never felt the need to prove himself to anyone, while I'd been trying to prove myself worthy from day one. Oddly, I didn't feel like I needed to prove anything to Don. The confidence he exuded seemed to spill out onto everyone around him, and now it was spilling over onto me.

The sheer size of my family and their exuberance could be overwhelming, but I figured he should get a picture of what I'm all about—that family means everything to me. When the party ended, I thanked him for coming and we went our separate ways—he, back to ABC and broadcasting for the Angels, and I, back to the East Coast to play for the Gems, where my frustrations with the WBL continued.

One of those frustrations was the high number of technical fouls and their resulting fines. The coaches were going to end up being bled dry if the players weren't careful. While the fine for a technical in the NBA and WBL was the same, $75.00, the WBL coaches were paid roughly $10,000 a year, and the NBA coaches were getting closer to

$250,000. The owners didn't seem to care too much about requests to reduce the amount of the fines, so nearly half of the WBL's coaches would end up being suspended at one time or another for unpaid technicals.

Those were the kinds of rules which seemed to lack common sense. In all likelihood, the high fines in the WBL were the result of a lack of understanding of the costs associated with running a national operation. They hadn't considered how expensive it was to rent NBA stadiums, pay salaries, and accrue travel expenses. We'd be traveling during the mid-season, and a game would suddenly get canceled. It was like the movie *Leatherheads*.

To highlight the point, we had one incident where we flew to New Orleans to play at Tulane University. The flight got in around 1:00 p.m. for a 7:00 p.m. game. After the game, we'd turn around and fly back to Jersey. The problem was what to do with us in those hours before the game started. We weren't about to spend six hours on the streets of New Orleans.

"What do you mean you don't have rooms for us?"

Our owners had nowhere for the twelve of us to hang out in until the game started. So I went to the other players and told them I'd pay for two rooms so we'd have somewhere to put our feet up...and mentioned that I'd take any contributions. Everyone started pulling fives and tens out of their pockets and duffle bags. Of course, this made the Gems management look foolish, so they eventually coughed up the money for two rooms at the Holiday Inn, which came to about $100.

Another time we were playing in Houston and didn't have time to shower after the game. They told us to throw on our sweats over our uniforms and to hightail it out to a bus, which had been assigned a police escort to the airport so we could catch the last flight out of Newark. The point was that it saved the Gems from spending money on hotel rooms. As female athletes, we were used to being treated like second class citizens, but the lack of organization and forethought within the WBL was hard to take, especially after spending time with the Pacers and seeing how things were done in the front office.

In retrospect, I think those involved on the financial end simply didn't understand the concept of a national women's professional basketball league let alone calculating the costs. It didn't take long before teams started folding, and more and more salaries went unpaid. It signaled the beginning of the end, and they were only their second year into it.

Not all my memories with the Gems were bad, however. Some of my teammates became good friends. Donna Geils, from Queens college, went on to become Donna Orender, the president of the WNBA for six years. She and I were a lot alike in that she could spend hours shooting hoops if something was bothering her, using that time to work things out in her head. Faye and Kaye Young were close to my heart because I'd played against them my senior year at UCLA and always thought they were nice and good players. They played for Hall of Fame coach, Kay Yow, at N.C. State. The Young Twins had a national commercial for Dannon Yogurt and became known as the Dannon Yogurt Twins. Their national exposure was helpful in promoting the WBL, which had little, if any, advertising budget.

The WBL loved it when any of its players received national exposure because it helped generate interest in the league. They used the model-like Young twins to its advantage, just as they had capitalized on two extremely attractive players, Molly Bollin and Jane Fincher. Unfortunately, even that became problematic for the league, as Kara Porter chronicled in her book *Mad Seasons*. The perception that attractive blondes were heavily favored in the WBL was becoming widespread, and cries of racism from within the ranks came up all the time, especially with regard to marketing. So it probably didn't help that I had done the 7-Up campaign with Magic Johnson, Sugar Ray Leonard, and some other big sports names, along with a Fuji Film campaign, which had my face on billboards across the country.

Various team owners had publicly commented that the promotion was a way to generate ticket sales, along with trying to counteract female athlete stereotypes at a time when engaging in aggressively competitive endeavors was still considered "unfeminine." Putting too much stock in my looks always seemed like an investment with diminishing returns. I was a basketball player, and I couldn't fathom that being sexy was part of the job description. Professional women's basketball, like professional men's basketball, may have been about putting players in the seats, but I wanted to do it with my talent.

As for the preconception that female athletes were, by and large, gay, that's still something that most women's sports have to contend with. In team sports, whether volleyball, basketball, softball, or soccer, there's a bond among the players which is no different than the men. They all just want to win. Sports, and especially team sports, creates a camaraderie, a tight-knit group of young athletes. Everyone may have his or her own role, but together they have a common goal. They are eating together, showering together, traveling on the road together, and I don't know whether this camaraderie leads to a *misperception* of same sex relationships, or whether it, in fact, engenders same-sex relationships. What I do know is the presumption that many female athletes were gay was never extended to male athletes in the 60s and 70s. If anything, it was just the opposite—male athletes were considered prototypes of masculinity.

If anyone had any questions about my sexuality during my time with the Gems, they were probably answered the first time Don showed up at a game in Jersey when he and Bob Uecker were sent to the East Coast to lay down voice-overs for ABC.

Ever since the party at Mark and Frannie's, Don and I had been talking on the phone at night after games or practice. It had been nice to have someone to share my frustrations with, to laugh with. Every day I looked forward to hearing his voice. It was even more thrilling to see him here, in the flesh, and the Gems had won, to boot.

It was nearly midnight by the time I got out of the gym. I'd showered and let my adrenaline simmer down so I could finally eat. Adrenaline is a great thing, and every player gets amped before a game. But knowing Donnie was there kicked my adrenaline into high gear. In addition to that, I had a routine of not eating four hours before a game, so by now I was starved. The only place open at that late hour was Howard Johnsons, so the three of us shared a brown plastic-upholstered booth and Formica table, ordered, and waited for our meals.

"Do you guys sit around naked in the locker room and talk about the game?" Only Ueckie could ask such a question.

I was taken aback and embarrassed until I realized it was a legitimate question. After all, that's what the guys did after a game, at least in Donnie and Ueckie's day. "No. I'm the only player from the West Coast and I guess I sorta keep to myself."

I heard the words come out of my mouth and immediately bit my tongue. I wanted to feel a sense of camaraderie with my teammates, so why was I keeping myself isolated? It was important to be able to talk about what happened after a game, to learn from it, to bond. If I was lonely in Jersey, it was my own fault. I'm sure there were teammates there who could have been possible allies in that impossible league, women who shared my frustrations, but I couldn't see that then. That's the problem with carrying a chip on your shoulder—it blocks your peripheral vision, making it tough to see the bigger picture.

But Ueckie went on as if he hadn't heard me. "When Don asked me if I wanted to see a game tonight, I thought maybe we were going to watch the Knicks." His smile widened. "Then when we got in the limo and headed out to Jersey, I thought maybe it was Seton Hall, Princeton, or Rutgers."

Don had told Ueckie he wanted to watch a player, but he hadn't told him *which* player. Not until the limo pulled into the Dunn High School parking lot and they walked into the Dunn High gym, did Ueckie figure out that it was some *girl* they'd come to watch. And not just *some* girl, but me.

The waitress came with our food, and I noticed the same thing I'd noticed in the Bahamas, that people instantly recognized Don and treated him with a near-reverent respect. But he didn't seem to care. He was equally nice to everyone, whether it was a young waiter who didn't recognize him or a die-hard Bums fan who knew him from back in the days when he was playing in Brooklyn for the Dodgers.

The conversation that night went in and out of sports, in and out of baseball and basketball, in and out of Ueckie's jokes. At night when Don and I talked on the phone, it was about so much more than the Gems. But when the topic did turn to sports, he always respected my opinion. He was different from other men that way. He understood we were both athletes, and he treated my view as being just as valid as his. Talking to him in person was wonderful. He looked good, and was obviously getting plenty of that California sunshine that I was missing.

Don was very kind, very confident, very handsome, very exciting and very smart. Unfortunately he was also still *very* married. Separated from his wife or not, I kept our relationship platonic because my Catholic guilt wouldn't have it any other way. And to his credit, he was a perfect gentleman. But as the weeks went on and our conversations continued, they became more personal and more frequent. Though I told myself we were just friends, deep down I knew I was falling in love.

14
Waiting It Out

"I never realized until later in life that women were supposed to be the inferior sex."
~ Katherine Hepburn

At the end of the '79/'80 season, I was named MVP alongside Molly Bolin. However, there was no fanfare, no publicity, and no celebration within the organization, whatsoever. I should have taken that to be another bad omen, but I still wanted to believe everything would turn out for the best. I returned to the West Coast for the off-season and got the shock of my life when a Gems' check to me for $10,000 bounced. I waited for them to make it good, but it wasn't going to happen, so I decided to sit out the following season's games until they paid me in full for the first season.

I also decided to take the *Superstars* up on their offer to compete in the upcoming event, and this time I would be ready.

I trained throughout the summer, well in advance of the December event, and let Papa's words ring continuously in my head: "Failing to prepare is preparing to fail." I didn't have time to prepare for the first go around because I was busy broadcasting for the Pacers and playing pro-ball with the Gems. But now I had a strategy. Not only did I know *which* sports to participate in, but just as importantly, the *order*.

Since I was sitting out all of the Gems' games, I was able to devote myself entirely to training for the *Superstars* event. As with everything that happened in the WBL, it seemed this, too, would be spun to my disadvantage. There was talk within the league and speculation among the press that I wanted to renegotiate my contract for more pay. "No one is quite sure where Ann Meyers is," wrote the *Post Dispatch*. "We'd like to know where she is, too," a spokesperson from the Gems told the paper. It was frustrating because management knew exactly where I was. I was waiting to be paid in full for the previous season.

My relationship with the WBL had been fraught from the beginning, yet I tried to make an earnest go of it. I'd made umpteen appearances for them and shown up for dozens of dinners and receptions with sponsors, all unpaid. I had no obligation under my contract to make these promotional appearances, but I did it because I knew how important it was to promote the league and the N.J. Gems, and in return they wrote me a bad check for $10,000. It was literally a federal offense.

I spoke to David endlessly about whether or not I should bite the bullet and return to play for the Gems and hope for the best. Part of me wanted him to say that I should return to New Jersey because I wanted to play basketball so badly. But there was a principle involved which neither David nor I could ignore. It wasn't about the money, but about how a professional player deserved to be treated, and the Gems treated their players like they were doing us a favor by allowing us to play a sport we loved.

Blaze tried to change my mind. "You gotta come back, Annie. With you and me, the Gems would smoke every other team in the league."

I sympathized with her because she had experienced her fair share of frustration. Blaze had made the '80 Olympics. however, with the boycott, there was no '80 team. Now that she had signed on with the Gems, she wanted me there with her.

"I want to, Blaze, I really do." And I meant it. She and I had played with and against each other on several teams over the years, and not only did I respect her as a player, but we'd become good friends. But that wasn't a big enough reason to go back. I talked over the situation with Don, whom I'd been seeing a lot more of since I'd returned to the West Coast. He agreed with me that I should wait for the Gems to pay me.

By now Don had told me he loved me, and I knew that I loved him, but I didn't know how things would turn out. Just like the untenable situation with the Gems, I had to have faith that things would fall into place between Donnie and me. I didn't worry about it. Instead, I directed my energy toward training for the upcoming *Superstars*. And there, I didn't need hope or faith. Now that I had developed my strategy, I knew I could rely on that and my ability coupled with hard work.

Since the Gems still hadn't made good on the money they owed me, I had the time to train for six to eight hours a day, preparing physically and mentally. It was a grueling schedule. I worked out with a swimming coach a couple of times a week, learning how to properly turn on the wall and stroke correctly. After that, I would drive up to L.A. and work with my old Olympic trainer, Gail Weldon, who owned a health club. She would set me up lifting weights and working with her for about an hour before I would go down to the local high school to run the stairs and the track.

One of the events I chose was rowing, so I ended my day by driving to Long Beach where my friend, Monica Havelka, was a rower. We'd get in a boat and row for a few miles. I also played a good deal of tennis with Dan Campbell, the tennis coach at Long Beach State, where he helped me work on my serve, backhand, and conditioning. I also hit hundreds of golf balls, working on my chipping and drive. By the time my second *Superstars* came, I was completely confident it was mine to win.

Among the other contestants that year were Martina Navratilova, Rosie Casals, the long-time rebel of women's tennis, who, along with Billie Jean King, was one of the driving forces behind equalizing award payments to female and male tennis players, and Lynette Woodard, an All-American basketball player from the University of Kansas who later made headlines in 1985 as the first female Harlem Globetrotter.

I couldn't help but smile when I learned Lynette began shooting baskets as a little girl using a stuffed sock. She wasn't the only one who developed fierce determination at a young age. Ironically, Trotter player, Fred 'Curly' Neal, first approached me with his idea of having a woman on the Globetrotters in the summer of 1984, but *TV*

Guide ran with the story prematurely. Ultimately, Curly and I decided that the team should remain all African-American. Lynette's cousin, Hubert "Geese" Ausbie, was a Globetrotter, and Lynette seemed the perfect candidate. During Lynette's tryout, she graciously told the press that it was my signing with the Pacers that gave her the courage to do it.

This year's *Superstars* took place in Florida, which was a perfect excuse for a Meyers family get-together. Of course Don and Ueckie were there broadcasting for ABC.

I hoped it would be an opportunity for Mom to get to know Donnie a little better. It was hard for me to tell whether she liked him as much as she did when she'd first met him. It was now obvious to her that we were becoming very close and I'm sure she worried about our age difference and his strong personality. She probably wondered if he was too fixed in his ways. It was true Don knew exactly what he wanted, and he usually got it, but I considered that to be an admirable trait. Mom saw things differently. She understood better than anyone how basically timid I was when it came to most things outside of sports and she had always been my protector because of that. I think she worried I might get in over my head with Don. She had no reason to worry, though, not about Donnie, or anything else.

Florida's heat and humidity weren't going to take their toll on me as had happened the previous year in the Bahamas. This time, I carefully considered the hour of the day that I'd have to compete in the most strenuous events. I chose the 100 yd. dash, the obstacle course, chipping, swimming, the quarter mile, and rowing. I ran a quarter-mile in under a minute, set an obstacle course record, won the tennis event, landed six inches from the cup on an 80-yard chip, and ultimately came in first overall to win that year's Women's *Superstars,* and the $50,000 purse. My win must have sent some executives' minds into overdrive because I was thrilled at what came next.

"How would you like to be the only woman ever invited to participate in the Men's *Superstars?*"

I couldn't believe what I was hearing. "Wow! Really?"

TWI and ABC, the event organizers, were asking me to do what I had loved, what I had missed, and what I had always used as a benchmark to judge my performance: compete with the guys. Well, they didn't have to ask me twice. Luckily they didn't bother looking for feedback from any of the other contenders—probably because they knew what their answers would be.

"Why the hell are they letting her compete with the men?" Rick Barry asked his wife and some friends at a table nearby. Sadly, he wasn't the only one cursing about my participation. ABC knew that asking me to compete in the Men's event would create a commotion, which would get them excellent press—and that was a good thing as far as any TV network was concerned. They also knew I was the only woman who would give the guys a run for their money. Unlike the Pacers tryout, there was no trial by media this time, just a good natured "let's see what she can do" attitude. That sure wasn't how some of the other competitors felt, however. Especially Rick.

Rick Barry was, and still is, considered one of the great small forwards of all time. He and I were good friends from our Vegas days playing tennis. But friends were one thing. He was a lethal perimeter threat, and he wasn't thrilled about my being one of his competitors—on national television, no less. Part of me understood. Then, as now, it's a no-win situation for a man to be seen as challenging a woman. To his credit, Rick wanted the same quality competition I was looking for, but why was he making the presumption that I would be his inferior just because I was a woman? First give me a chance.

The Men's *Superstars* followed directly on the heels of the Women's *Superstars,* which meant I would have no time to calculate the weaknesses of my opponents or train for some of the events, like the soccer kick, or be able to devise an overall strategy.

Mom had overheard Rick's remark and was hotter than a wet hen. "He's got some nerve. I heard other comments, but Rick is supposed to be your friend."

"Oh Mom, don't worry about it. It's no big deal."

He hadn't hurt my feelings. It was simply par for the course, something I'd run up against time and time again, and nothing to get riled about. But she was still fuming. We hadn't been inside the room but maybe a minute when the phone rang. It was Rick asking me if I wanted to play tennis.

"See?" I told her, "He didn't mean anything by it."

The male ego can be an unpredictable apparatus. Like a light bulb improperly screwed into a socket, it can go on and off without warning, and I'd learned early on to tread lightly around it. The funny thing was that Rick was one of the most confident guys I'd ever met. He had this highly unorthodox, but incredibly accurate, underhanded free-throw shot. Had we both been allowed to compete in the Hoop event, the press might have had a field-day with the two of us, including Rick's style "shooting like a girl," and Rick wouldn't have cared one whit. He'd grown up being ridiculed for that shot. But when you were as good as he was, it didn't matter because it was natural for him. And, in fact, it's a more natural way to shoot the ball. Wilt was known to do it as well on occasion. But when someone tried to teach Shaq to throw underhanded, his ego wouldn't allow him to try. Rick didn't care. He knew the ball was going in, and that's all that mattered.

Some of the other men competing against me and Rick that year were Edwin Moses, the Olympic sprinter who had run hundreds of races in a row without losing once, New England Patriot's football player, Russ Francis, and Renaldo Nehemiah, the 110 meter hurdler world-record holder and the first man to run the high hurdles in under thirteen seconds.

Before the event, I received a card from Yvette Duran, a former roommate at UCLA. She had hand-written the letters 'WO' and 'S,' in strategic places, turning the gender specific sentiment upside down on its chauvinist head.

Life's battles don't always go to the strongest WOman; but sooner or later, the WOman who wins is the WOman who thinks She can

I taped it to the mirror in the bathroom and fixated on it every morning and night while I brushed my teeth. I knew if I didn't believe in myself, I didn't stand a chance. I was like Demosthenes, only I had toothpaste foam dribbling down either corner of my mouth instead of marbles tumbling out. Even if I didn't come in first, I knew I wouldn't lose.

From the events I chose, I did well in the swimming and the soccer kick, and equally as well in tennis and running. The men's obstacle course was much tougher than the one for the women, and I was up against a couple of the world's greatest track athletes. Still, I gave it everything I had. I didn't come in first at the Men's *Superstars*, but I didn't come in last. I was in the money. Should I need one, my war chest was growing.

I flew back to California, where I proceeded to dig in my heels and wait out the full amount due me for the first season with the Gems, who were in the process of repossessing the car they'd given me, and which I'd driven out over the summer. It was clear we were at an impasse.

I flew to Omaha to talk to the owners of a new WBL franchise. I wanted to play and I didn't care how much they paid me. As I went through the practices, I couldn't help but notice that the other players seemed skeptical. I guess I couldn't blame them. After seeing two year's worth of headlines calling me everything from a savior to a demon, no doubt my name left a bad taste in their mouth. Ultimately, I'd never suit up because the owners felt signing me presented too big a risk because the New Jersey Gems were still claiming me as theirs and telling everybody they were just waiting for me to return before they'd pay me.

The owners shrugged in frustration. "They could yank our franchise, Annie."

Meanwhile, I was waiting to get paid before I'd return. Good thing I didn't hold my breath. More and more signs were popping up that the WBL was not long for this world, and this time the rumblings appeared on the West Coast. *The Orange County Register* had done an expose on the California Dreams team, which had enrolled its players in the John Robert Powers Charm School the previous season. The players weren't at all pleased about being made to learn how to walk, talk, eat, dress, and apply make-up. No doubt it was another lame attempt to doll-up team members in order to debunk sponsors' fears that the players were simply too unfeminine and/or too unattractive.

It was a replay of what had happened forty years ago, when the All-American Girls Professional Baseball League required players to attend Rubinstein's Evening Charm School Classes during spring training. The league, which was formed as a way of keeping baseball in the American zeitgeist while its players were off fighting the Germans, also required that the women wear lipstick under the three strike rule. The first infraction cost $5, the second would put a player back $10, and the third got you suspended. Here we were forty years later and nothing had changed.

Far more scathing for the WBL than reports of the charm school, however, were players' complaints that they hadn't been paid and were refusing to play. Little waves soon spread throughout the sports world of the WBL's financial instability, which tainted the possibility of endorsements and television contracts — something the league desperately needed if it was going to stay afloat. And then the tsunami hit. *The New York Times* reported that the WBL was showing only "feeble flickers of life," having racked up $14 million in losses in its three years. Among their many unpaid obligations was the better part of my $145,000 contract.

An arbitration ruling was issued in May of 1981, but by then I'd long since given up any hope of resolving the situation, and the league was on the verge of collapse anyway. Besides, the money wasn't the issue; it was the principle of the thing.

Just as I was coming to terms (or, rather, not coming to terms) with the Gems, David decided not to re-sign with the Milwaukee Bucks for a sixth season. The GM of the Bucks, Wayne Embry, called Coach Wooden. "Why isn't Meyers signing with us? Does he want more money? Is he really that greedy?"

Papa's response was simple. "You really don't know David, do you?"

David was coming off a back injury, and he wanted to spend more time with his family. He had also become more involved in his church and decided to take a job teaching in Temecula. Sure, the money from basketball was great, but Dave and I played basketball because we loved it, because it was as vital to us as sunlight is to a plant. And Papa knew that.

It would be an odd thing that my relationship with John Wooden would develop more deeply after we had both left UCLA, though I don't know that he ever *really* left. What he did there was unrivaled with his ten championships in twelve years, and I think that until the day he died, UCLA remained as much his home as the house he shared with Nellie. Papa used to say that the importance of basketball was small in comparison to the total life one lived, and that the only kind of life that truly won was a life that placed itself in the service of others and in the hands of God. His love of UCLA had more to do with the friendships he made there, and for that reason he could often be found on campus walking the track or just hanging out in his office long after his coaching days.

It was wonderful that I and anyone who loved him knew where to find Papa, whether for guidance or just a chat. Either way, his Pyramid of Success and his 'Woodenisms', which had as much to do with how one lived one's life as with how to play basketball, were never far away:

"Work hard constantly to improve."

"Be quick, but don't hurry."

Sometimes we would talk about family or career, but always it boiled down to contribution—contribution to the family, to the team, to society, and to the world. And that included the small world of Southern California and their multitude of charity fundraisers.

Then, just as now, most all So Cal athletes were part of a tight-knit group that knew each other well. Being on the board of the California Sports Council and the So. California Olympic Association, I commonly ran into local athletes at various events. Along with family, I had missed seeing these friends while I was on the East Coast. Finally, I was once again enjoying that same wonderful camaraderie and making some new memories to go along with the old ones—like the time Hugh Hefner held a fundraising event for Mayor Tom Bradley at the Playboy Mansion.

I had asked my brother, Mark, to come with me. We arrived in my Toyota Corona, which seemed out of place on a street lined with Bentleys, Ferraris, Porsche's, and limos. At the party, Rosey Grier and Elgin Baylor recognized me and came over to talk with us. At the end of the evening we all left the Mansion together and both men groaned about how they'd parked far away. Since my car was close, I offered to give them rides to their cars. Mark was 6'3", Rosey was 6'4", and Elgin was 6'5", and somehow we all managed to stuff inside my little Corona for thirty seconds.

The Southern California athletes weren't confined to fundraising in, or for, Southern California charities. Every year Howard Cosell held a dinner in New York to raise money for the families of the slain Israeli athletes of the '72 Olympics. In 1981, I was one of the athletes being honored. I had already met many famous people by this point and been on *The Tonight Show*, the cover of sports magazines, and featured in every newspaper and rag from *Time* to *Playgirl*. But that evening, when Muhammad Ali walked in late with Don King, it was as though the Messiah himself had stepped through the door. I had never seen anyone with such charisma, such magnetism. He was like a vortex, sucking all eyes his way. And it wasn't simply that he was the most famous athlete in the world. He was overpowering in terms of sheer presence. Who needed ten rounds when you had a hypnotist's ability to transfix your opponent before sending him to the mat with a well-timed jab.

As remarkable as it was to meet Ali, there was still nothing quite like that warm feeling of running into a fellow-alum like Mark Harmon. Mark had played football for UCLA in the early 70s, and was now beginning his television career hosting a local talk show. He had invited Ron Howard and me to appear. Before the couch discussion, he taped the two of us playing one-on-one basketball. Ron loved basketball, was a huge fan, and he wasn't a half-bad player. He came in second.

Of course, I liked to tell Papa all of these stories. Like Mark, Tom Bradley had been an athlete at UCLA running track before going on to become Mayor of Los Angeles. Papa always enjoyed hearing about UCLA athletes who were going on to do other things. Now it was I who was getting serious about a new career.

Since the WBL had folded, there was no way for a female basketball player to make a living doing what she loved, and I didn't see how my sociology degree would net me what I'd made as an athlete. Mark's dad, Tom Harmon, the great 1940 Heisman-winning Michigan football player and broadcaster for the Raiders, took me under his wing and suggested I get into broadcasting. While I had taken Art Friedman's classes at UCLA and had already broadcast a couple of the UCLA Men's games with Ross Porter for Prime Ticket when it launched back in '79 before broadcasting for the Pacers, I hadn't decided to really pursue it until now. Don said if I intended to get serious, I should enroll in the Don Martin School of Broadcasting in Los Angeles. He said it was the best.

There were a few actors I recognized, but I don't recall seeing one woman there. Broadcasting was still very much a boys' club. We learned to work both sides of the camera, and I immediately felt comfortable because I had broadcast professionally for the Pacers.

But *feeling* like a pro was what mattered. I had to believe in myself in front of the camera the same way I believed in myself on the court. I learned to center my voice, never let a sentence trail off at the end, and became aware of how subtle nuances like tone, inflection, and depth affected the credence others gave to our words. For instance, more credibility was placed with a deep voice as opposed to a high, thin voice. But it was especially important that as a female broadcaster, who naturally had a higher voice, I learned to center my words.

Don knew I hoped to broadcast basketball for the networks, so he arranged an appointment with an agent in Hollywood. I'll never forget what he told me. "Well, Annie, you're going to have to grow your hair and nails." His expression conveyed that he thought I was crazy for not thinking it myself. I'd summoned all the confidence in the world before marching into his office, and now I felt like I was auditioning for Miss America.

I could feel that confidence plummeting. "But I have a lot of knowledge about the game," I said, centered voice and all.

"I'm sure you do, but come on, everybody knows sex sells."

I could feel myself crawling back into my shell, the one that I'd constructed as a child the first time someone made fun of the way I dressed, or that I preferred to play with my plastic horses over Barbie dolls. I smiled and thanked him for his time.

He sensed that his suggestion had deflated me. "You never know. You might get a break."

I extended my hand — with its naked, unpolished nails — and we shook.

There were a lot of variables in the world of broadcasting that I couldn't control. I thought about trying to conform to the tastes of whoever might hire me. Everybody knew that you had to be attractive if you wanted to work on television, but I thought I was okay looking. I'd already jumped through hair-hoops in high school (though it was in the opposite direction) and they still didn't accept me. As for my nails, well they just wouldn't grow, no matter what, and I wasn't about to have those fake things put on. Instead, I decided I'd have to become as good a sports broadcaster as possible.

I became aware of diction, proper pronunciation, and hitting my mark. I learned that when covering a game, it was vital to research the players beforehand and take note of interesting details so I could relay them back to the audience in a succinct and comprehensible way. As a shy child, I'd always been observant, peering in from the outside. Only now, I discovered what I'd long considered a weakness was, in fact, a strength. I wasn't going to grow my hair and nails, but I was going to find my voice off the courts now.

After sending out what must have amounted to miles and miles worth of demo tapes, I finally received a call from KGMB, the station that covered the University of Hawaii's men's basketball games. I had no contacts there, but someone was willing to give me a chance. The Sunday Sports section of the *Honolulu Star* ran a picture of me smiling, wearing headphones, and a lei. The caption read, "Ann Meyers—She's Pretty, But Effective" as though it were an oxymoron. "She knows a zone press isn't a device for ironing," the piece went on to say. It was hard to keep from groaning.

When I was doing the color commentary in Hawaii, I explained the game in layman's terms, and if I felt there was a bad call, I wasn't afraid to say it. I made sure it was always about the players, never about me. Still, my stint there didn't sit too well with a lot of the folks. I knew there'd be people who expected to find a man doing my job. What I didn't realize, however, was that the former men's coach had been doing color for the games for years, and neither he nor his players understood why he was suddenly being replaced.

For my part, I was just grateful to land a paying job in the world of broadcasting, and grateful someone at KGMB had decided it was time to mix things up at the station. But there were other frontiers, namely network television.

Once the season contract was up, I decided to leave Hawaii and set my sights on a national broadcasting gig. I headed back to California and continued to train for the upcoming *Superstars*. While I was trying new things, I also decided to test my luck at a new sport.

Golf was possibly the only sport I didn't play as a child. I remember that on the one occasion I tagged along with Patty to a golf course, I swung the club, and it went further than the ball. I'd chipped away endlessly in preparation for the previous *Superstars*, and now I was beginning to hone the other parts of my game by playing with Donnie.

Once I got good enough, Don introduced me to Lou Rosanova. Lou had played football for the Cleveland Rams in the 40s before buying a golf course in Savannah, Georgia, and then later the Calusa Country Club in Miami. Donnie said Lou was a great teacher and since he often traveled to the West Coast, maybe he could improve my game. I was eager to play with him at the L.A. Country Club, but hit an unforeseen snag.

"I'm sorry, Ms. Meyers, but women aren't allowed to wear slacks on the range, or the course."

I couldn't believe it. I was going to take my first golf lesson with the great Lou Rosanova, only I couldn't because I was wearing pants! It was just like being out on the school playground again and people were telling me I couldn't do this or that because I was a girl.

"Well, what am I supposed to wear then?"

"We have lovely golf skirts you can rent."

RENT?

Coming from a long line of hand-me-down recipients, I wasn't opposed to wearing used clothes, but *leasing* them sounded plain weird. Not seeing any other choice, I rented the skirt and marched out onto the course—club in hand, smile on my face, and white socks pulled up to my shins.

Lou bent over laughing as he stared at my socks. "You look like a Polack!" Lou was 6'1" with a full head of gray black hair and an Italian accent. He reminded me of Luca Brasi in *The Godfather*.

I shrugged. "They said no slacks."

"Well, at least fold your socks down."

I didn't realize the first lesson would be on fashion. *Note to self: High socks are not in vogue. Pants are poison.* I wanted to tell Lou that I *was* a quarter Polish on my Dad's side, but I didn't want to embarrass him. Turned out the only thing that embarrassed Lou was a missed shot, mine or one of his other students. Lou never missed.

Lou was brash, unrelenting, and confident. I liked him immediately. I flew to his golf course in Florida, and we practiced eight hours a day. In two weeks he was getting golf magic from me. If he wanted a fade, I'd hit a fade. If he wanted it high, I'd hit it high. I learned to hit the ball low into the wind, or high over a bunker— whatever he told me to do, I could do it. He was a terrific teacher, and I wanted so badly to please him. I quickly got down to a six handicap and began loving the game the way you have to if you want to go pro. Lou had conjured up the same kind of magic from LPGA players Dale Eggling and Hollis Stacey. Now he was encouraging me to follow in their spikes.

15
Gal's Got Game

"How good does a female athlete have to be before we just call her an athlete?"
~ *Anonymous*

I returned to California where I played in various celebrity golf tournaments and did quite well. In the spring of 1983, I was invited to play in the Dinah Shore Golf Tournament as a celebrity. Until that point it was exclusively male celebs who had been invited to play, and I was the first celebrity woman to be invited (other than Dinah). Of course, to me, all of the LPGA players were celebrities.

It was a shotgun scramble format, which meant you played as a team of four amateurs and a celebrity. Each player on the team would drive, with the best drive used by all players on the team as the spot for taking the second shot and so forth, with the team always playing the best ball. I got to hit from the women's tees, which gave my team a huge advantage since I could drive the ball just as far as the lady pros and land on the green.

"What are you letting her do that for?" some of the guys on the other teams would yell. Between my driving and a couple of my partners' putting, we were unbeatable.

I continued to play golf, entering several charity tournaments in Beverly Hills, Las Vegas, Bel Air, and I kept playing with Lou Rosanova and Tom Harmon. The fact that Lou got me down to a six in two weeks made me think that, perhaps, I really could join the LPGA. *Was I nuts?* Maybe. But Donnie was behind me all the way, even though we both knew it would mean my going on the road. I had already done that with basketball, and I knew that trying to go pro would be a huge commitment. And even *if* I got my card, it didn't mean I'd necessarily win tournaments. After much thought, I chose to stay in California and spend more time with Donnie. He was a hard man not to want to be around. I also began doing more broadcasting and promotional work for Buick and Fuji, two of the upcoming Olympic sponsors, and I was working for Sports Channel in Chicago. This turned out to be terrific because Don was broadcasting the Chicago White Sox games, so we could spend lots of time together. When Don's season was over, I stayed with my dad who was now living in Chicago with a lady friend. While I was glad to have a place to lay my head, it put me in that same conflicted situation familiar to every child of divorced parents.

During my off season, I continued to train for the upcoming *Superstars*. The ABC Sports Show had been airing since 1973, and it had seen its share of famous Olympic athletes attempting to shine in sports they weren't known for, and nearly killing themselves in the process. I still shudder over the time Joe Frazier nearly drowned. In the very first event, the 50 meter swimming heats, Frazier was clearly in trouble. After he was retrieved from the pool, he admitted to commentators that he didn't know how to swim. When asked why he would choose that event, Frazier replied, "How was I to know I couldn't unless I tried?"

It's hard to argue with that logic.

By now, I had won the previous two women's events, and while I'd helped drive up the ratings in 1981 competing in the men's event, the rules said that once you won three *Superstars*, you were done, so I knew this would be my last. In the months leading up to the event I kept getting sick. I'd been running around so much and working out so hard that I was continuously getting sick and not getting better.

My doctor suggested I have my tonsils removed. *Do I leave them in and continue to get sick, or have my tonsils out right before the Superstars knowing I won't be able to eat for awhile afterward?* I decided to have them yanked. I was twenty-seven. Don was working in Chicago, so Mom stayed in the hospital with me.

My sister Cathy came to see me a week before the event and noticed I'd lost weight. "You're too thin! How do you expect to compete?"

I knew I'd also lost a little strength, but I was still hitting tennis balls, running hills, and taking swimming lessons in preparation for the event. I had to. I was counting on that purse from the *Superstars*. The event that concerned me the most was the obstacle course.

Each competitor would run, hit a wall, climb the wall, high-step through tires, swing through monkey bars, then jump over the water, run to the high jump bar, roll into the pit, roll out, do two hurdles, and cross the finish line. The high jump bar was only 4 ft. high. Most athletes would jump over the bar and somersault into the pit.

I knew I could save time by jumping over with both feet tucked underneath me so I could quickly hop out of the pit, rather than have to get up after rolling. Lynnette Woodard was competing again in this year's *Superstars*, and she was the one I had to beat. She was like a race-horse, she was so fast. Even though I'd lost some of my strength, I was able to shave seconds off my time at the high jump.

That year I placed in the swimming, came in second in tennis, won the quarter, placed top three in the 100, came in first in the golf, got points in rowing, and won the obstacle course. I came in first overall, and won my third and final *Superstars*.

The show remained popular for a few more years before losing its appeal. Once you've lost your audience, it doesn't matter if conjoined twins are competing because it's hard to resuscitate a thing once it's run its course—whether it's a basketball league, a TV series, or a marriage.

Don had been married to Ginger Dubberly for nearly twenty-five years. Don's divorce was official now, and he asked me, again, to marry him. My heart said *maybe*, but I worried that his parents and his grown daughter, Kelly, might think he was rushing into things— or worse, that I had been the cause of the divorce. Everything was fine just the way it was.

While I intended to stay Ann Elizabeth Meyers a little while longer, I still wanted to spend time with Don, so I began looking for a place to buy in Palm Springs, the golf capital of the world. Don had maintained a home in nearby Rancho Mirage for years. I'd been living at home with Mom and my younger siblings in La Habra since returning from New Jersey, but between the *Superstars* winnings, the money from the Gems, and the KGMB gig, I'd earned enough to buy my own place. Several of my siblings had places or timeshares in the desert. My family knew it was good vacation spot. There was golf, great weather, smart real estate, and, of course, there was Don.

By now it was pretty clear to my family that we were getting very serious. It turned out that my sister-in-law, Frannie, had suspected we'd end up together from the first day she met him, and confided in me while we were out house hunting. "I told Mark I could see from the way he looked at you in the Bahamas, 'that's the man who will take care of our Annie.'"

I never did end up buying a place in the desert. Instead, I ended up buying a condo elsewhere, which turned out to be a great investment. But I still spent time with Donnie out in Palm Springs working on my golf game.

"What are you doing here, big guy?" I teased him one day out on the course. "Shouldn't you be shooting from the *men's* tees?"

"These *are* the men's tees," he said, pointing out the large black-painted cement representations of golf balls on either side of the divot-marked swath of grass.

"Well, then I guess we'll *both* be shooting from the men's tees."

When I first started out playing golf, Donnie was supportive and offered good advice. "You're not keeping your head down," he'd tell me if I hit a shot I didn't like. "You've got to swing through the ball."

"When you're shooting even par, *then* you can tell me what to do," I'd say back. I was no longer a six handicap since I wasn't working regularly with Lou anymore. Now I was about a ten, but I was still giving Donnie a run for his money.

I remember one time we'd just teed off, and I'd landed right in the middle of the fairway, a good 220 yards out from the tee box, 150 yards away from the green. I took out my six iron, swung, never taking my eye off the ball, and landed on the green not far from the pin. Donnie smiled. He was supportive alright, but he was also every bit as competitive as I was.

"Beat that," I said.

"In golf, you're competing against yourself. It's you against the course," he told me very matter-of-factly, as he had so many times before. But this time he wasn't smiling. He looked through his bag and finally grabbed his Wilson 8 iron. *Ping!* The club made solid contact, sending that crisp pop that's music to any golfer's ear down the length of the fairway, right along with the ball, which landed on the green right next to mine. Okay, so Donnie could give me a run for my money, too.

We were pretty well matched on the golf course, but I was always looking to do something athletic, like a rabbit hopping around. I'd often go out for a run. "Why don't you come with me?" I asked him one day

"I did all that when I was with the Dodgers," he'd say. "I don't need to do it anymore." Of course! The poor guy had a bad shoulder and a bad knee from his baseball days.

Baseball had defined Don's life from the time he was a young boy. That he would grow up to define how the games' players were treated was something I'm sure he never could have imagined. The Drysdale-Koufax 1-2 pitching combination had helped win the World Series in '63 and '65, but it was the Big Holdout of '66 that became a defining moment for baseball players. Don and Sandy had formed their own mini union to negotiate for better pay. It was a calculated, ground-breaking move, and it rattled the baseball world like nothing before. The games' two best pitchers were refusing to sign unless each could get paid what he believed he was worth. I was only eleven at the time, but everyone's parents had read about it, sometimes quoting sportswriters who cast the two as villains. To the players, however, they were heroes.

That year, Donnie took me back to his home away from home in Vero Beach, Florida, where the Dodgers held fantasy baseball camps every year for adults who wanted to play with giants like Duke Snider, Carl Erskine, PeeWee Reese, Roy Campanella, Don Newcombe, and Don Drysdale. Following the fantasy camp, the Dodgers held a Hall of Fame camp with guys like Hank Aaron,

Brooks Robinson, and Sandy Koufax, all of Don's friends from the baseball world. The first time I went, I couldn't believe it.

Dodgers Owner, Peter O'Malley, was the Walt Disney of baseball. There were basketball courts, tennis courts, an Olympic-sized pool, and a carnival day. In February, Mr. O'Malley had Santa show up to hand out Christmas gifts, and he saw to it that everything was done in a family atmosphere. There were theme nights like Western Night, where everybody would wear jeans and hats and eat BBQ. It was surreal seeing baseball icons sitting around a fire, licking their fingers while recalling the old days. They were men in their twenties right up through their seventies, and everybody wanted to rehash old games. It was Dodgertown, and they were inviting me to become part of the Dodger family.

Donnie and I went back every year, but it was in 1983, when I was shooting hoops, that Tommy Lasorda first came over and challenged me to a game of pick-up. As manager, he'd helped the Dodgers win the World Series two years before, and he was feeling pretty darn good about himself. "Come on hot shot, show me what you got."

Though Tommy was quite a bit older than I, he still thought he had game. He'd just come off the diamond pitching batting practice and now he was willing to see if he could beat me at basketball. On offense, he couldn't get the ball from me. He'd get frustrated and talk trash, and knock me down to the ground. He figured if he was physical with me, I'd back down on him. A few people started to gather, including the Dodger photographer, who took some pictures. Tommy's face started getting a little red. He was getting winded and that made him even madder. The more he tried to knock me down, the more I went past him and scored. By the end a nice little crowd had gathered and some of the guys started razzing him.

"I want a rematch," he said. "You didn't play fair."

I loved that Tommy was so tough, so competitive. He was great.

All of the camaraderie aside, regardless of where we were—Florida at Dodgertown, or in Chicago with the White Sox, or at home in California—when Sundays came around I went to Mass.

"It's her thing," Donnie would say if anyone asked where I was. Going to church on Sundays was more than just my thing, it was something I couldn't get away from, even when I tried. My first time away from home playing with the Women's National Team, Juliene Simpson ended up dragging me to Mass on Sundays when we were on the road. Here I thought I'd finally caught a break from going to church, being out of Mom's sight, but Juliene was a devout Catholic, and she wouldn't dream of letting my soul get dusty, even for a weekend. By now my faith had become ingrained.

Hope and faith had seen my family and me through so many near misses from as far back as I could remember. Without it I'd have been like a dingy adrift in a storm. Instead, God looked after us. There was the time my younger brother, Jeff, and I suffered third degree burns over most of our bodies. We were five and three, and had been playing too near an open water heater flame with the gas can my dad kept in the garage for the lawn mower. There was a big explosion and the next thing I knew doctors were pealing away the dead skin, strip by strip. It was painful, and the stench of burned hair and flesh is something I'll never forget. To this day, we're amazed that neither of us has any scars.

Then there was the time Dad was driving home from a basketball game in Chicago and his Corvette skidded on black ice and careened into the guard rail on the overpass, preventing the car from crashing down onto the freeway below. His feet went clear through the floorboard, and his ankle bones clear shot through the skin. The doctors told us the frigid temperatures kept him from bleeding to death, but they also said he'd never walk again. Mom, who was eight months pregnant with my little sister, Kelly, nursed him to health, and he was up and back to work within three months. But Mom was so paralyzed with fear over the accident that her body literally shut down, and Kelly was born five weeks overdue—beautiful and healthy. Yes, God looked over us. But in August of 1983, our faith was tested like never before.

"Yes. I have a daughter named Susie. Is everything okay?"

Mom had been ironing in La Habra when the phone rang with a woman's voice on the other end claiming to be a sheriff in Mexico.

"Was your daughter, Susie, in Mexico?"

"No, but my daughter, Kelly, is in Mexico."

"Do you have anyone there with you now?"

"Yes, my son, Jeff, is here."

"Please, wait there for us to call you back."

Mom prayed everything was all right, but deep down she knew better, the way every mother knows when something has happened to one of her children. How could anything have happened to Kelly?

Kelly had always been invincible. We always said she was the Meyers with nine lives. She relished adventure, once rolling a jeep during an off-road ATV escapade only to step away without so much as a scratch. From the moment she came into the world a month late, it seemed Kelly had been determined to make up for lost time. She had a zest for life and a beguiling way of enchanting everyone she met without ever trying. When she was only six, Mark brought Frannie home to meet the family.

Kelly looked up at her with her big blue eyes and said, "You don't really like my brother do you?" which melted Frannie's heart on the spot. Since that time, Kelly had grown into a beautiful, vivacious, young twenty-year-old who had the world at her doorstep.

It was summer break and Kelly was about to start her third year at Pepperdine University, where my sister, Patty, was coaching her on the basketball team. A friend invited Kelly down to Mexico in his old Volkswagen bus for a short vacation. Our youngest brother, Bobby, had wanted to tag along just like I had always wanted to tag along with David when I was young. Kelly was all for the idea, but Bobby had broken his ankle playing basketball the week before, so Mom didn't think he should go. Reluctantly, Bobby stayed home. For some reason Kelly had Susie's drivers license with her.

When the sheriff called again, this time Jeff answered. "May I speak to your mother?....Mrs. Meyers, I'm afraid your daughter, Kelly, is deceased." Jeff saw Mom's face and he knew immediately Kelly was gone.

The Volkswagen bus she and her friend had been traveling in got a flat, veered off the road, and tumbled into a ravine, killing them both instantly. I was at a car show in Detroit doing promotional work for Buick, one of the sponsors for the upcoming '84 Olympics. Once I got the news, I flew home immediately, as did my dad who was living in Chicago, and the rest of the family.

Neighbors flooded the house, bringing food and words of condolence. Kelly's friends camped out for days in the backyard huddling together, swimming in the pool, sleeping at night on the chaise lounges, unable to leave each others' sides until the funeral provided some sense of closure. But there could be no funeral without a body, and the body was still back in Mexico.

At the time, my brother, Mark, was working as a bailiff for Judge John Flynn, our neighbor and close friend. Judge Flynn did what he could to expedite things with a government known for dragging its feet unless someone offered to grease its palms. Meanwhile, a Rosary Mass was said. Five days later the Mexican government finally released Kelly's body so that a funeral could be held.

Time can be measured in breaths, heartbeats, waves rolling on and off the shore, little bits of expansion and compression, little births and little deaths, the unending dance of new green shoots with wilting ones, over and over. But a life is measured in memories, friends, moments of excitement, sorrow, joy, or fear. And they say when we come to the end of our lives, it's those things we didn't do that we regret—the adventures we were too afraid to try, the secret loves we were too timid to approach. Where I had been stubborn and introverted growing up, Kelly had been just the opposite. She was open and vivacious. Kelly grabbed life by the lapel and danced.

We took comfort in the knowledge that she had been so loved by so many, and that she had lived a great deal in her short life. I wanted to believe she had no regrets when it came time for God to take her back. But that's hard to do when someone dies so young.

The holidays would be approaching soon, and it was going to be a painful time for all of us.

Don's daughter was also named Kelly. At first, it was very hard for me to hear him say her name when she phoned. When a loss is still so raw, just hearing the person's name can make your heart ache. I know that in her own way, the same was true for Don's daughter. I'm sure hearing my name hurt her. She and I weren't far apart in age, and we still hadn't figured quite how to relate to one another.

16

My Big Broadcasting Break

"Do not go where the path may lead;
go instead where there is no path and leave a trail."
~ Ralph Waldo Emerson

"She is quite possibly this country's top all-around athlete. But who knows the name Ann Meyers?" Such was the beginning of the November, 1983 issue of *American Way* magazine's profile piece, titled, "All Suited Up With No Place To Go." On the opposite page was a full-page picture of me holding a basketball inside an empty locker room.

I was struggling to make $50,000 a year from broadcasting, doing product endorsements, and teaching basketball at youth camps, and now anybody traveling cross-country on American Airlines with five minutes to spare knew it. "A man at age twenty-eight who is labeled 'the best' commands a $1,000,000 contract and legions of fans," wrote George Harrar.

Tell me about it, I thought.

My brother, David, had made $350,000 a year, and I was just as good an athlete. But like I told Harrar, "It's a man's society. Still, I have no right to complain. I was born with a lot of God-given talents." And the truth was, I knew there was more to life than fame and money, especially now. If I had commanded a $1,000,000 paycheck that year, I'd have been overjoyed to give it up if it meant I could have my sister back. As for it being a man's world, well, who didn't know that? There was no point in moaning about it, other than it sometimes just felt good. And feeling good was something the Meyers had in short supply that fall season.

The holidays had come, and we were all looking for ways to get through them, to appear cheerful, when inside we were still reeling over Kelly's death. I had spent Thanksgiving with Donnie and his daughter, his parents, Scotty and Verna, and his sister, Nancy, and her family. It was wonderful to get to know them better and to see how close they all were. It also meant a lot to see how important it was to Donnie that they liked me and that I liked them. Though his divorce was finalized, there still remained a bit of awkwardness between his daughter, Kelly, and me.

Still, being back home for the holidays would have been much harder. A few of my siblings were still living there with Mom, who had become more and more depressed. Dad's leaving delivered the first blow, and Kelly's death was the knockout punch. While I'd grown up with a mom who had been to each of my games, making every one of my lunches, and taking me to doctor appointments, my younger brothers and sisters now had a mother who was barely able to do any of those things. Several of us older kids tried to help out financially as much as possible, but we all had obligations of our own. While my father hadn't totally dropped the ball in that department, his checks were always late. While no one was destitute, both parents were MIA when it came to providing emotional support for my younger siblings. It was a tough time for everyone.

Though it seemed to take forever, December finally passed. 1984 offered at least a distraction with the Summer Olympics in Los Angeles. President Reagan branded the Soviet Union an "Evil Empire" and making the case for deploying NATO nuclear armed missiles in Western Europe as a response to the Soviets installing new nuclear armed missiles in Eastern Europe, which meant there'd be little chance the Soviet athletes would compete. Even without an arms race, we had snubbed them at the 1980 Olympics, and now they were playing tit for tat.

The response was that nearly all of the Eastern European Block countries announced they would not be participating in support of the Soviet Union, which meant the U.S. women's basketball team would probably take the Gold. I had brief pangs of nostalgia more than regret. It was hard. Part of me wanted to be out there competing, but rules were rules. I was no longer an amateur athlete. By now I was a broadcaster.

I'd done some work with ESPN, broadcasting with Robin Roberts in her early career. I also worked with Sports Channel Chicago, where I was their #1 analyst for most of their college sports, both men's and women's, while Don was broadcasting the Chicago White Sox games and doing ABC's Monday Night Baseball.

Word had gotten out that ABC was considering hiring a woman to broadcast the Olympic women's basketball games, which was a big deal because it had never been done before. I had hoped they would hire me for the job, since I was a local athlete and knew many of the athletes participating in 1984, like Jackie Joyner-Kersee, Carl Lewis, and Mary Lou Retton. I'd been a UCLA Olympian, competed in the Pan Am Games and other events leading up to the '80 Olympics. I was also well known by the folks at ABC because of my *Superstars* trifecta. As one of sixty-five Olympians appointed by the Mayor to the Olympic Committee, I'd hoped my selection to broadcast would be a natural, logical decision. So I was beyond thrilled and honored when I found out I had the job. It was a broadcasting breakthrough for me and for all women.

As the front man of the XXIII Olympiad, Peter Ueberroth was smart not to confirm that Soviet athletes would not be participating. Instead, he kept the men's and women's basketball schedule under wraps. Normally, the public would have been notified six months out which Olympic teams were competing, and their playing dates, so they could make travel arrangements and purchase tickets ahead of time. But Peter played it close to the vest, knowing that few would care if the U.S. teams were scheduled to play Africa because the odds were that the African teams would lose by a hundred points. However, everyone wanted a ticket to the U.S./Soviet games.

I didn't know the lineup of the women's basketball teams, and much to his chagrin, neither did ABA President, Bill Wall, the man who had underwritten our bid for a berth to the '76 Olympics. He and his secretary ended up standing outside selling tickets right before the games. Yet, they would always sell out.

In Los Angeles, there was no need to build ambitious structures as Montreal and Moscow had, since the Coliseum, USC, and UCLA provided ideal venues. One of the big fears everyone had leading up to the bid was that there would be too much traffic congestion in a city already choked by smog and freeway delays. Peter jumped that hurdle by convincing large and small Los Angeles businesses to divide the workforce info shifts from 8a.m.-1p.m. and 2p.m.-7p.m., thus freeing up the freeways and allowing LA workers to attend many of the games. All the events were packed.

The women's team had an excellent lineup. Cheryl Miller was the big local draw having played for USC and nabbed her second NCAA title. On par with Cheryl were Denise Curry, my former UCLA teammate, and Lynette Woodard, who had made the '80 Olympic team only to be denied competing. Lynnette, of course, had also competed in the *Superstars* with me. Rounding out the team was eighteen-year-old Teresa Edwards, the youngest player on the team, who would eventually compete in four more Olympics. Pat Summitt and Bobby Knight, who had both coached at the Pan Am games in '79, were the women's and men's coaches now.

Broadcasting the '84 Olympic women's basketball games were especially exciting for me because they were being held in Los Angeles. It was a wonderful honor. It was also another seismic shift for women in broadcasting, but apparently someone forgot to mention that to a couple of guys at ABC.

I worked with Keith Jackson doing color. ABC had paid millions for the rights to broadcast the '84 Olympics and, as a result, Roone Arledge decided not to spend much time on the events that he didn't feel would bring in a huge number of eyeballs for the sponsors. This meant that other than women's track, swimming, gymnastics, and volleyball, little time would go to many of the women's events, including basketball. Television was expensive, and live television, especially so.

ABC decided they were going to come to Keith and me for about a minute on a cutaway featuring the women's basketball. Although very few of the women's events were getting any coverage, and this piece was only a minute or so, the director didn't ask me one single question. We did a practice run-through and the entire time, all I heard was him asking Keith questions in the headset.

"You have to have Annie say something," Keith finally said. "I'm not going to sit here while you ask me questions and not have your expert say a word!"

The director hadn't thought to get a female Olympic basketball player's take on the team. Keith made sure that wasn't going to happen when we went live. "She's the pro. Let her talk." It's something that I will never forget, both the director's disinterest and Keith's response.

In retrospect, I shouldn't have been surprised. When it came to basketball, the broadcasting booth was very much the boys' sandbox, even as the emerging gender gap was being thrown onto the national scene in a big way. If Geraldine Ferraro could be the first woman added to the presidential ticket by a major party, then this was a perfect time to open the doors in broadcasting. But clearly, there were still those who hoped the women on the teams would keep their pretty little mouths shut.

Well, I wasn't about to keep my mouth shut. Not when I was being paid to do the exact opposite. When they came to us on the live shot, everything went off without a hitch. Keith was a real pro and, by that point, I probably knew more about women's basketball than anyone. But more than that, I was finally comfortable speaking publicly and giving my opinion.

My shyness off the courts and in front of the cameras made it surprising to more than just the other journalists that I would want to get into broadcasting. It was a shock to friends and family, too. It was a challenge, but there was nothing I loved more than a challenge — and I'd learned from the best.

In typical Los Angeles fashion, the Games opened to eighty-four pianists in white tuxedoes playing "Rhapsody in Blue," while three-hundred dancers performed. But the most compelling moments featured one single man: Rafer Johnson

Rafer had become a good friend of mine, and my heart burst with pride when he took hold of the torch that day. Though many were too young to realize what Rafer had accomplished both as a decathlete and as a man in his lifetime, they still got the sense that they were witnessing someone very special. Rafer obviously felt the weight of his journey to sports history because he didn't feel as calm and collected as he seemed. There had been three or four rehearsals for the opening ceremonies, and he told me that something had gone wrong every time. First the stairs didn't open properly, then the unicopter crashed in the grass, Rafer got a cramp, the blimp lost its sign. There had always been something. But now it was the real deal, and it came off beautifully, and without a single hitch.

Being a UCLA track athlete himself who also played basketball under Papa for awhile, Rafer and his wife, Betsy, had followed my career both in and after school. Rafer and I played basketball together for a charity fundraiser each year that pitted a group of celebrity athletes against the Rams or the Raiders, whoever was the LA football team at the time. We'd play against Deacon Jones, Howie Long, Marcus Allen, Jim Plunket, and Merlin Olsen. When Rafer was voted team captain, which was most often, he was so nice about choosing me as his first pick.

"You're the best player on this court," he'd say, whether we won or lost.

He was generous with his praise, his spirit, and with his time, which was largely spent on many of the same boards and committees I sat on. The Special Olympics board was our favorite. He had long been the face of the Special Olympics (along with Eunice Kennedy). When an event was held at UCLA my freshman year, I became a volunteer. By now, we had come to know each other very well.

Rafer and I often talked about how there were no individual athletes, even in individual sports. There was always a talented coach who could say just the right thing at the right time, a loving supportive family, teachers, and so many others who were responsible for helping an athlete fulfill his or her full potential. Now, both of us hoped to inspire and help others.

When he reached the top of the stairs on Opening Day, he held the torch out to the crowd before lighting the flame, which passed through to set ablaze the huge Olympic Rings, specially designed for that purpose. Within days, the U.S. women's basketball team was holding the gold.

17
Goodwill Toward All

"We need people who can dream of things that never were."
~ John F. Kennedy

Once the Olympics ended, I flew to Cooperstown with Donnie to watch him be inducted into the Baseball Hall of Fame. We'd found out while playing in the All American, a golf tournament put on by Lee Iacocca. The MC, Don's good friend, Howard Cosell, had announced it when Don came up to the first tee. Sandy Koufax was at the same tournament and was pleased to hear that his pitching partner, who'd been passed over a few times, was now going to join him in the Hall of Fame.

It was exciting being in Cooperstown with Donnie, but being anywhere with him was always exciting because he knew so many celebrities from his playing days with the Dodgers.

Just like Pauley Pavilion during the Coach Wooden Era, Dodger stadium was *the* place to be during the 60s, and 70s. Hollywood and baseball were very much intertwined back then, and it wasn't at all unusual to see the likes of Richard Burton and Elizabeth Taylor, Doris Day, Cary Grant and Dyan Cannon, Frank Sinatra, Charlton Heston, and Tom Selleck. Afterward, Donnie would join some of them for a night on the town.

Donnie had played golf with Frank in the Bing Crosby at Pebble Beach, and was there to tee off when Frank started the Frank Sinatra Celebrity Golf Tournament. It was pretty cool when Donnie introduced me to him, and so many others. He would take me to hear Frank sing before going backstage to say hello. One time Donnie brought me to a gathering at Frank and Barbara's house in the desert, where I met Clint Eastwood, Chuck Conners, Robert Wagner, and

Gregory Peck. Even though I didn't run around in the same crowd, I'd competed at the Olympics, and had done enough commercials, and had my face plastered across enough billboards, that they seemed to know who I was. More to the point, they understood and appreciated what I'd accomplished in women's basketball. It was impossible not to be flattered.

They always wanted to know what it was like to compete in the Olympics and wanted to hear my side about my Pacers tryout. I'd tell them it probably wasn't too different from how they felt when they went on stage to perform in front of tens of thousands. Athletes and entertainers have a few things in common; we always want to give our best, we get butterflies before a performance, and we want a suitable platform in which to perform.

For athletes, that means worthy competitors, which is one reason why the first Goodwill Games was so successful. The absence of the elite Soviet and Eastern Block athletes had impacted the level of competition at the '84 Olympics, so Ted Turner created the Goodwill Games in part to provide that level of competition that everybody hungered for—athletes and spectators alike.

In 1985, I was one of seven Olympians chosen as Goodwill Ambassadors to travel throughout Europe promoting TBS and the Goodwill Games, which were to take place the following year. I'd be doing double duty because I was also broadcasting the Goodwill women's basketball games. I was grateful to get another high profile, prestigious gig because I'd had to hustle to sell myself again as a broadcaster after coming off the Olympics. Oddly it was always the same thing, "You just worked for ABC doing the Olympics, we can't afford you." For an entire year, all I'd wanted was a job, and now they were telling me I was over-qualified? But with the Goodwill Games, I finally had that job. But it also meant I'd be spending a lot of time away from Donnie.

Carol Lewis, Terry Shroeder, Teder Bitmore, Rowdy Gaines, Nancy Hogshead, and Willie Banks were the other Goodwill Ambassadors chosen, and together we traveled to Spain, Germany, France, Italy, and England, covering five countries in ten days. We'd fly into Rome, stay two days, then fly into Madrid for dinner, get up the next morning to do a press conference, then leave without spending a second night because Juan Bautista was heading up a revolution. As Goodwill Ambassadors, we didn't want to get in the middle of that mess.

And that wasn't the only hotbed of political uncertainty. NATO missiles were being set up in Western Europe and used as bargaining chips by Reagan during arms talks with the new Soviet leader, Mikhail Gorbachev. It wasn't the greatest time to be traveling abroad, and I was glad when the press tour was over. However, I returned to devastating news.

One of my business managers, told me that the $250,000 I'd earned from the *Superstars,* the ´84 Olympics, and the contracts with Fuji and Buick, was gone.

"I'm so sorry, Annie, I don't know what to tell you. Everyone's been wiped out," he said, breaking the news as gently as possible.

Donnie and I, and about 900 other athletes, doctors, lawyers, and businessmen, many from the Palm Springs area, had invested in a company that only a few years before seemed to be a sure thing.

Technical Equities board of Directors read like a who's who of the day. Robert Campbell, CEO of Newsweek, and astronaut Eugene Cernan, were among them. High profile players in the world of finance were so certain of TE's return that they happily sunk large sums into the company. When prominent doctors and athletes we knew in the desert did the same, we followed suit. Now word on the street was that the company was filing bankruptcy.

The Bernie Madoff of his day, Harry C. Stern was the founding partner and manager of Technical Equities. Jurors would find that every tax return from 1969 to 1986 had been false—nothing more than one big Ponzi scheme.

My quarter of a million dollars had gone up in smoke. It was a clobbering unlike anything I'd ever experienced as an athlete. If I'd lost a game because we'd been outplayed, or came in second in an event because of an injury, at least there was some sense to it. This was inexplicable. Like a car accident, it came from out of nowhere, causing instant destruction.

I'm young. I can recoup. I've still got my broadcasting career ahead of me, I told myself. I was still living with Mom when I was in California, so I didn't have the expenses and responsibilities compared to those whose finances had been decimated and feared they couldn't possibly *ever* get that money back (Many years later 60% of investors' funds were returned). I thought about older couples and people who were raising families, like Raiders player, Pete Banaszak, who according to *Sports Illustrated* had lost nearly twice what I had, and was counting on that money to put his kids through college. I felt terrible not just for me, but for them.

Money and I had already established a sketchy track record. I'd botched my $150,000 deal with the Pacers by canceling the contract and then sat out the second year with the WBL waiting to get paid for the first year, not realizing the organization would fold in its third year. I was starting to think maybe I didn't have a green thumb, or a green anything else. *Was this just par for the course?* I'd worked hard to earn what I'd made, but I wondered if fate had decided that money and I simply weren't meant to be together.

However far and wide the Technical Equities' financial meltdown was felt in the world of American athletes, that February, a global meltdown with far more serious and greater reaching repercussions was about to take place in a part of the world I was preparing to visit.

On April 26th, 1986, the Ukraine's Chernobyl Nuclear Power plant's reactor #4 melted down, spewing large quantities of radioactive contamination into the atmosphere. The plume drifted over much of the Western Soviet Union and Europe. Thirty-one deaths were directly attributed to the accident, but everyone was aware of the potential threat the toxic air posed for those living in the region. I had turned thirty-one the month before, and now I was heading to Moscow to broadcast the Goodwill Games for TNT. Like everybody else who found themselves heading to that part of the world, I wondered how my own health would be affected.

When I arrived in Moscow, the first thing I decided was that I wouldn't eat the local food, fearing contamination. There was a microwave in the hotel, so I existed on popcorn and orange drinks bottled somewhere else. I steered clear of milk, vegetables, fruit, and meat. I'd always been able to eat whatever I wanted and not gain a pound. Now I wondered how long I'd last. I missed American food. Heck, I missed food! I also missed home and Donnie, and I wondered when I'd wake up and start missing that $250,000. I wasn't in the greatest of places in my head. But then, the earth wasn't in the greatest of conditions in the universe.

The 1986 Goodwill Games were designed to accomplish something very noble, but because of the nuclear disaster and the escalating arms race, they were playing out against a dark backdrop. Those first few days, I could never have guessed how everything would end up. It had been eleven years since the two countries' athletes had competed on such a world stage—eleven years since the Soviet women had shredded us by thirty-five points.

I was announcing with my old pal Rick Barry and 1956 Gold Medal Olympian and Boston Celtic great, Bill Russell. Like Rick, Bill was also a friend. As basketball greats, they were very familiar with the Soviet women's global domination on the court. But having never lost to the Soviet women themselves, they weren't quite as invested in seeing the U.S. Women's team succeed like I was. That year, 6'8" Anne Donovan was playing for the U.S., and she would negate the size of the Russian giantess, Semjonova. On July 11, under Coach Kay Yow, Donovan, Katrina McClain Johnson, Denise Curry, Cheryl Miller, and Teresa Edwards trounced the world champions 83 to 60, breaking their 152-game winning streak that had lasted twenty-eight years.

I was through the roof and over the moon, and nearly unable to keep my emotions in check. It was a historic day and a long time coming. I had always worn my patriotism on my sleeve, but probably never more than that day. There was a changing of the guard, and it was palpable. I began to tear up at the end, knowing that not only had the U.S. women's team finally beat them, but we'd done it on their home turf. It may have been a game of goodwill, but we were still archrivals, and the competition in Moscow in '86 was as fierce as it had ever been.

Before I did the interview with Anne Donovan, I put on my highest heels so that the cameraman could get us together in the shot, but she still towered over me. I was so proud of her and her teammates. Some thought the Goodwill Games may have even helped pave the way for peace, as Turner had hoped. Months later, Reagan would make his famous speech in West Berlin urging the Russian leader to open the gate and "Tear down this wall." Eventually Reagan and Gorbachev would sign a pact to reduce nuclear arsenals and eliminate intermediate and shorter-range nuclear missiles — an atomic-age first.

But for now, the U.S. would simply be happy with our showing in Moscow. Among the 142 Gold medal U.S. winners, was Jackie Joyner-Kersee, who broke the heptathlon record with a score of 7,148 points. She would later write in her autobiography that she had decided to attend UCLA after seeing me play on the UCLA Championship Team on TV and after seeing Evelyn Ashford run track and field for the Bruins. Watching two women who had both already become Olympians, each wearing the UCLA jerseys, sold her. I was happy and proud of Jackie, just as I was elated for the US women's basketball team, but more than anything I was glad to be returning home. I was looking forward to some good old American meat, bread, potatoes, and milk. Mostly I was looking forward to seeing Donnie.

Our long phone conversations weren't possible while I'd been traveling. There was no Skype, email, or cell phones. We had both been so busy, and the time difference made it near impossible to connect, so I wrote him letters. The flight home was long. I thought about how I had missed him, how he had asked me so many times to marry him over the years and how I had always said, "just quit asking me." Even after his divorce, I said no. It was largely because I worried about what he would tell his parents and his daughter, and I didn't think it was a good idea to rush from one marriage straight into another. It had been six years since we had first met, and a tiny part of me wondered whether he would ever ask again.

After the plane touched ground, I made my way through the international terminal to Customs, and there he was, with that great smile and disarming manner that made everyone want to be his friend. We hugged, and all I could think of was how much I had missed him. After we collected my luggage, we drove to a hotel nearby LAX. On the way, I told Donnie about how I'd been surviving on microwave popcorn since the Chernobyl disaster had scared me away from trying anything grown in the region. I told him about the press conferences, the games, how the U.S. women did us proud.

Even with all the traveling I'd done playing basketball, I'd never been to all of the places I'd seen in just the last year. Rome, Paris, London, all of the most romantic places in the word, and at each stop, all I could think was how I had wished Don were there with me. But I'd never missed him more than I had in Moscow.

Finally, we were together after what had seemed like forever. About a half a mile from the hotel, with his left hand gripping the wheel, he reached into his pocket with his right hand and pulled out a little box and handed it to me.

"What do you think?" he said, letting a little grin play out on his face. My mind took a mental picture of how the street lights illuminated the small dimple on either side of his cheeks and the tiny cleft in his chin, and the bits of grey in his full head of hair shimmering.

"What are you asking me?" Of course I knew what he was asking me, but I wanted to hear it again. I wanted to make sure this was really happening, and that this time I was actually, completely ready.

"Will you marry me?"

Hearing those words now, I knew it was right. I knew I couldn't have been more ready. I was so excited that I reached over and gave him the biggest hug and kiss I could muster, almost swerving us right off the road.

18

Juggling It All – Life With Don and Our Children

"Those who dance are considered insane by those who do not hear the music."
~ George Carlin

On November 1st, 1986, Judge John Flynn presided over another wedding ceremony in which more than half the guests were Meyers, this time at the Club at Morningside in Rancho Mirage. Never before had so many Bloody Mary's been served before noon. Everyone was on vacation in a place where wildflowers bloomed in autumn and the only high-rises for miles had palm fronds shooting out the tops.

I wore a cream-colored lace, knee-length dress with short puffy sleeves that covered my shoulders and a garland made of pink carnations and baby's breath in my hair. Don wore an off-white sports jacket and a tie which was perfectly appropriate, since this wasn't a big church wedding, though I know that's certainly what my mom would have preferred. But Don would have had to fill out a three-hundred-page annulment document in order for the two of us to be married in the Church, and that sure wasn't going to happen.

The Club at Morningside on that sunny November day was as beautiful as any bride could hope for. Its huge windows looked out past a sea of perfectly manicured fairways, which framed the mountains off in the distance. We'd been living there in the home we bought on the 8th fairway behind a lake. Donnie knew the country club owner, Don Johnson, and the golf pro, Vern Fraser, so it just felt right.

Donnie's best man was his good friend, Gene Mauch, one of baseball's greatest managers. I chose my oldest sister, Patty, to be my maid of honor. It was a tough choice because I was so close to all of my sisters and I had many good friends. But Patty was my oldest sister, and I hoped everyone would understand.

We'd set the date for November because it was after the baseball season, and Donnie was still broadcasting the White Sox games out of Chicago. It didn't give us a lot of time, but luckily everything had come together quickly and easily. Many of Donnie's good friends were there, like Chuck Connors, Sparky Anderson and his wife, Carol, and Gene Autry and his wife, Jackie, who owned a home in the desert. Don's daughter, Kelly, parents Scotty and Verna, and sister Nancy and her husband and family were also there, making it the perfect opportunity for our two families to become better acquainted.

I knew the guests would be expecting my dad to walk me down the aisle, but my relationship with him had always been complicated. I didn't want Mom to be any less involved in my wedding, so I asked them both to walk me down the aisle. They hadn't seen each other since Kelly's death.

There had been plenty of Meyers events since then, of course, but none with as much laughter. Everyone danced while the drinks flowed. At one point, after Bob Uecker gave his toast, Donnie and I were dancing when Ueckie came up and tapped on Donnie's shoulder. Thinking that Ueckie wanted to dance with me, I turned toward him, but he grabbed Donnie's hand instead and the two of them waltzed around the room, a couple of clowns grinning from ear to ear while everybody howled. It was like the Bob Hope/ Bing Crosby *Road To…* films, with me as Dorothy Lamour.

It was impossible for anyone to spend much time around these two and not find their belly sore from laughing so hard. And it was good to see Mom smile. That night, there was every bit as much laughter as there had been that first night when we all had dinner together in the Bahamas, but this time instead of stewing about how I'd done in the *Superstars*, I was laughing, too.

After the reception Ueckie and his wife, Judy, got in their car and followed Donnie and me to Dominic's, a great old restaurant about two miles from The Club where we'd planned to have dinner. On the way, Don drove through a yellow light and Ueckie followed behind just as the light turned red. One of Rancho Mirage's finest stopped Ueckie, who explained that he was in Don Drysdale's wedding party.

"Have you been drinking?"

"Well, my best friend just got married. I hope so."

"If I let you go, do you promise not to have another drink while you're in there?"

"I promise."

"You better not, because I'm going to follow you, and when you come out, I'll be at your car, waiting."

Of course Ueckie proceeded to have a couple of drinks during dinner, and when we finished he and his wife headed out to their car, and sure enough, there was the officer, waiting.

"After you, my dear," Ueckie told Judy, opening the driver's side door so that she could slide in behind the wheel and drive them home. There was nothing the officer could do but smile. Ueckie and Donnie had that effect on people.

They had first met when they were in their twenties down in Vero Beach, Uecker at his first spring training with the Braves, and Donnie playing for the Dodgers. Donnie gave everybody a nickname and soon 'Ueckie' stuck. Ueckie liked to tell about the first time Donnie threw a pitch to him and it went over his head. "I had no idea what a bad pitcher he was." Of course, Ueckie realized soon enough that Donnie had done it as a joke. They loved to tease each other whenever they could, but never on the field. "He'd bean his own mom if she swung at one of his good pitches," Ueckie always said. "You never messed with Don when he was pitching."

When the two slap-happy friends weren't behaving like Bing and Bob, they were acting like Felix and Oscar. I don't know that I'd call him fastidious, but Donnie was certainly proud of our home in Rancho Mirage, which looked out beyond the lake onto the pass where the San Jacinto and San Gorgonio mountains converged. I'd watched him oversee the building of several homes, and he was particular about what he chose and how the place looked. Our desert home was beautiful, and Donnie wanted to keep it that way. Especially when Ueckie came to visit.

Donnie would make drinks, put them down on coasters, and during the course of conversation, Ueckie would casually pick up his drink, take a sip, then purposely set it down on the glass table, right next to the coaster. Donnie would grab a towel, wipe up the ring, then place the drink back on the coaster, from which Ueckie would move it again. Then Ueckie would get up, walk around, touch a window or move a trinket or a piece of furniture, knowing that Donnie would be right behind him, straightening up, oblivious to the fact that Ueckie was doing it all intentionally.

Donnie had worked hard to get where he was. He'd been a smart investor who'd owned restaurants in Hawaii and properties in California. But his divorce had been costly. When he asked me to sign a pre-nup, I had absolutely no problem doing it. I wasn't marrying him for his money. I knew I could take care of myself. I didn't need a man to provide for me. I needed him only to love me and to laugh with me. And, occasionally, to compete with me.

Donnie and I loved to compete at golf. And there was no such thing as a friendly game. As much as I loved playing golf with Donnie, I still played pick-up basketball and tennis.

We weren't married for long when I became pregnant with our first child, but I continued to compete and broadcast. There wasn't a lot of free time, but when we found it, we played golf—and my swing never felt better. I had to slow down and go around my tummy. When I was pregnant, I ate well and took good care of myself, especially when I was on the road broadcasting. But I knew that exercise was good for me and the baby, so I ran and played basketball, working clinics here and there. I also knew that when the big day arrived, I wanted Donnie to be in the delivery room with me, so I asked him a few months into my pregnancy how he felt about that.

"I've watched colts and puppies being born. I'm good, thanks." Donnie had been on the road with the Dodgers when his daughter was born, but it wouldn't have mattered since hospitals didn't allow fathers in the delivery room in those days, something he was probably grateful for. Now things had changed so much and at age fifty, Donnie was becoming a father all over again, so I put out the offer to be involved in the birth of this child. But he made it sound like he'd just as soon pace a spot in the waiting room carpet.

Several months later, while we were in Chicago staying at the Lake Point Towers Downtown, which is where we stayed when Donnie was working for the White Sox, I was a week past due. Mom and Patty had flown into Chicago a few days earlier expecting the baby to have already been born. It was a sweltering July 22, but the three of us spent that whole day walking up and down Lakeshore Drive, hoping to get the baby moving. Late that night I went into labor.

The next morning was Don's birthday, the same day our son was born, weighing 7.5 lbs. As it turned out, the man who'd seen enough animals born for a lifetime couldn't keep himself away. We both watched in awe as this small being emerged, barely enough hair on his scalp for us to be able to tell that he was blonde.

"Mr. Drysdale, would you like to do the honors?" The doctor handed Donnie an instrument to cut the umbilical cord. We were so excited to have a healthy child. We had talked about names, and Donnie had been very definite that if we had a boy, he didn't want to name him Don, Jr. Don had friends he'd played ball with who had named their sons 'Juniors,' and it had put a lot of pressure on those kids. But, amazingly, our son had come into the world on Don's 51st birthday, and we decided that if the good Lord had arranged that kind of a gift, then how could we name him anything else? Donald Scott Drysdale, Junior was typed onto the birth certificate, but from day one I called him D.J.

The year D.J. was born was Donnie's sixth and last year broadcasting the White Sox games. White Sox owners Jerry Reinsdorf and Eddie Einhorn had become dear friends, as had so many other people we met in Chicago. But now it was time to move on. Long-time announcer Jerry Dogget was retiring and Dodger's owner Peter

O'Malley had asked Donnie to come back and join the organization in the booth with Ross Porter and Vin Scully. It was a dream job for Donnie to work side by side with the same man who had announced his shut-out games so many years ago. It brought his career full circle.

We looked for a place to rent in the La Canada/Pasadena area so we could stay close to the stadium during baseball season. We found a beautiful place fifteen minutes from the ballpark and, unlike our desert home, it wasn't wall to wall mirrors—a great touch if you're trying to bring nature's beauty indoors and make a place look bigger, not so nice if you've just given birth and everywhere you look there's a reminder that all the baby weight didn't magically disappear just because the baby was born.

As an athlete, I wondered how long it would take me to get my body get back into shape. The well-toned machine I'd spent my entire life tuning and tweaking so it could run faster and jump higher had served a miraculous function. All of the awards, trophies, and firsts I'd racked up to that point paled in comparison to this achievement. But looking in the mirror now, I saw that, like anything worthwhile, it came at a cost. I assessed the damage and calculated the number of crunches, lunges, and pull-ups it would take to put things back in order.

DJ's birth was natural, so I was able to start exercising pretty soon, and because I continued to work out during my pregnancy, I snapped back to my original size easily. I was back on the courts and the courses inside of a month. Donnie and I also spent a lot of time in the pool teaching D.J. to swim, using the Esther Williams video *Swim Baby Swim*. Between the summers in Pasadena when Donnie was working broadcasting for the Dodgers, and the off-season months in the desert, it seemed like we were always near a pool. At seven months, D.J. could hold his breath under water and swim.

When we were back in Rancho Mirage, Donnie had a baby seat built into our golf-cart so we could take DJ out on the links with us. Wilson Golf gave DJ a little 5 Iron, and when he was old enough to walk, I would take him out onto the driving range where he would hit balls. Meanwhile, my golf lessons continued with Verne Fraser at the Morningside Club. Donnie and I would go out and play a round, sometimes just the two of us, sometimes with friends who would come out to the desert to visit.

Donnie had many friends from his playing days who still liked to come by and spend time with him, and they were all great. But I have to say I was fascinated the first time Sandy Koufax came to visit. I'd read and heard so many things, I wasn't sure what to expect. Drysdale and Koufax were names that had been long linked together by writers who were looking for a good story. If there wasn't a good story, they made stuff up. Why let reality get in the way when you can fabricate conflict between the two superstar ballplayers. The only truth was that Don and Sandy had always been great friends.

Watching them share stories and laugh about the old days was fun for me, and I could tell it was a tonic for both of them. As different as they may have been—Donnie, the right-handed blonde from California and Sandy, the Brooklyn-born, Southpaw—they made each other better as players back then, and they made each other smile now. Most people didn't realize that Sandy was also a great basketball player and played both baseball and basketball at the University of Cincinnati. It gave the two of us something to talk about.

And I'd just received some exciting news to share in that department. I'd been named the first Bruin women's student-athlete to be inducted into the UCLA Athletics Hall of Fame. It was 1988. By the year's end, I received more good news. I'd become pregnant with our second child.

On August 23, 1989, I was visiting Don's daughter, Kelly, in Manhattan Beach while Don was out of town working for the Dodgers in Montreal. I started having what felt like contractions. The baby still wasn't due for a couple of weeks though, so I called Mom. "I think I'm having contractions but they don't feel the same as they did when I had D.J."

"It's probably a false alarm, probably just Braxton Hicks contractions." Mom had been pregnant enough times to know everything there was to know about being pregnant.

"Well, I think I'm going to head back home just the same. You don't mind do you?" D.J. and I had spent the previous night at Kelly's, and I was planning to head out to La Habra to see my mom.

Instead, I returned to our home in Pasadena since I didn't feel well. I had our nanny, Valerie, a sweet Irish girl from a family of nine, watch D.J. while I went upstairs to lie down. That's when my water broke. I felt down between my legs and there was something there that didn't feel like the other pregnancy. I called Kelly and asked her to call her dad, then I drove to the hospital. I don't know how I made it there, but I slammed on the breaks, grabbed myself with both hands, and ran in. They put me in a room and tried to contact my doctor's partner. My obstetrician was on vacation...naturally.

"Somebody better get in here," I shouted loud enough to wake the dead. While I'd been lying in the room, I'd felt a foot pop out, and now I was really scared. The nurse stuck her head in and, within a fraction of a second, her expression changed from annoyance to panic. Then the other foot popped out. Meanwhile Don had caught the first plane to L.A. Kelly, who was staying in touch with the hospital, convinced the airline to relay updates from her to her dad via the pilot.

When the doctor arrived, he performed an emergency episiotomy. I nearly jumped off the table, but there was no time for drugs to deaden the pain. The baby was coming fast and the chord was wrapped around its neck. I was alone and incredibly scared, but I had no idea the baby's supply of oxygen might be compromised. I prayed our baby would be okay. Like a bolt of lightning, I suddenly realized that a hair's breadth lie between giving life and losing it.

With a worried look that I'll never forget, the doctor instructed the nurse to push down on my stomach while I bore down with all my might at the same time. It was touch and go for a while, but thank God the little guy who'd been in such a hurry to get here had lungs strong enough to let us know everything was fine. It was the sweetest sound I'd ever heard. Kelly got a message through to the pilot that a healthy baby boy had been born, weighing 6.5 lbs, with all ten fingers and ten toes intact. Apparently the whole plane cheered.

When the nurse handed me my son, I was more relieved than anything else, relieved and grateful. Tears streamed down my cheeks as I held my beautiful little bundle. He was perfect. I wanted to name him John after John Wooden, John Havlicek, and John Wayne, but Donnie didn't want two boys named Don and John because the names rhymed, and he thought that would sound silly. A friend of his, Darren Johnson, had recently passed away after battling cancer. We both loved the name. It was a Gaelic word that meant both "great and strong." Thus Darren John Drysdale was christened.

I had been playing basketball into my seventh month in the John Wooden Adult Camp while I'd been pregnant with Darren, just as I'd stayed active throughout my first pregnancy, but Darren never did turn. My doctor would put me on my side and try to maneuver the baby's head down. He suggested I spend the remaining months of my pregnancy being less active, but I didn't like anyone telling me I couldn't play basketball. I would swear Papa had been talking to my doctor because he'd say, "Annie, what are you doing out here?" when I was about to take a charge. My mentality was that the baby was well-protected inside of a miraculous creation capable of making life and baskets all at once.

The first several days after Darren's birth were difficult. Because he was jaundiced, he had to stay in the hospital an extra day. It was so hard to be away from my newborn that night. When he did come home, we needed to keep him under a special light to remove the extra bilirubin. The nurse would stop by and draw blood to check his levels. Here he was only a few days old and bleeding from all these needle pricks. That didn't sit well with Don.

Added to that, was a strange sensation that crept in from out of nowhere, until it filled the house like a plague. Don and my family couldn't understand my teeter-tottering emotions, and I couldn't explain them any better. One minute I was crying, the next laughing. Apparently God's miraculous creation had some post-partum kinks that no one had warned me about. Thank God for Valerie. She helped me so DJ wouldn't feel like he was being replaced. The two boys were only twenty-four months apart. At night I could bond with

Darren and the daytime was dedicated to giving DJ the attention he needed. Somewhere in between I tried to rest.

Eventually the fog that enveloped me, and the surplus of iron that was making Darren's skin look so olive, dissipated. It had been a very difficult patch for a while, but we all got through it.

Don was a wonderful father. He was known throughout the world of sports as a man's man, and yet he knew how to change a diaper. As the boys got older, he would take Darren in the pool and teach him to swim, just as he had with D.J. He'd also take the boys out in the backyard to play catch and learn to hit a ball. Don was also such a fundamentally good person. He helped friends out when they were struggling financially, yet he never let anyone know about it. It was the same when he would quietly send money to charities. He was very much like his friend Frank Sinatra in that way.

And Don was a team player. Donnie was broadcasting the game with Vin Scully when Orel Hershiser was in the midst of pitching for the record, eventually breaking Don's 58 2/3 scoreless innings streak by one. I asked Donnie how he felt about the possibility of having his record broken. He would explain how he had been encouraging Orel after the games. Whenever Orel expressed misgivings to Don about the position he was in, Don would guide him, offering advice on how to shut-out the batters. "You can strike this guy out with a fast ball on the inside corner if you let him think you're throwing a slider." In Donnie's mind, records were meant to be broken, so long as it was a fellow Dodger. Lesser men would have clung to the past, but not Don. He was good at moving on.

Even with the children, we both stayed busy traveling and broadcasting, but we worked during different seasons so there was always one of us home with the kids. When we were apart we would talk to each other six to eight times a day, just to hear each other's voices. Every phone conversation ended with, "I love you." If it was at night we'd add, "Sleep tight, don't let the bedbugs bite, and if they do, get your shoe, and smack them with your crackers and stew." When we were together again, it always felt like we were on our honeymoon. Everything was perfect, and it only seemed to get better.

On February 3, 1990, in Pauley Pavilion, Denise Curry, Bill Walton, Kareem Abdul-Jabbar, and I watched as our jerseys were the first in the school's history to be retired. My family was there along with our coaches, Billie Moore and John Wooden, Donnie, and our two boys. My Jersey, #15, had been framed and was now being handed to me as a photographer from *Sports Illustrated* clicked away. The picture to appear in the magazine featured Kareem, Bill Walton, and me on either side of Papa. The two players dwarfed the aging coach, whose shoulders were beginning to stoop a little. To us, however, he remained every bit the giant he'd been in college. But he would always be larger than life in spite of his enormous humility and increasing frailties.

It was such a special day for so many reasons. As a Meyers, we've all supported one another during occasions like these, but now I had my husband and my two sons with me, and it was the first time Don had ever been inside Pauley Pavilion. Growing up in Van Nuys and playing baseball with the Dodgers, he hadn't had many opportunities to catch a UCLA basketball game during Coach Wooden's championship winning era. Now he was here for me.

I felt proud and blessed.

19

That Four Letter Word I Hated More Than Any Other: Loss

"I am but waiting for you, for an interval.
Somewhere. Very near. Just around the corner."
~ Henry Scott Holland

That summer after broadcasting the '90 Goodwill Games, I returned to discover I was pregnant. I was just as excited about this pregnancy as I had been with the boys, but Donnie and I decided to keep it quiet during the first trimester, which wouldn't be too hard because I never started showing until after then anyway.

Don's parents adored D.J. and Darren, but Scotty and Verna had questioned their son's decision to have more children. "Aren't you a little old to be having babies?"

Don's demanding schedule broadcasting and traveling with the Dodgers concerned them, and they wanted to make sure he considered the toll of having more children, and whether he'd have the necessary time to devote to his children.

At about eleven weeks into the pregnancy, we were at our place in Pasadena when something felt off. Luckily, I was already scheduled to see the doctor. He turned on the ultrasound machine and together we watched the monitor transform sound waves into what looked like a Rorschach test. Every time he moved the gadget around my bulging tummy a new design appeared, but unlike the other two pregnancies, each picture was stagnant. I realized I'd put off going to the doctor's office longer than I probably should have, but having had two healthy babies, I knew the drill. In fact I considered myself almost a pro by that point. After all, my mom had had eleven babies and all were born healthy.

"Well Mrs. Drysdale, I have some good news and some bad news," the doctor said. "The good news is you have twins. The bad news is you've lost them. I'm sorry."

"I've lost them?" I repeated, unable to process what I'd heard, wanting proof that this wasn't some sort of weird dream. He was so casual. Maybe he was joking. This was the doctor who had delivered Darren, the hero who'd appeared at the zero hour to save the day. Wouldn't he at least want to touch my hand, show some sign of sympathy? Wasn't that part of the whole Hippocratic oath thing? Or maybe I was just too much in shock to recognize whatever bedside manner there was.

"Stop by the counter before you leave and the nurse will schedule a D&C."

But how? Why? What happened? I wanted to scream, but he was already gone. I put my clothes on, and then, half-dazed, asked if I could use the phone to call my husband. The line was busy. I tried his car phone, but it just rang. I called the house in Pasadena where Don was with my mom and the kids a few more times, but I still couldn't get through.

I propped-up my arms on the counter near the nurse's station so that my legs wouldn't give way beneath me. I was supposed to fly out to Carolina that evening to broadcast an NC State game for ESPN. *What am I supposed to do?* This feeling of helplessness was something I wasn't accustomed to. I wasn't like other girls when I was little. I hadn't dreamt of growing up to marry a prince and having babies and, therefore, had never considered that something might go terribly wrong with that scenario.

Even if I had, that dread of the worst happening would never occur to me because I'd long since trained myself not to give negative possibilities any room to grow. I'd always plucked them out before they could take root. But now the worst *had* happened. I found my keys and my bearings then made my way to the car and drove myself home, empty and alone, an internal kind of autopilot kicking in the whole way.

"Annie, are you okay," Mom had come out to spend time with the boys who were four and two, but she had no idea about this pregnancy.

"Where's Don?"

I had to let him know what had happened before I could tell anyone else, even her. My mother had always been there for me through everything, she was my protector and my inspiration. I felt guilty about keeping such a huge secret. As much as I wanted to run crying to her now, explain everything and be comforted by her, I knew that I had to tell my husband first. Don was my emotional anchor. He would make everything okay. He was still strong enough to take a fastball to any part of his body and pretty much laugh it off. Donnie loved to laugh. I prayed his strength would make me strong. I opened the door to the office where he was talking on the phone. The moment he saw my face he knew something was wrong.

"We've lost …," I started a sentence I couldn't finish and Don hung up the phone without saying goodbye.

I don't like to cry, but I cried that day. I felt hollow, like a failure. I also felt guilty. *Had I done something wrong for our babies not to make it? Was it because I hadn't told anyone about the pregnancy?* Don held me in his arms and tried to console me. It was hard for him too, but even harder for Mom.

When I finally told her, I had to explain everything; why I hadn't shared the news with anyone but Don, that I'd been carrying twins, and that now they were gone.

"I suspected as much," she said. "You can't hide that kind of thing, not from your own mother. But twins. Oh my."

I imagine it brought up so many unpleasant feelings inside her. Her own mother had died after giving birth to twin girls when my mother was only six. It also made her think of my sister, Kelly. My pain was so minor compared to what Mom had been through. By the time Kelly died, Mom had the chance to wash her face, kiss her cheeks, tuck her into bed and soothe her fears and hurt feelings a thousand times in a thousand different ways. My loss paled by comparison, but I could relate to that very horrible pain she had endured.

"It simply wasn't…"

"…meant to be," I said finishing her sentence, knowing somewhere deep, deep down that she was right. That God must have had His reasons. "I know."

I realized I still had to catch the flight to Carolina. It was too late for ESPN to find anyone else. That was so difficult though—the flight out, doing the game, coming back, waiting for my hospital appointment once I got home, and the whole time carrying a different kind of secret.

After the D&C was performed, Don and I decided to accept the fact that there would be no more children. He was fifty-five, I was thirty-six, and we had two beautiful, healthy sons. There was no need to ask for anything more. But once again, just when I thought I had everything planned, life let me know it had a mind of its own. One day when we were out on the golf course in Rancho Mirage, I told Don that I didn't feel quite right. I thought maybe something had gone wrong with the D&C. This time we went to the doctor's office together.

"You're expecting," he told us.

"How'd that happen?" Don asked.

"Well, don't look at me," I said.

Certainly, we were both surprised and overjoyed, but while I was more careful with this pregnancy by visiting the doctor more often, I still played basketball, tennis, golf. And I still ran.

"Maybe we should give her some crumbs or some candy to drop along the way in case she drops the baby. Then at least we'll know where to find them." Ueckie was always good for a joke. He had come by to visit us at home in Rancho Mirage one morning in early February, '93. I was nearly eight months pregnant with our third child and about to head out for a jog after making breakfast for the boys. That's when the phone rang. Don answered. It was The Naismith Memorial Basketball Hall of Fame.

"You're in," Donnie told me, giving me a big hug. I didn't scream like I had after the call from Sam Nassi. I'd been passed over several times before, so I knew not to get excited. Papa always used to say that you can't get too low if you don't get too high. Love and Balance were his two favorite words. I remembered that now. Inside, though, I was beaming.

I'd already been inducted into the International Women's Sports Hall of Fame and the UCLA Athletics Hall of Fame, but this was Hoop Heaven, where the immortals of the game were enshrined! There was *nothing* in the world more prestigious for a basketball player. Luckily, the enshrinement ceremony wouldn't take place for a couple of months yet. I hoped our third child would come when it was due. The first had been late and the second one early. They say three's a charm. I was counting on it.

On March 10, 1993, at the Desert Hospital in Palm Springs, the nurses outside my room seemed more than just a little excited over my husband's imminent arrival. They didn't realize I could hear them. "Don Drysdale just called. He said he'll be here any minute."

Donnie had taken me to the hospital hours earlier. We knew months ago that if the baby wasn't born by March 10, we'd have to induce because I had to fly into Nashville to broadcast the first round of the Men's NCAA tournament for CBS on March 17.

They started the I.V. drip when we first got there, but nothing much seemed to be happening, so Don decided to run over to Jensens' Market to grocery shop. In the meantime, thanks to the pitocin I.V., my contractions came on suddenly, fast and much stronger than with my first two deliveries. However, there was *no way* this baby was going to be born without Don there. He'd been at one birth and missed another. We'd planned for this birth, and he wasn't missing it. Everything was on hold — including my pushing — until we could find him. Donnie had just called the nurses' station for an update and was told to hustle on back. The nurses were in a dither as the news spread about Don's arrival. I may have been the one about to give birth, but he was the one they were waiting for.

I suppose it couldn't be helped. Everyone was familiar with Don's career, both as a baseball player and a broadcaster. I'm fairly sure these ladies neither knew nor cared much about what his wife had accomplished. It was OK, I was used to it. I'd always said it was a man's world. At least now another female had come into it, to help balance things out.

Drew Ann Drysdale weighed in at 8.5 lbs. Like her brothers, she was born with a healthy set of lungs. Unlike her brothers she was also born with a thick tuft of jet black hair.

"Whose kid is this?" Donnie blurted out. "The boys weren't dark."

"Well yours of course!" I shot back. He liked to tease no matter where we were, even in a hospital room after one of us had just pushed a new life into the world after waiting for the other to get back.

We knew Drew would be baptized into the Catholic Church, just as her two brothers had been. Don wasn't Catholic, but he wanted the children to have a strong religious foundation. He also wanted Mom to like him. They'd had a tenuous relationship. After everything, she still worried about my marrying someone with such a strong will and who was much older. The fact that he had accepted the children being raised Catholic helped smooth things between them, to some degree. If the way to a man's heart was through his stomach, the way to a mother-in-law's heart was often through her faith… that, and ample mother-in-law's quarters.

By now we'd moved out of our place at the Club at Morningside and been living for past two years in our dream home—an 8,000 square foot custom home off Clancy Lane in Rancho Mirage with plenty of room for guests and family. When Ueckie came to visit, Don watched him even more carefully now.

Since our home was near a golf course, I continued to play more and more golf. It was nice to see how my game had improved through my pregnancies. Speed and quickness were assets on the track and courts, but on the golf course they could be liabilities. My three pregnancies had demanded that I slow my swing down enough, so by now it had become habit.

The previous year I'd competed in the Celebrity Golf Association Championship up in Tahoe. No woman had ever been invited before, so the standard questions were, "What tees will she be playing off?" and "What kind of a handicap is she getting?"

At this point in my career everybody knew there was no way I was coming in last at anything, which meant that, just like with the Men's *Superstars*, I was going to beat some of these guys. And none of them wanted to lose to a woman.

I knew I'd be playing in the next CGA Championship, so after returning from the NCAA tournament, I reconnected with Lou Rosanova to work on my game.

In between strengthening my golf swing and taking care of the kids, I continued to broadcast. My career was finally taking off. While ESPN, CBS, and other networks kept me busy, I was especially thrilled that TNT asked me to do a third encore appearance at the upcoming Goodwill Games. I also continued doing some basketball camps and speaking engagements. All the responsibilities made it interesting playing the balancing act with being a full-time wife and mother. But mostly I held my breath waiting for June when I would officially become a member of the Basketball Hall of Fame.

Donnie was working for the Dodgers covering a Cubs series in Chicago when June finally came, but he flew out to meet me in Springfield. My family was already there, and I had brought DJ and Darren, who were five and three. Drew was still too young to care about anything like this, so she stayed with Don's folks. When Don got to the hotel, we looked out the window and saw a crowd below begin to swell. By the time he and I were dressed and ready to go over for the enshrinement ceremony, I had never seen so many people trying to get Don's autograph. It was a little bit scary. The NBA Commissioner, David Stern, recognized how crazy it was and how it might be impossible for us to get to the bus let alone walk to the auditorium, so he had his limo come around the back. Who knew there would be so many baseball fans in Springfield?

Julius Erving, who had long since become more like a brother than a friend, was also being inducted that year, along with Bill Walton, Calvin Murphy, Dan Issel, and Walt Belamy. It was the biggest class ever to be inducted. Protocol was such that each inductee needed a resident Hall of Famer to present him or her. Bill Walton and I had asked Coach Wooden, unwittingly causing quite a predicament for the man we both loved and admired. Papa wouldn't choose. He told us that at eighty-three, he didn't want to fly cross-country, but I think it was just his way of not hurting either one of our feelings.

I selected Pete Newell, another coach whom I admired very much. Known for his Big Man Camps, I first approached Coach Newell back in '77 after Anna's Banana's had won our first of three AAU Championships and asked him to do a Tall Women's Camp. The camps were mostly about footwork. Years later, while pregnant with Drew, Pete and Pete Jr. invited me to be a coach at USA Basketball. Pete gave a demonstration on how to set a pick, so I ran into him, barreling him down. Nobody outside family knew I was pregnant, so I chose that night at dinner to share the news.

"Imagine that," Pete said, looking dazed. "I can't remember ever working a pregnant woman so hard."

The only other woman to be inducted that year was someone I hadn't seen since 1986, Uljana Semjonova. The Russian Giantess who had been my rival on the courts was now my comrade, of sorts. She and I suddenly belonged to an exclusive club. Don had been inducted into Cooperstown nine years earlier, which meant he and I were now the first married couple to be enshrined in our respective sport's Halls of Fame. For me, it was the crowning glory to an athletic career that had been a dream come true. And yet, now it feels like a lifetime ago.

After the basketball enshrinement, I flew to New York with Donnie for the Baseball Hall of Fame dinner at the Waldorf. It seemed this hotel kept popping up in my life. I'd stared out the door at its famous façade when I'd stayed across the way at a smaller hotel the first time I played USA ball. Now I was staying at the place as a wife and mother—who'd just been inducted into the Hall of Fame.

When we got back home, it was nice to relax after the whirlwind of activity, but Donnie and I only had a few days together before he had to go on the road again, this time to Montreal.

On Friday, July 2, I turned on the television before the Dodgers game so the boys and Drew could see Daddy on TV, something I did often, especially when the team was playing away and I knew he wouldn't be home to tuck them in. Don would come on before Vinny, do the opening, and the kids would go up to the TV and kiss him, often asking why Daddy didn't say hi to them.

I thought Don looked good, if a little tired, but I didn't think much of it. He said he'd popped a blood-vessel in his eye from a fall at Dodger Stadium a few days before, and I figured maybe it was bothering him.

"How'd they do?" I asked him about nine 'o clock that night. It was three hours later in Montreal. The Dodgers had played the Expos, and Donnie had just gotten into his room after riding up the elevator with Ross Porter.

"We came in first." Donnie would usually put it that way. They came in first or second, but they never won or lost. "Have you gotten anything for Kelly, yet?" The following day was his daughter's birthday, and the boys and I were going to Kelly's place for her party.

"I ordered the flowers. I'll run out tomorrow and pick something out."

"Make sure it's something special. Wish I could be there with her and you and the kids."

I couldn't have agreed more. "We wish you could, too, but we'll see you when you get back."

"I love you," he said. The sound of his voice still made my heart sing. "Goodnight, sleep tight, don't let the bedbugs bite. And if they do, get your shoe…"

"And smack them with your crackers and stew…" I finished the limerick with him, told him that I loved him, and hung up.

7:30 the next morning, I called knowing it would be 10:30 in Montreal, but there was no answer. I figured he was off having coffee with an old acquaintance or working a business deal. I put the kids in the car and headed up to Manhattan Beach. It was the 4th of July weekend, so we knew the place would be packed. I planned to drop Drew with Kelly so they could have time together, while I took the boys to the beach. When I got to her place, I asked if she'd heard from her dad. She said no. Now I knew something was wrong. He would have called to wish her happy birthday. Before heading out, I tried phoning Don again. Still no answer. *What's going on?* It was noon already. By now we'd normally have spoken at least two or three times. I didn't know whether to be mad or worried. I called Mom and told her that if Don called looking for me, she should tell him to ring Kelly's.

It was a perfect beach day; yet as beautiful as it was I couldn't help but feel uneasy. By the afternoon, the boys were covered with sand. When we got to Kelly's I saw her standing there holding the baby.

"Has your dad called yet?" I asked, taking Drew into my arms.

"No."

The game was about to start, so I couldn't try calling him now. I headed to the TV to turn on his broadcast so the kids could watch Daddy and Vinny, but with party guests arriving, Kelly didn't want the TV on.

At about 4:20 p.m. I received a call from my sister, Cathy. "They've been looking for you Annie. You need to call Mom." When I called she gave me Peter O'Malley's phone number and told me to call him immediately. *Why's Peter calling me?*

"Don's had a heart attack," Peter said.

My heart started racing and an acrid taste lined my tongue. My first thought was that I needed to make sure he had the best doctor. "What hospital?" I asked, trying not to sound as frantic as I felt. "I have to get there, so I can take care of him..."

"No, Annie. He didn't make it."

"What? No! I need to be with him," I insisted. I don't know what I was thinking. My mind alternately went blank, and then raced with thoughts of plane flights into Montreal. Every cell in my body ached to be near him. *If I could just be with him, he would make everything okay.*

"I'm sorry, Annie. I didn't want to have to tell you like this. We've been trying to reach you all day. I didn't want you to hear it on TV..." Peter went on to explain something about other news channels already broadcasting his death and Vinny's announcement that night—how they'd tried to postpone it. Peter's voice was just a jumble of sounds now, and I was off somewhere too far away to decipher any of them.

How can I tell Kelly? And Don's Parents? How will they survive it? Kelly could see that something terrible had happened, so her friend, Alex, took the phone and talked to Peter, then broke the news to Kelly.

The children were in the back room playing, so I turned on the T.V., and there was Vinny. "Friends, we've known each other a long time," he said slowly, "and I've had to make a lot of announcements, some more painful than others. But never have I ever been asked to make an announcement that hurts me as much as this one. And I say it to you as best I can with a broken heart."

As Vinny continued, I prayed that Scotty and Verna weren't watching, but of course, I knew they were.

20

Fly Me to the Moon

"Grief is the price we pay for Love."
~ *Queen Elizabeth, II*

I took the boys into Kelly's bedroom, sat them on the bed and talked to them. It was one of the most difficult things I have ever done in my life. I knew I couldn't break down because it would only scare them. I told them as gently as I could that Daddy was in Heaven. D.J. understood more than Darren did, but Darren could still sense that something terrible had happened. When both the boys started to cry I pulled them in close to me and held them tight as tears streamed down my face.

Meanwhile, the details came flooding in. The Dodgers had sent Billy Delury, the longtime Dodgers secretary, to look for Don when he didn't show up for the game. He had died in his room of a massive heart attack.

Donnie died on July 3, 1993, on the 34th birthday of his oldest child, Kelly. His number was 53; the two boys were five and three. The baby was three months.

My mind sped ahead in a fogged haze. In a few weeks D.J. would be turning six. The previous cakes all had Don's name on them as well as D.J.s because they shared the same birthday. I couldn't suddenly leave Don's name off this cake. Before I could worry about any of that though, I had to make it through the funeral.

I called Ueckie and asked him to speak, but I told him I wanted him to keep it upbeat. I didn't want it to be any more difficult for Don's parents, our children, and everyone else who loved him than it already was. There had been no warning, nothing to prepare any of us. Donnie had needed an angioplasty a few years earlier, and two of his uncles had died from a heart attack in their forties. But Donnie always seemed so invincible. He was this strong, hulking man who was in great shape and so full of life. And he was so happy. He loved me and his children. Everything seemed so perfect. Even when I couldn't reach him that day, I wouldn't allow myself to think that something terrible had happened. And I think part of me still refused to believe it.

On July 12, with D.J. on one side and Darren on the other, I carried Drew in my arms as we made our way to a designated area in the first pew at the Hall of the Crucifixion-Resurrection, an auditorium large enough to accommodate eight hundred people at the Forest Lawn Cemetery in Glendale. Several Dodgers had already been laid to rest at Forest Lawn. Three weeks earlier, Donnie and I had been there for Roy Campanella's service. I remember sitting there with him, and for no reason, he suddenly turned to me and said, "Don't hook me up to wires. When the time comes, let me go quickly." Now I felt numb.

I walked up to the lectern to thank everyone for coming. *Just focus on the words.* I didn't want to break. I read ten or twelve lines, never looking up, keeping my eyes glued to the paper that trembled with my hands.

Then Ueckie spoke. He talked about Donnie knocking him on his rear end, and what a great guy he was *out* of his uniform; but in it, how he'd bean his own mother if she was standing at the plate. He talked about how competitive he was and how if you put the two of us together, Donnie and me, you had yourself a small army. He also told the glass story, how Donnie would clean up after him whenever he came to visit. He made everyone laugh, and for a moment it felt like Donnie was right there alongside me, just like always. When reality set back in, the tears rolled down my cheeks. And then after a moment, a wave of peace crept over me, strong at first, then diminishing, as though Donnie were squeezing me tight and then relaxing his embrace the way he always did whenever I was upset. Whether it was the power of the mind, or the power of love I'm not sure. A little of both probably.

After Ueckie, Vin Scully gave a beautiful tribute. Vinny had watched Donnie's career, calling his historic shutout for the fans, while marveling at the feat himself. Then, much later, Donnie would get a feel for Vinny's side of the game along with Ross Porter. Game after game, the trio formed their own little rotating team of partners, a family wedded by baseball. Now Vinny and Ross had lost one of the family.

"The tragedy of life is in what dies inside a man while he lives," Vinny began, "There was only life in Don and an awareness to feel the pain and glory in others and himself."

He went on to finish, and I know it was hard for him. It was hard for all of these guys. They had lost a close friend. I suppose everyone expected Sandy to speak next, but he wouldn't. He couldn't. Donnie and he had practically been boys starting out, and they ended up changing the way players were treated forever. I imagine, for Sandy, it might have felt like losing a brother. Gene Mauch, who had been Donnie's best man at our wedding, didn't want to speak, either, but he did. It was tough for all of us when his voice started to crack a bit. Same thing with Tommy Lasorda.

Toward the end, we played Donnie's favorite song, Frank's version of "Fly Me To The Moon," against a backdrop of video clippings and stills from Donnie's years with the Dodgers and family snapshots.

It was a maze of sad faces who had come to honor a wonderful man—Al Michaels was there with Dick Enberg, Don's family, my family, and all of Don's teammates, Ross Porter, who had read a beautiful poem, Orel Hershiser, Duke Snider, and so many others I don't even remember. After the service, we all filed into limousines and buses to make our way over to the Clubhouse at Dodger Stadium where a reception was being held. It was mid July. The sky was blue and everything else, green.

"You'll survive this, Annie," Mom said squeezing my hand. "I promise." But we both knew there was no easy way she could rescue me this time.

The entire funeral had been orchestrated from beginning to end by Peter O'Malley and his sister, Terry Seidler—from bringing Don's body back from Montreal, to arranging the transportation now. They had done the same for Campy three weeks earlier.

The Dodgers were family.

The next day, I contacted Tommy Lasorda. We all called Tommy, 'Izzy' because that's what Donnie had called him, and asked if the boys and I could crash the team's batting practice sessions.

"Of course," he said. "And I'll throw them pop flies."

The boys loved Izzy, and he was remarkable after Don's passing. While we were at the Pasadena rental house, we were close enough to visit him in the stadium every day until school started back up. Izzy would let the boys into the clubhouse and dugout before each game. It was as I'd hoped, Dodgers Stadium made me feel like Donnie was just away somewhere, working.

That first day, though, we did something Donnie would have never allowed. I palmed three baseballs in my left hand, and pitched them underhanded, one at a time to the boys who stood ready at home plate. Donnie never let the boys on the field while he was broadcasting. He felt that it was wrong, since he was no longer a player himself. But I sensed now he was giving us his blessing, *Go ahead. Just this once.* As we left the field, four-year-old Darren said, "Carry me like Daddy did," loud enough for Izzy to hear, and it made him cry.

There was a lot of crying that first year. D.J. had refused to blow out the candles on his sixth birthday cake that bore both his and his father's name.

And when we released white and blue balloons up to Daddy, one at a time, which was our way of blowing kisses to him in Heaven, D.J. decided he wanted to stop. He had also refused to take the mound in Palm Springs when we were invited to throw the first ceremonial pitch for the California Angels' Class A Team.

"Why can't I die and go to Heaven to be with Daddy?" D.J. would ask. It was the inevitable question. It must have seemed a logical solution to a six-year-old. Once he even tried to open a car door while it was in motion. "I want to die so I can be with Daddy," he kept saying that first year.

I didn't know how to console him. *How could God take the only man I'd ever loved when we still had three young children who needed him? How could Donnie be gone when just a few months ago had been the happiest time of our lives? How can I console my young son when I'm inconsolable myself?*

I don't know how I made it through that first year. In fact, I don't remember much of those first few years, except that there was an endless outpouring of kindness. Several NBA teams asked me to broadcast for them, including the Chicago Bulls. This was during the Michael Jordan-Scottie Pippen era. The Bulls had just won the NBA championship two years in a row, and our dear friend, Jerry Reinsdorf, was offering me a huge amount of money—money that I was not currently making.

I liked Chicago and I loved Jerry. Heck, I'd grown up outside of Chicago and had lived there for six years with Don while he was broadcasting for the White Sox and I was broadcasting for Sports Channel. I loved it—even during the frigid winters, when a biting wind could whip over the lake and chill to the bone.

If I took this position, I knew I'd be committing to living in a city without the support of my family and Don's. I knew I would be at the arena every day by 5:00 p.m. and not home until after midnight. I knew I would be in for long seasons because the Bulls routinely played well after the NBA's 82 game schedule ended. I said no. Jerry continued to ask me and I'll always appreciate him for that. There were other lucrative offers from several other organizations, and I said thank you, but no, to each of them. My children came first.

That autumn, Don's daughter, Kelly was overseeing the Don Drysdale Charity Hall of Fame Golf Tournament in Newport Beach for a seventh time. Hall of Famers from every sport arrived to shoot fifty-six holes and to grieve. The kids and I had moved back to the desert home for school, but they came out to watch the tournament. Don's friends meant well when they told D.J. that he was the man of the house now, but it was incredibly frightening and overwhelming to a six-year-old.

Meanwhile, the phone continued to ring with offers which I still felt I had to decline. And each time the president of some team called, he heard Don's voice saying there was no one home and to leave a message. My excuse was that changing the outgoing message wasn't a high priority. The truth was that I didn't want to erase what I had left of him. I couldn't touch his clothes, or get rid of any of his belongings. Some nights I'd grab a sweater that still held his scent and hold it next to me in bed, and just cry until I fell asleep.

My dreams were much kinder. Donnie would appear vividly and I could feel him there with me. And then I would wake up and, just as quickly, he was gone. On those mornings it was especially hard to get out of bed.

I needed Don. But I had to go on because my kids needed me.

I had never been a stay-at-home-mom in the traditional sense, but without Don, I didn't want to commit to anything that would keep me away from the children too long. I begged out of covering the '94 Goodwill Games for TNT, giving them plenty of time to find another broadcaster. I knew I would have to do something to help support us and to help me move on. I didn't feel like doing much of anything, though, especially that first holiday season.

In December, Mark and Frannie celebrated their 25th wedding anniversary, and they threw a huge celebration. I knew I had to go, but it was difficult. The pain of losing Don was still so raw. I tried to put on a good face, and everyone was extremely gracious and conscientious of my feelings, but that almost made it worse. I could tell some of the guests felt uncomfortable about celebrating Mark and Frannie's long, happy marriage in my presence. I clapped when they blew out the candles on their cake, willing a smile that didn't want to be there. Guests came over and offered me their condolences, and it felt like each kind word was chipping away at my carefully constructed emotional dam, until I thought it might break. As much as it hurt, I told myself that this had to be part of the healing process.

On Valentine's Day, friends dragged me out to the Charthouse, a one-time Rancho Mirage landmark restaurant that had been chiseled out of a large rock formation that hugged the hillside. The inside was dark wood and rock, keeping with the cavernous, inconspicuous feel, and I'm sure my friends figured it was a good place to bring someone who was reluctant to go out. They didn't realize it was the first place Donnie had taken me back in 1980 when I visited him in the desert.

We hadn't been seated long when I noticed Frank and Barbara Sinatra dining at a table nearby. I didn't want to go up and say hello, even though I knew that's what I should do. However, I had long ago promised myself I wouldn't let opportunities pass me by so that I ended up thinking *I wish I would have done this or said that*. The little regrets that stack up during the first half of a shy person's life can be wonderful motivators later on.

Frank and Barbara had always been very gracious when I'd visited their home with Donnie, or attended the Frank Sinatra Celebrity Golf Tournament. And when each one of the children was born, they sent beautiful Tiffany rattles and frames. But when Donnie died, Frank wasn't at the funeral.

They were just now finishing up, so I knew I wouldn't be interrupting dinner. I went over. "Hello Barbara, Frank."

The way Frank looked up at me said everything. "It's not the same without Donnie, Jilly, and Chuck."

There was genuine pain in that deep wonderful voice. Jilly Rizzo passed in 1992 and was Frank's closest friend. But Frank had carried special affection for Donnie and Chuck Connors, who went on to star in the long-running *The Rifleman* after ending his baseball career. I suppose Frank must have wondered how the three of them could be gone, when he was still there. As fitting, Frank mourned Don's passing his way.

As for me, I decided that rather than mourn the future we had planned, I would watch the sunsets, make birdies on the golf course, and raise our children to be strong, capable, contributing members of society for both of us. I wanted my kids to remember their father, and I would often sit with Drew, who was still just a baby, and point at pictures of her dad. "Who's that?" I'd ask her. "Is that Daddy? Do you see Daddy?"

21
Moving On

"Time is a dressmaker specializing in alterations."
~ *Faith Baldwin*

In May of 1994, our business advisors suggested that I put the Rancho Mirage house up for sale. The annual air conditioning bills alone on an 8,000 square-foot home were enough to put one of the kids through college, never mind the cost of keeping over a half-acre of grass in the desert. Facts were that I wasn't bringing in the kind of paycheck Donnie had commanded. Peter O'Malley had generously honored the rest of Don's contract for the year, which was a huge financial help, and Don had left us well provided for. However, I knew that from here on out I would be the sole person responsible for everything. I didn't want to uproot the children, but I was a thirty-eight-year-old widow with three kids ages six and under, and I felt the need to simplify our lives as much as possible. It was a lousy time for anyone to have to sell a house, though.

Home prices in Southern California had jumped during the 80s only to plummet in the 90s. The bubble popped in real estate, which affected affluent areas like Beverly Hills and resort cities, like Palm Springs. Clancy Lane in Rancho Mirage was, and still is, considered about as high-end as it gets in the Palm Springs area. Our home, along with all the others near Clancy Lane, had declined in value. Adding to my confusion was a condolence letter from a woman who lost her husband years earlier. She advised against making any big decisions in the first year of a spouse's death because we're grieving, and not emotionally stable or rational enough.

While I knew it was good advice, I ultimately decided to go with my gut. I loved Rancho Mirage; where Don's parents, Scotty and Verna, had been a great help in providing love and support to the kids, but now Scotty and Verna had moved to Hemet to live in a house Don had bought for them two years earlier. Most of my family was in Orange County, and I needed to be near them. I also wanted to be near Dodger Stadium. I reasoned that spending time there would be like sleeping on the right side of the bed when Don was on the road. It would fill a void. Orange County was much closer to Dodger Stadium than the desert. I put the Rancho Mirage house on the market and kept my fingers crossed.

The kids and I stayed with Mom in La Habra that summer while my real estate agent/sister-in-law, Frannie, helped me find the right place for the four of us in the surf capital of the world. Huntington Beach wasn't far from La Habra or Dodger Stadium, and I knew the boys loved the ocean. By the time school started, we were moved into our new home just down the street from Mark and Frannie.

We weren't in the house long when Drew, who was a little beehive of activity, climbed up the stairs while no one was watching and fell, catching her leg between the banisters. There was my seventeen-month-old dangling from the second story, screaming. That night I kept her with me in bed. She was too young to communicate, but the way she whimpered I knew she was in pain. It was late, though, and I didn't know any doctors in town and I didn't want to call my family. I'd imposed on them so much already and, frankly, I didn't want to hear any more disapproval. I waited until morning. When I took her into the emergency room, the doctor said the poor little thing had broken her femur. I couldn't have felt like a worse mother. I knew if Don had been there, things would have been different. I wasn't always good at making decisions by myself.

There were so many other mistakes I made. I'd pushed the boys into public schools with twice the amount of classmates than they were used to at their private schools. Poor Darren was only four and becoming more withdrawn, and D.J always seemed angry. To make matters worse, Drew's cast from the accident on the stairs had barely come off when she fell while we were shopping at the South Coast Plaza and broke her arm.

I missed Don. I needed him to help me raise the children. I didn't know if I'd be able to do it without him.

They say getting through the first year after the death of a loved one is the tricky part. But for me the first three years were so difficult. Amazingly, though, you somehow do it. You get up, brush your teeth, comb your hair, and go on. Some call it a testament to the human spirit. For me it's a testament to my faith and my family. And every time it got really hard, or I screwed up, I thought of Papa's words: "No Whining, No Complaining, No Excuses."

I had to be there for my children. I had to be strong. Moving into the new home in Huntington Beach helped, and with the kids enrolled in a new school, there were plenty of distractions. I continued to force myself to get out there. I'd already committed to doing the CGA Championship again up in Tahoe. This time I brought the kids along with family to help.

I'd begun preparing for it with Lou after Drew's birth. The problem was that I'd stopped training when Donnie died, and I'd lost a lot of weight. If I could hit the ball 150 yards with a five iron before, now it was twenty yards short of that. Over the four days, I shot in the high 80s and 90s, but still finished ahead of plenty of the guys, including Bryant Gumbel and Charles Barkley, but beating those two might not have been that impressive. I won some cash, and along with it, bragging rights.

By now I was working with CBS covering the men's 1st round of the NCAA Championships, and a job with ESPN doing color for the women's games. It gave me flexibility. That March, I was in Kansas City working for ESPN and Mom was staying with the children. She called me to say that Darren had brought a knife to school and that the school was threatening to expel him. He was only in kindergarten. *How can a child be expelled from kindergarten? Especially when all he did was share something of his father's with his classmates?*

Before I'd left, I took out Don's toiletry set, which included a razor, a fingernail clipper, small scissors, and various other manicuring devices, and showed them to Darren. It was just one more way to keep the memory of their father alive. Once I removed the blade, I let Darren hold the razor, so that he could pretend to shave. "Remember how Daddy used to shave his face every morning?"

I knew that at some point I would have to become a father as well as a mother to my two little towheads, who looked a lot like Don as a child, and I figured there was no time like the present. While I was on the road, Darren had taken the all-purpose tool to school as something cool to show his friends. The school, however, wasn't amused and pointed out their no-knife policy.

"It was my fault," I told the principal. "I guess I just wasn't thinking."

"I understand completely," she said after learning that Darren was in a new home and a new school after recently losing his father. Darren was also shy. He was quiet and often let his older brother, D.J., speak up for him.

D.J. was like Don, and Darren was more like me. I worried about being gone with everything the kids had been through, but it was unavoidable. I was the breadwinner now. I had to make a living the only way I knew how, which at this point in my life would undoubtedly involve broadcasting or basketball; and the idea of a pro women's league had been on the rebound.

Women's basketball remained a small sorority where everyone knew each other, so I wasn't surprised when the ABL contacted me about coming on as an adviser of their new women's league. However, in the course of discussions, I began hearing that the commissioner of the NBA was thinking of forming a women's league under the NBA umbrella, so I informed the ABL I would have to pass on their offer.

I was intrigued with the idea of the WNBA, which was a natural progression spawned, oddly enough, from failure. After taking Gold again in '88 Olympics, the U.S. women's Olympic basketball team came in third in '92; and they were greatly overshadowed by the now all-pro men's Dream Team. So in a much-prayed for act of even-handedness, USA basketball decided to do something similar with the women. They persuaded Stanford coach Tara VanDerveer to swap her university gig for a paid year coaching Lisa Leslie, Teresa Edwards, Dawn Staley, Katrina McClain, Rebecca Lobo, and Sheryl Swoopes, to name a few.

In 1995, they ended up going 60-0. Nothing like that had ever happened before. They were the original women's Dream Team in my opinion, and a sure way to win the Gold at the next Olympic Games. But more than that, it confirmed the NBA Commissioner's suspicion that the time was ripe for a WNBA league.

In early April of 1996, the NBA Board of Governors officially approved the formation of the WNBA, which was announced at a press conference, with the face of the league, Rebecca Lobo, Lisa Leslie, and Sheryl Swoopes, in attendance. The exposure they garnered in the upcoming '96 Olympics in Atlanta, where 30,000 fans screamed for more, helped further launch the new league.

I'd been asked to coach or be the GM of several teams, but that presented another time commitment conundrum, so I was grateful when NBC signed me to a six-year deal to broadcast the games, instead. I had Dick Ebersol to thank.

Dick had been a good friend. The summer that Don died, Cooperstown invited me to attend the Hall of Fame induction, where they planned to honor Don posthumously. I needed to go, since many players were unable to fly out for the funeral. They expressed their condolences and told me wonderful stories about my husband that I'd never heard. Their memories brought him back to me for a short time. It was during the flight back that I met Dick, who had worked with Don when he was broadcasting *ABC Monday Night Baseball*. They were buddies, and Ebersol was now the President of NBC Sports.

Dick was the Olympics Shaman, heading up U.S. Olympics programming since the '88 games in Seoul. During the plane ride, I had hoped to convince him to hire me for the '96 Olympics in Atlanta. But when I dropped out of the '94 Goodwill Games because Don had just died, TNT hired Cheryl Miller. Now it was even more natural that the '96 broadcasting gig should go to Cheryl, since her brother Reggie was on that team; and go to her it did.

By invitation from NBA Commissioner, David Stern, I went to the Olympic Games, along with Juliene Simpson and several other past Olympians, to be introduced at half-time. Juliene and I walked to the Georgia Dome to watch the games, cutting through the Olympic park from the Ritz Carlton, where we were staying. One evening, after we'd returned to the hotel, Juliene was awakened in the middle of the night when her husband, Michael, called, frantic. All over the East Coast, the news was reporting that a bomb had gone off in the Olympic park, and he wanted to make sure his wife was okay. It had detonated fifteen minutes after we'd arrived back at the hotel. We were lucky.

And my luck didn't stop there. When I returned home, Dick Ebersol called me to do the NBC *Hoop It Up* Three on Three event in Dallas, which opened the door to my covering the WNBA games now. As with so many things that had happened in my life, it was all about coming full circle.

The first game pitted the New York Liberty against the LA Sparks at the Western Forum in Inglewood. It was nationally televised by NBC, with over 14,000 fans in attendance. No one had expected ticket sales would be so high, and they had to open up parts of the Forum to allow for the overflow. The League president at the time, Val Ackerman, threw the toss. The two teams tipped-off, while Hannah Storm broadcast the play-by-play, and I did color. It was the first time a major television network had paired two women to cover an event. Like me, she also had Dick Ebersol to thank. Dick also insisted that as many women work behind the camera as in front appointing *Iron Man* producer, Lisa Lax, to call the shots in the truck.

Hannah and I announced the action, and the country watched as a whole new generation of female basketball players seemed poised for a type of job security that had been illusive for decades.

With eight teams, everybody was excited. The plus was the greater sense of credibility under the umbrella of the NBA. They had sponsors, TV networks, and infrastructure already in place. Of course, the birth of one league meant the demise of the other. The

ABL folded after lasting three years just as the WBL had, and this left many of the ABL players jumping ship to climb aboard the new league.

In the West, there was Phoenix, L.A/Sacramento, and Utah. The East had New York, Charlotte, Cleveland, and Houston. Like the nascent perceptions, the league would evolve and grow. Teams would move, players would be traded, and I would continue to broadcast, bringing at least one of my children with me every time I went on the road. It was a great way to have one-on-one time with each of them.

At home in Southern California, the local games aired on Prime Ticket (Fox Sports channel) where Chick Hearn called the action, with me as his wingman. Chick had come over from the Lakers, where he had worked with Stu Lantz for so many years that he would often refer to me as Stu. We would be tossing to a commercial break and he'd say, "Some game, huh, Stu?" And I would just smile.

If Vin Scully was the voice of baseball, Chick Hearn was the voice of basketball. He had coined the term "Air-ball," along with a dozen other 'Hearnisms' like, "20-foot lay-up," which he used to describe a jump shot by Jamaal Wilkes. Others were "put him in the popcorn machine," and "put mustard on the hotdog." When the game was finished he'd say "The game's in the refrigerator, the door's closed, the lights are out, the eggs are cooling, the butter's getting hard, and the Jello's jiggling." He'd say the whole thing every time and never miss a beat.

Chick had earned his nickname while playing AAU basketball at Bradley when teammates surprised him with a shoebox containing not shoes, but a dead baby chick. By the time I had the honor of working with him, he had seen more practical jokes than he could count. He'd been working for decades in a business populated with men. I figured being called Stu occasionally was a small sacrifice to work with one of the greats.

Chick had a hard time with names, in general, and specifically the women's names because he wasn't as familiar with the WNBA as he was with the NBA. There was a huge Chinese player on the

Sparks team, Zheng Haixia, and Chick spent the first few seasons getting her name right. After awhile, he wouldn't even try, instead calling her "The Big Chinese girl." One time we did five takes on a toss to a commercial so that Chick could say her name. Each time he called her "The Big Chinese Girl." Another was Mwadi Mabika, which is pronounced like it sounds, yet he butchered it. But then, Chick had trouble saying *quesadilla*. He was lovable and wonderful, a hard worker, and I sensed that he liked me as much as I liked him.

He sure knew the game—the men's game. One of the consistent complaints I heard from Sparks' fans was that Chick would always call the players "girls."

"But they *are* girls to him. He's in his 80s," I'd explain. Women are okay with calling each other" 'girls," but they don't want to hear men say it. I knew it was never malicious with Chick. To him it was the "girls' game."

"The word 'women' has two syllables,' I'd tell the fans. "It's just easier for him."

One time, I'd just flown in on the red-eye after broadcasting a WNBA away game for NBC, when Chick and I prepared to do the weekend game. I had Drew with me, who was about five, sitting behind us. During half time we were supposed to show the highlight reel from the first half, which I was to cover as the color announcer. Halftime came and Chick started talking about something, I can't remember what. After a few minutes, Susan Stratton, long-time Lakers producer, whispered into my headset, "Annie, whenever you get a chance, just break in there so we can do the highlight reel." But there was no way I was going to interrupt Chick.

"Don't forget about the highlight reel," Susan finally said to Chick in the headphone.

So Chick turned to me. "Okay, Annie, they're telling me we got to do this darn highlight reel."

He was old school, that Chick. Now he had a woman in his left ear and a woman in his right, and he was calling a bunch of other women's plays down on the court. I'm sure growing up, he never dreamt such a thing could happen.

I never believed it couldn't.

Regardless of whom I was working with, or whether I was covering the women's games or the men's, when it came to doing the color, I was careful not to compare the players' instincts, reactions, or decisions to my own in similar instances.

I had learned from the best.

"If I thought the guy shoulda thrown a knuckle ball," Donnie used to say, "I'd never add 'cuz that's what I woulda done.'" He knew you could talk about your days as a player, but you couldn't compare plays.

"Kid could benefit from learning the two-foot jump stop," I'd say, instead of criticizing her for not passing the ball before she'd gotten to a certain position. I knew the players and coaches were reviewing the tapes from the televised games as learning tools so, wherever possible, I'd try to be constructive and point out possible alternate scenarios, rather than label someone as being at fault. I needed to help the fans recognize what was happening, though, and in doing that I knew I would offend someone. "She just wasn't hustling on that play," I might say, and whoever *she* was wasn't going to like it. But by now, I knew one thing, for sure: You can't please everybody.

If I had to try to keep the way I played out of my color, I never worried about any personal regrets creeping in up in the booth. I was never one to think *what if*. "What if you'd been born later, you might have played today?"

I'm asked that question often, but I played at a great time in the game's history, and I'm grateful for that time. After so many years, and several false starts, a women's pro league had finally arrived. It didn't matter that I wasn't playing on it. It was here to stay, and if I'd contributed in some small way to its creation and was now able to be involved as a broadcaster, well, that was more than enough for me. I still call the games with every bit as much enthusiasm and pride in women's basketball as I'd ever had.

Basketball was basketball. It was the game I loved and I'd always said that no other country's men or women played better than ours. I remained every bit a fan of the NBA players as I'd ever been. In less than a year after I began broadcasting the WNBA games, I became the first woman to announce an NBA game on network television for NBC. Again, thanks to Dick Ebersol. I announced with Dick Enberg up in Utah covering the Jazz, who, ironically had partnered with Donnie years earlier for the Angels Broadcasts. Who knew Dick and I would end up together when he and Donnie were so close? But like Women's basketball, broadcasting is a small circle. Men's basketball—on the other hand—well there's never been anything small about that.

The number of spectators at the NBA games dwarfed the average WNBA game, and the ratings crucified the women's games. But I figured it would only be a matter of time. There was no doubt the women's game had finally arrived. And now it even had its own Hall of Fame.

It had been a long time coming. When the Women's Basketball Hall of Fame was finally erected that June of 1999, I brought my daughter, Drew, with me to Knoxville where I became a member of the inaugural class to be inducted.

My good friend, Robin Roberts, was the MC for what would be the largest class ever. It was wonderful to see old pals Juliene Simpson, Pat Summitt, Lucy Harris, coaches Billie Moore and Sue Gunter, and the rest of the '76 Olympic team. We were all inducted, along with so many others whom I had played with or against over the years. As we'd approached the building, Drew, who was now six, looked up to see the largest basketball in the world. The Baden Ball measured thirty feet tall and weighed ten tons. Inside, there were artifacts, memorabilia, and other iconography which had been painstakingly collected over the years and was now in one place for posterity.

"Mommy, I want to go home," Drew said the next day, one hand tugging on my shirt, the other holding a rainbow ice-cream cone; purple stains framing her little mouth. We'd been sightseeing in downtown Knoxville all morning, but every now and then a stranger would stop me.

"Can I have your autograph, Ms. Meyers?" People were often stopping me on the street, wanting to discuss the Final Four teams, the coaches, or my history. That got old fast where the kids were concerned. For the past few years, I'd been bringing one of them with me each time I travelled for some special one-on-one time, but they noticed when my attention was being diverted, even for a moment. Now Drew was looking up at me with these big, blue eyes that reminded me of her dad.

"Of course we can go home, honey. We can do anything you like," I bent down and kissed the top of her head, which was covered in auburn locks. As a single parent, I was always trying to do double-duty, and it hurt when it felt like I was falling short. But I still had to travel, and I knew that keeping myself and the kids busy was part of the healing process. When we returned to California, I still missed Don, but I could feel the haze lifting. It would not lift for long, however.

I came back to find that my 80-year-old father, who had been battling dementia for the last year or so, was worse. He was in and out of various facilities because he'd wander off and sometimes become abusive with staff, so invariably the facility would call us in and tell us that things weren't working out.

He'd forget to eat, forget to take his pills, and he'd get angry that everyone was telling him what to do. He couldn't remember much of the present, but he would tell us things from his past, stories we'd never heard, and it was so interesting. I didn't remember him being so talkative when I was younger. It was nice. Other times, though, he'd become convinced we were stealing his money and demand that we take him to the bank.

Mark and Frannie were there a lot, along with Patty, David, Jeff, Susie and Colleen. Sometimes he recognized us, and sometimes he didn't. But it didn't matter. We were family and that's what family does.

That same year, my oldest, beloved brother, Tom, who was a favorite uncle to all of his nieces and nephews, had grown increasingly sick after having contracted HIV years earlier. Mom was taking care of him in La Habra, where we'd all grown up. She watched her 6'3" first-born, hulking son, who had been able to tackle anyone on the football field and been nicknamed "The Mayor of Newport Beach" because of his larger-than-life personality and generosity, whither away. In 1999 Tom died. Mom had now lost two children.

Then, in early 2000, my dad passed on. As an athlete, one of the first things you learn is how to go on after a loss, how to pick yourself up, go out there and battle all over again. This was different though. I had never dealt with such an unrelenting opponent.

I was glad that the father I'd loved, despite everything, was finally at peace. So was Mom. For her, Dad's passing represented closure. The little death that had occurred for her so many years earlier, way back in 1979, when Patricia and Robert Meyers had officially divorced, was now finally being laid to rest. Whenever I felt sorry for myself that Don had died, I thought about my parents. It made me realize there were so many worse ways a marriage could end than in the death of a spouse. My mother had been living with an open wound, which would finally be allowed to heal.

The kids and I were also on the mend. It had been seven years since Don had died. I had faith that the new millennium would usher in only good things for all of us.

22
A Single Mother

"You have a lifetime to work, but children are only young once."
~ Polish Proverb

"Mrs. Drysdale you have to come down to the school, fast." I was doing some research for an upcoming broadcast, when I got a call from D. J.'s Junior High telling me that he had hurt his arm playing football during lunch, and that I should come quickly.

"Well... okay..." I remember feeling a bit put out, like maybe they were making a mountain out of a mole hill. He wasn't a little kid anymore, he was almost 12. I figured if it were a real emergency, they'd have called the hospital. I almost told them to give him two aspirin and have him lay down—basically the same line Mom would give us when we were younger and got hurt. I'd been raised that if you fell down, you pulled yourself up and tied-up your bootstraps. If that philosophy was good enough for me, it was good enough for my kids.

D.J. was less impressed. "Mom, you didn't come forever," he said, when I finally arrived.

After we got home, I sent him to bed to rest, and went back to what I'd been doing. But I could hear the different groans he was making, and they didn't sound right. As a mother you can tell when your child is really hurt. You've heard him cry from anger, frustration, or pain enough times to know the difference. This sounded like agony.

When I took D.J. to the doctor, sure enough, he had broken his humorous bone, the one between the elbow and shoulder. The doctor said it was one of the hardest bones to break. I felt like I'd dropped the parenting ball yet again.

Now I was supposed to leave for Sydney and the 2000 Olympic Women's Basketball Games. Dick Ebersol had hired me to do the color. But Drew was only seven and Darren was ten. After what had happened with D.J., I didn't want to leave them for three weeks while I travelled halfway around the world. So I pooled my airline miles and was able to bring them. Mom, my brother David, and my sister, Cathy also came, and it turned out to be the most amazing trip for everyone.

Darren, my brother, David, and D.J. stayed in one hotel room, while Mom, Cathy, Drew and I stayed in another. Things were different since FIBA had changed the rules in 1989 that allowed professionals to compete in the Olympic Games. The catalyst may have been when the US Men's team finished with only a Bronze at the '88 Olympics. The '92 Olympics had ushered in the first Dream Team. Since then, no other country stood a chance. (Women's 'Dream Team' came in 2000.)

These were also the first Olympics in which WNBA players would compete. There was a fierce rivalry between Australian basketball player, Lauren Jackson and our own Lisa Leslie. The Games were played at the Sydney Superdome, and both the U.S. Men's and Women's teams took the Gold.

When we returned to the States, I continued to do the NCAA Final Four for ESPN, and when I wasn't broadcasting, I worked various basketball camps and did some motivational speaking. Offers kept coming to coach or work in the front office with various WNBA franchises, just as they had when the league first started up, but I still said no. I wanted to wait until the kids were off to college.

Sometimes I wondered if my youngest would ever make it. By now, in addition to breaking her femur and arm, she seemed like she was always hurting herself whether it was splitting her chin jumping backward into the pool or breaking her wrist while competing with a boy to see who could jump highest. She was nine and reminding me more of myself when I was young. Nowadays, I didn't run and jump the way I had then. Now, I had to make time to exercise along with every other broadcaster who hoped to keep their backsides from turning to mush from sitting in the booth too long.

By 2004, I realized I'd been broadcasting for twenty-five years. That spring, after attending a Baseball Hall of Fame luncheon at the White House as Sandy Koufax's guest, I flew into New Orleans to do color for the NCAA Women's Final Four with Mike Patrick who was now calling the play-by-play. It was there that I received a phone call requesting that I fly to Los Angeles to attend the Cy Young Awards. I was asked to represent Don. All of the other Dodger Cy Young Award winners were invited to be there when Eric Gagne was presented with his award. I wanted to go and I knew my children would be there, and I wanted to be with them, but arranging for a flight back and forth in time would be difficult.

That same week the *L.A. Times* ran a piece, "Meyers At Home in Final Four." I'd been featured in the *Los Angeles Times* a lot over the years, but what made this article so special were the nice things my colleague, Mike Patrick, said about me. "I've never met anyone who doesn't rave about her. You never hear an unkind word spoken about her from anyone."

For the most part, I got along well with all of my broadcasting colleagues. They'd been so nice to me over the years, and Patrick, especially so. "Not since Ann Meyers had anything so great come to TV," he was once quoted saying when asked about the advent of HD Television, and I'm still so flattered that he would say something so nice.

But now, when I was feeling like I couldn't be at the right place at the right time, like maybe I was letting too many people down, it was especially great to read something like that. It was beyond gratifying to learn that colleagues considered me to be a decent individual in a business that was often driven by ambition and greed. I'd always taken pride in my work, always wanted to deliver and be the best without being cut-throat about it. To know now that I was respected and liked by my peers felt good.

That July, I left the children to travel to Athens to cover the 2004 Olympics, again for NBC. Just as it had been in 1984, it was still an incredible honor to be broadcasting the Olympic women's basketball games, for which I, once again, had Dick Ebersol to thank. This time, though, we were warned not to bring our families. It was still so soon after the terrorist attacks of 9/11. The fear was that the 2004 Olympics would be a dangerous place, especially for Americans.

Without the kids there, I was better able to focus on my work. A lot of the players from other countries had tricky names. I was working with one of the best play-by-play announcers out there, Mike Breen, with whom I'd worked covering WNBA games for NBC. Together we studied the pronunciation of each player's name so we could avoid stumbling during the broadcast. While I was working color for the women's games, Doug Collins was working color for the men's, and Mike was doing double duty calling both the men's and women's. Afterward the whole crew would go to dinner at the same beautiful open air restaurant with its gentle sea breezes. We'd be there until one or two in the morning and the place would remain packed. It seemed Greece came alive at night. The basketball banter would go back and forth, and we'd remember past Olympic games, and it always made the food taste better

We all had a great time and as it turned out, it couldn't have been safer. The staff in charge of security was hyper-vigilante, and I regretted not bringing the kids. Then again, hindsight is a lovely thing. How many times I have wished for a crystal ball, so I'd never make a wrong step. Most of all, you always want to be there. But later that year, I learned that even being there was no guarantee that the worst wouldn't happen.

In late November, Dick and Susan Ebersol's fourteen-year-old son, Teddy, died. The family had boarded a small, private jet in Colorado that crashed moments after take-off in icy conditions and poor visibility. Dick suffered serious injuries, as did the rest of the family, but Teddy had been ejected from the plane, dying instantly. He had been the youngest of five, an altar boy, who had spoken at his 8th grade graduation the previous year by saying, "The finish line is only the beginning of a whole new race." My Darren and Teddy were only a year apart.

Those of us who knew Dick and his wife, actress Susan Saint James, could not imagine the heartbreak they were going through. There were no words to heal their pain. Dick had been instrumental in the careers of so many. His protégés were scattered throughout the broadcasting world, most of them flourishing, many of them owing their livelihoods to him. He was pivotal in launching my Olympic broadcasting career for NBC, and he'd given me the honor of being the first female to broadcast a nationally televised NBA game, in addition to hiring me to work the WNBA games. Now I and so many others could do little more in return than pay our respects and offer up our prayers at his son's funeral.

It was appearing more and more that the peaks of life were impossible without its valleys. When I got back home, I'm sure I hugged the kids much harder and longer than I normally do when returning from a trip. Then I called Mom. As parents, we are programmed to protect our kids, not to bury them, and this was something she understood all too well. After we talked I reminded D.J., Darren, and Drew that however difficult things were for us without their dad, there was still so much to be grateful for.

During this same period, I tried to spend as much time as possible visiting Papa. He was always on my radar and I'd often call him whether I was on the road or at home. He was in his nineties, but still managed to get to plenty of the UCLA games at Pauley Pavilion when he was feeling well. He always sat in section 103B in a seat behind the home bench. And he always managed to give out autographs. Even as frail as he had become, his signature was as pure and clear as it had been forty years earlier, just like the heart and soul of the man himself. He had never sought the limelight or all the attention. He'd been a teacher in his early career, and that's always how he thought of himself, a teacher first and foremost. When he started coaching back in the 30s and 40s, and then at UCLA in the 50s, he was one of the few coaches out there who would play black athletes. In 1947 he'd refused an invitation to the Final Four Tournament in Kansas City because of the NAIB's policy banning African American players.

This was well before they began calling him the Wizard of Westwood, a moniker he didn't appreciate because he'd tried so hard to teach his players that success could only be achieved through commitment and hard work. The press was making it sound as though it were as easy as magic for him. We, who knew him, never used that term. And if he'd have let the press know how much he disliked it, they would have stopped using it, too. That's how strong a sway he held over people. Even in the twilight of his life, his influence was such that when he appeared on Charlie Rose with Bill Walton and Bill Russell, Russell admitted later that the only reason he went on the show was to be near Papa. We all wanted to be near him whenever we could.

And I wanted to tell him my news; and get his advice.

Robert Sarver had called me from Arizona asking me to act as General Manager for the Mercury. The Phoenix Mercury was the one WNBA team that called year in and year out. They had been relentless. I'd just received the Ronald Reagan Media Award a few months earlier, placing me in the company of Howard Cosell, Bob Costas, Keith Jackson, Frank Deford, and Rupert Murdoch. It was a personal victory for me because I was such an introvert unless I was performing as an athlete, and I considered it a triumph over nature to think that I had been given an award in the name of one of the greatest American communicators of the 20th Century. Whether or not I would consider Sarver's proposal depended on a couple things. I wanted to know that I could take the job and continue to broadcast and, more importantly, whether my children thought it was okay. I wasn't about to uproot them again.

Sarver had just purchased both the NBA and WNBA Phoenix franchises a couple of years earlier from Jerry Colangelo, who was instrumental in supporting the WNBA league in 1997. A self-made man at twenty-three, Sarver had been the youngest to found a national bank. Now, nearly twenty years later, he hoped to make both the Suns and the Mercury as profitable as all of his other endeavors. Not long after he stepped in, the Phoenix Suns tied a record for the NBA-Best 62 wins. In September of 2006, Robert hoped that by bringing me onboard he could do the same thing for the women's team.

I needed to talk to someone who understood the rigors of being a GM, so I turned to Don's good friend, Buzzie Bavasi. The Hall of Fame GM with the Brooklyn/LA Dodgers, California Angels, and San Diego Padres, was a wealth of information. Of course, I also spoke to Papa, and my family. Before presenting it to the kids, I wanted to make sure I understood all the ramifications myself.

By this time, D.J. was nineteen and a senior at Cushing Prep Academy in Massachusetts, Darren was seventeen and in high school, and Drew was thirteen, in junior high. They were getting older, but I still wasn't sure if it was the right thing to do. They were the first ones I asked. I had to know how they felt. A few months earlier we'd all been invited by the Dodgers to see the premier of the movie, *Bobby*, the fictionalized account of the hours leading up to the assassination of Robert Kennedy on June 5th 1968—the same day Donnie had achieved his sixth straight shutout. It was filled with newsreels from the day, and though much of the dialogue revolved around Donnie's shutout, they never did show footage of him.

"Gosh, Mom, the whole way through I kept thinking they were going to show Dad," Darren said.

Darren was just three when Don died, an age where memories of his father were only just beginning to form. Now Darren was trying hard to recall what he could. It reminded me of when he was younger and how frustrated he would get when he couldn't remember the same things about his dad that his older brother, D.J., could. I would wonder when all the little scars from Donnie's death would finally disappear, leaving us with only beautiful memories.

Now we had watched a movie that had taken us back in time to a day that was so terrible for the nation, and yet historic for their dad. It was one of Don's greatest achievements.

"As proud as he was of that day, I know he'd be twice as proud of you two now," I told Darren and Drew after the movie, and I believed it with all my heart.

Though they didn't show Don, the comments from the other characters in the movie had been enough to give the kids a good idea of what their Dad was like as a younger man. There were so many things even I learned about Don from that film. When I think about it now, in some ways it was probably good that D.J. was at prep school instead of being with us that night. If Darren had faint memories of his father, and Drew had none, their older brother was living with a ghost.

D.J. carried his father's name, his eyes, and so much of Don's personality. When he'd been younger, many adults would come up to him and say, "Are you going to grow up to become a baseball player like your dad?" They'd ask both the boys, and I know it bothered them, just like it bothered Drew when someone would ask if she wanted to become a basketball player like her mom.

But everything seemed to resonate just a little bit more with D.J., and I think it's because he remembered his father and how much it had hurt those first several years after his death.

Afterward, Izzy and some of the other Dodgers told the kids stories about Don back in the day. The movie had brought us a little closer to the man we all loved. But for children, a movie reel is a lousy stand-in for the real thing. I thought back on that night now and worried about whether or not my taking the GM position for the Mercury would be the right thing.

We had a family discussion, and they thought it was a good idea. They told me they were aware of how many opportunities I'd turned down up to that point. We all decided that Darren and Drew would stay in Huntington Beach rather than come with me to Phoenix. This would allow them to finish school with the same friends and teachers and be near the ocean.

Drew was playing soccer and running track, and Darren was playing soccer and running track as well. Their lives were in Huntington Beach. I had the help of Mom, Patty, and Frannie, and other family members who took turns staying at the house while I was away. And Phoenix was just a short plane ride away. My sister, Cathy, was already living there, so I knew I'd have family nearby. I looked at each of my kids head on, trying to read their faces, hoping that they really meant what they were saying, wondering if it might finally be all right.

23

The Road to the Boardroom
Is Through the Locker Room

"If you want something said, ask a man. If you want something done, ask a woman."
~ Margaret Thatcher

"This is Ann Meyers, the new GM of the Mercury." Robert introduced me to everyone in the front office. We shook hands, exchanged pleasantries, and then Robert cleared his throat. "Oh, yeah, and she's also going to be Vice President of the Suns." When I heard that I gasped right along with everybody else. We had never discussed the VP position or my responsibilities. I couldn't have predicted in a million years that he was going to spring such a totally thrilling, surprising prospect on me. The title alone would open up doors.

The next thing I knew, I was out scouting for the Suns, and I loved it. I also scouted for the Mercury. The Suns continued to dominate, and the Mercury finally started to heat up.

They'd always had the talent, the nucleus of a winning team. Diana Taurasi, Cappi Pondexter, and Penny Taylor were three phenomenal players. They were missing the fourth leg. I knew their coach, Paul Westhead, because I'd broadcast some of his games when he was coaching at Loyola, and he'd also been head coach for the Lakers during the 1980 Championship with Magic and Kareem, and I knew the assistant coach, Corey Gains, because he'd played for Coach Westhead.

But it was in the front office that Jay Parry, COO/President, and Amber Cox, the Marketing Director, and I clicked. The three of us had an instant chemistry, which made each of us better.

Through a bizarre bit of luck, when Jay and I went back to New York for the WNBA meetings, they also had the lottery for the #1 pick. We could hear the ping pong balls popping inside the machine. The Mercury had the worst odds, so everyone was stunned when the ball popped up and we got the first pick overall.

When it was time for the draft, I made a tough decision, but one I felt was necessary. After discussing it with Coach Westhead, we traded the first pick to Minnesota for Tangela Smith. No one had ever traded away the number one overall pick before, not in the NBA. And there were a lot of people who believed I'd made a big mistake, including Jay and Amber. But I felt that going with a seasoned pro like Tangela was a smart move. She was the missing piece of the puzzle. I had broadcast Tangela's games when she was in college, and then in Sacramento, and Charlotte when she went pro. I knew she could play, and more than that, Coach and I knew she'd fit into the system he ran. The chemistry among the teammates could now work to create a whole greater than the sum of its parts.

Papa used to say, "It's amazing what you can accomplish when nobody cares who gets the credit." When you think of competitive athletes, altruism seldom comes to mind. But I knew that to have a winning team, they had to play for the *team*, not themselves.

All for one and one for all had been my motto as a team member, but I had refrained from saying "we" as a broadcaster. In part, it was an attempt to remain impartial. Even when broadcasting the UCLA games, I tried not to say "we." But now, as a representative of the Suns and the Mercury "we" was all I said. "Group think" would also be accompanied by a lot more orange and purple clothing in my closet. It was such a great organization with so many wonderful people, and they made it easy. Jerry Colangelo had built it from scratch and Sarver had come in with so much passion. Mike D'Antoni, Rick Welts, Alvin Gentry, and Steve Kerr on the NBA side were behind me a hundred percent.

But behind the decision to trade our #1 pick or not, even the fans could see that the players began communicating better on the court and making the extra unselfish passes necessary to build a championship team without losing the individual heart and drive it took to be great. They chalked up their first-ever 23-win season, the first regular-season Western Conference Championship. At the same time, the kids and I flew to Madrid, where Dean Smith, Bill Russell, and I would become the first Americans to be inducted into the FIBA Hall of Fame. It was an enormous honor, but the whole time I hated the thought of missing a play-off game. We flew back to Phoenix in time for game 4 in which a last-minute shot by Cappie Pondexter forced a decisive Game 5. And though on the road, in 2007, at long last, the Mercury clinched their very first WNBA Championship, beating out the favored and more playoff-experienced Detroit Shock. Detroit's coach, Bill Laimbeer, tipped his hat. We had beat him, and on his home turf. It was another WNBA first.

If I'd been juggling before, now I felt like I was juggling on a unicycle. But at least I was on a peak.

The following June, I found myself in the East Garden of the White House. President George W. Bush had invited the Mercury in celebration of the previous year's championship. I had met him several times in the 80s when he was part owner of the Texas Rangers. They'd come into Chicago to play the White Sox and he'd met with Don.

I brought D.J. with me. He was attending Arizona State and interning for the Mercury and the Suns. The President had asked him to stand during his presentation—he wanted to see if D. J. resembled Don as much as he'd heard. "He does kinda look like the big right hander," he said before proceeding with his congratulation speech to the team.

Next, it was my turn. "Mr. President, we know your support for the Phoenix Mercury is genuine because of the influence of the women in your life."

"Yes," he said.

"All first ladies—your graceful mother, your classy wife ..."

"Thank you..."

"...your very strong-willed daughters." When I said this, everybody laughed—as I expected they would. The twins had recently been featured in the news as big-time party-girls. They were just displaying typical, (some may have said irresponsible) teenage behavior. It was harmless, unless your dad happened to be the president.

"That's why my hair is white," he quipped, and again there was a big laugh. Up until that point, his standard response to the press' questions about his daughters had been, "That's why my *mother's hair* is white," but he'd obviously rethought the wisdom of that, deciding to make himself the butt of the joke, instead. After all, he was playing to a primarily female crowd.

Clearly, the leader of the free world enjoyed making people laugh. I'd met his father and mother with Don when Bush, Senior was in the White House. Don had known all of the presidents from the Kennedys on up, and as an Olympian I'd met President Ford. Now, however, I was here with the Mercury, and I couldn't have been prouder. I continued my speech, and then Diana Taurasi and Cappie Pondexter, our team captains and two fellow Olympians, presented him with a Phoenix Mercury jersey and a replica of our championship banner.

The president finished and came over to say hello. When D.J. went to shake his hand, the President smiled, took D.J.'s palm, closed the fingers, and gave him a little fist bump. He was laid back and friendly, and it might have been my imagination, but it was almost as though he sensed that D.J. had had to act like a grown up for far too long, and he wanted him to relax and enjoy himself, at least for an afternoon. The three of us must have spoken for a good fifteen minutes before his security finally came up and took him away.

Afterward, D.J. and I headed back to our hotel, the Mohegan Sun in Connecticut. The team had a game that night. The hotel's casino had about a half-dozen shops and boutiques, one of which was filled with celebrity memorabilia. Something of Don's was there, but that's not what caught my eye. In the window, there was a framed picture of Mother Teresa with a letter written and signed by her.

"Mom, we have to get that for Papa," D.J. said the moment he saw it. Mother Teresa had been one of Papa's greatest inspirations.

Back in the 80s, former LSU basketball coach, Dale Brown, had arranged a meeting between Papa and Mother Teresa when she was in California, but Papa had fallen sick. Dale loved him, as so many of the coaches and players did, and he knew how much the meeting would have meant. Papa had never asked for anything. He didn't need anything. But I knew how much he regretted not being able to meet her that time. I hoped this would help. I couldn't wait to get home to give it to him. He had far more yesterdays than tomorrows, yet he lived each day as his masterpiece. It had always been his credo.

I thought about Papa's philosophy that July, as I left for the Beijing Olympics. This time I brought the kids with me. The flight was long, and when we finally arrived, the room was small. The four of us had to stay in one hotel room. I had no problem sharing a bathroom. I was used to that having grown up in a big family. But for the kids it was something new. Drew and I shared the bed, while the boys slept in a bed and a roll-away. The accommodations couldn't take the shine off our thrill to be in Beijing. The eyes of the world had turned to China, which was proving to be the new superpower while billing itself as the best of the old and the new. Beijing was every bit as metropolitan and high tech as I'd heard. I'd also heard about the choking smog, and that was no lie either.

We'd only been there a few days when Drew complained about her throat hurting. She had tonsillitis earlier and now I was afraid it might be back. She didn't want to miss any of the sight-seeing, though, especially The Great Wall. She knew this might be her only opportunity to visit China, so she came out with us every day and was a great sport. But the air quality was so noxiously bad in Beijing, especially during the summer, that a year earlier there had been speculation in the U.S. press about whether or not some of the events would need to be postponed. Now factories were closed, construction slowed and it was reported that one million of the city's 3.3 million cars were banned from the roads by China's government as a precaution.

They had spent nearly 40 billion dollars to remake the capital in anticipation of being on the world stage. Image was important. The basketball games (which were very popular in China, because of Yao Ming's participation in the NBA) were indoors, so the players were more or less unaffected. But the highly anticipated track and field events took place in the Bird's Nest national stadium. You might be able to disguise the pollution for the cameras, but with over 550,000 foreign visitors and about 22,000 accredited members of the media descending upon the city, there were bound to be plenty of people who noticed athletes complaining about the air quality — athletes, and visitors recovering from tonsillitis.

Toward the end of the trip Drew was really sick. When I looked inside her mouth, her tonsils were so swollen that I couldn't see the back of her throat. We found the nearest clinic in Beijing where a doctor who spoke some English gave her an herbal remedy which, luckily, worked right away.

All in all, it was a great opportunity for the kids. The Opening Ceremonies were some of the most spectacular I'd ever seen. The U.S. Women's basketball team had an excellent showing by defeating Australia 92-65 to take the Gold, in large part thanks to a team of WNBA players twelve deep, as compared to Australia's seven WNBA players. Among the U.S. team were two of the Phoenix Mercury, Diana Taurasi and Cappie Pondexter. And three-time Olympian Dawn Staley, a point guard for the Houston Comets, was selected to carry the flag. That another woman, and basketball player no less, was selected to carry our country's flag made me proud.

Back home, the Suns were continuing to dominate. Two-time MVP, Steve Nash, could knock down shots from any point on the court, and as one of the best passers in the league, he was one of the NBA's big ticket draws. But it was the WNBA Fever - Mercury Finals that changed the way the country was coming to view the women's game. The Indiana franchise had been hemorrhaging cash so badly that there was talk that it might fold. Pacers President, Larry Bird bought $5,000 worth of tickets for the fans in support of the team, and then Steve Kerr, GM of the Suns, bought $5,000 when they were playing in Phoenix. All of the Finals were sold out.

Away games three and four of the finals had produced full houses of over 18,000, giving the Fever a much-needed financial infusion. On the Mercury team—in the bleachers during games, and in management—we all felt it was a historic series. *The New York Times* agreed. A piece appeared in early October likened the WNBA finals between Mercury and the Fever to the Lakers - Celtics rivalry of the 1980s, with Diana Taurasi in place of Magic Johnson, and Tamika Catchings instead of Larry Bird.

It had been thirty years since I'd felt like a woman without a team, since I'd spent three days playing with some of the NBA's best only to find myself, ultimately, playing with ladies who could barely pass a ball. Now women's basketball had finally arrived. I was contacted by a *Sports Illustrated* reporter asking me for my take on whether a woman might finally play in the NBA.

NBA Commissioner, David Stern, had been quoted saying that he thought it was a good possibility that we would see a woman playing in the NBA within the next ten years. That idea had been heresy in 1979. Suddenly, with the way the finals had played out, the commissioner was suggesting that it was likely. The irony, of course, was that now that women finally had a league of their own, playing on a level to par the men, they didn't need to go out for the NBA (although there were and are all sorts of issues as to the huge disparity in compensation.)

When the Mercury won the Championship again in 2009 in another exciting five game series, we were invited to the White House a second time. This time, I brought my daughter, Drew, to meet President Obama. He didn't spend nearly as long with the team as President Bush had, but I suppose the world had changed so much in that short period and he had a busy day ahead. I will say I was disappointed that he didn't spend more time with us.

After he left the podium, the president took a group shot on stage with the team. As he left the stage, Corey Gaines, now our head coach, jumped off the stage and ran up to the president, rousing security. "My mom would kill me if I didn't get a picture with you."

After half-scaring the President to death, Corey got the photo he knew would make his mother proud and explained that his mother was also from Hawaii. Hopefully, it was a bit of levity for a man dealing with a country in turmoil.

The crash in the housing industry and resultant bank failures were being felt far and wide and as near as Vero Beach. The Dodgers spring training camp for sixty-one years was suddenly no more. Florida's 220 acres of practice fields with their intersection of Vin Scully Way and Don Drysdale Drive became an antique over night. The new owners, the McCourts, thought it would be more cost-efficient to build a new facility in Arizona rather than try to coordinate the team's long trek cross country from L.A. to Florida.

Vin Scully called Dodgertown his "memory factory," and I'd been taking the kids back every year as a way of staying in touch with their father's memory. The final game was set for March 17, the traditional St. Patrick Day game where the players wore green caps and ran around green bases. After that, the camp was moving to Glendale, a suburb outside of Phoenix, where the Dodgers would share a training site with the Chicago White Sox. While it was certainly closer for me and I would be able to reconnect with all the friends Don and I had on the White Sox team, it just wasn't the same. They didn't even serve Dodger Dogs! But still, it would be convenient, and that was a good thing.

When I looked at my calendar these days, it was like a completed crossword puzzle—no empty spaces. Of course, I loved being busy and had gone at life that way from the beginning. I didn't want to play just one sport, I wanted to play them all. While it was a great way to avoid burn out, I think there was also this sense that time was always running out. *Do as much as you can Annie, for as long as you can, especially when you're relatively young.* Not working hard while you still had your health seemed to me like an athlete not competing in her prime—it was squandering leverage. After all, life was short. And even when it wasn't, it was still too short.

On June 4, 2010, John Robert Wooden died. He was ninety-nine years old. We all knew it was coming. He was looking forward to it. He had been waiting a long time to see his Nellie again. The man who started out his career known as Rubberneck for his dives on the hardwood at Purdue had ended it as The Greatest Coach Ever. The man who had instilled the necessary discipline and knowledge to what would become some of the most talented, celebrated athletes in the world, had now left it. He'd been adored by athletes, and yet his heroes were not sport stars, but icons of integrity. His famous Pyramid of Success was based on acting with integrity and kindness. Even though I know he would have never described himself that way, honorable is exactly how I and so many others shall always remember him.

My brother, Dave, along with my freshman coach, Kenny Washington, and too many others to list, attended his funeral. After the services, they spoke for a while and I overheard Kenny tell Dave that Papa used to quietly come into our practices once in a while and sit high up in the rafters where no one could see him so he could watch me. "I never told her." Kenny said, then added, "Wooden may have gotten Kareem, but I got Annie."

The truth was, we all got Papa.

The same year that John Wooden passed, I was made President of the Mercury. It was a strange feeling when I got the news. I picked up the phone to call Papa and share it with him, and then I remembered he was gone.

In addition to my promotion, I continued to act as GM and retained my responsibilities as Vice President of the Suns. I also continued to broadcast for Fox and do motivational speaking engagements when my schedule permitted. In 2012, I broadcast the Olympics women's games for NBC. But, now, as priorities change I've decided to relinquish the positions of President and GM to remain V.P. for both the Mercury and the Suns, thereby allowing me more time to focus on other things, including broadcasting.

Sometimes it's hard to keep all the balls in the air, but in terms of gaining insights for our players—having had the various perspectives of GM, VP, and President, and the ability to go between the NBA and the WNBA—it has been invaluable. In terms of broadcasting, my day-to-day interaction with the players keeps me in the loop with everything from new tricks, to new terms, to new trades. But I'll still always believe that knowing the fundamentals trumps everything.

Of course, the hardest job is still being mom. The kids are all off to college, doing what they love, and trying to find themselves. I know they've enjoyed a certain amount of independence over the years, but I also know they've felt abandoned at times, and that is a guilt I will carry with me forever. Still, I try to remind myself that because of baseball and basketball, they've had the opportunities to travel, to meet people in sports, entertainment, and politics. They realize, firsthand, the importance of treating others with respect, and of always trying to give back. Most importantly, they've learned to be grateful for what the Good Lord has provided for all of us. In 2011, the two boys threw out the first pitch at Dodger Stadium in honor of what would have been their father's 75th birthday, and the following month Drew sang the national anthem there for her dad. Donnie would have been proud.

All in all, I have been very blessed. I know that God only gives us as much as He thinks we can handle. It's been a full life, full of blessings and heartache. But if I know one thing for certain, it's that 90% of life isn't about what happens to you, it's about how you respond to those things. Character trumps circumstances every time. One you can control, the other you can't.

In my bid for the Pacers, when it felt like the eyes of the world were on me and things didn't go my way, and the press was ridiculing me, I was still grateful for the opportunity. And given the chance, I'd do it the same way, all over again.

So many athletes fear failure. I don't like it, but it doesn't scare me. I know that failing is not just part of life, it's fundamental to success. To achieve greatness, you can't be afraid to fail. When I think back on my life, I wouldn't change a thing, except to have Don back. Not a day goes by that I don't miss him. But I also believe that life doesn't end because Don is gone, or my children are grown, or jobs change. Life does get better. Like Papa used to say, "Live each day as your masterpiece."

24

Where We Go From Here

"To throw obstacles in the way of a complete education is like putting out the eyes."
~ Elizabeth Cady Stanton

When I was at UCLA with my brother, Dave, we became instant human interest stories, so the media seemed to like me until I went out for the Pacers. But someone has to be the first to open the door for others. A lot of rookies got cut that season and while most of the NBA players, GMs, and coaches believed there was no woman on earth who could have made any of the twenty-two NBA teams that year, or any year, I also know there were some who were rooting for me in spite of their bias.

The Pacer's assistant coach at the time, Jack McCloskey, who would go onto become the GM of the NBA Champion Detroit Pistons said this about my playing, "Fundamentally, Annie is better than half the guys out there."

Atlanta Hawks coach, Hubie Brown, said of a woman's bid to make the NBA, "If there is to be an exception, I wish her a good deal of luck because it couldn't happen to a nicer person."

I'm still the only woman to sign a free-agent contract with an NBA team, and I'll always be proud of the way I played during those three days and grateful that Sam Nassi had the courage to let a woman tryout for the team. It was never about publicity for me, it was about seizing the opportunity. Do I believe that a woman will be signed to an NBA team by 2020 as NBA Commissioner, David Stern, suggested? With the WNBA providing a viable professional outlet, I don't know that it's that important anymore. The question shouldn't be will women play in the NBA, but rather will women be commensurately compensated? And will young women continue to be given the same opportunities in school to pursue their athletic dreams as young men?

Before Title IX was passed forty years ago, less than 300,000 girls nationwide played competitive sports in high school, and athletic scholarships for women were non-existent. Today close to 3,000,000 girls are competing athletically at the high school level and many are going on to college, largely as a result of this legislation. Yet every year Title IX comes under attack. Given that so much is learned in competitive sports, it's very sad that there are still schools which remain non-compliant. Where else can girls learn about hard work, self-esteem, perseverance, teamwork, leadership skills, the world won't end because you lose a game, and you can compete with someone and still be friends off the court? It's a given that all of these traits in excellence are beneficial in the business world, but also in life.

Where would we be without Title IX? Would we have a Mia Hamm or a Lindsey Vonn, or a Lisa Leslie, Michelle Wie, or Misty May? I'm not sure where I would be without it. And I was one of the lucky ones.

I'd been born into a wonderful family where we'd all been encouraged to spend the better part of the day playing sports outside whether in the snow of Chicago or the 75 degree weather of Southern California with parents who stoked the flames of our competitive natures rather than squelch them for harmony's sake. My father, in addition to being very athletic, instilled in us a single-mindedness of purpose and an intensity that demanded we learn from our mistakes—the girls no less than the boys. My mother bred in us a ferocious work ethic and unyielding loyalty both to others and to whatever pursuits we embarked on—the girls no less than the boys. But it was Title IX which gave me a full ride to a Division I school. If not for Title IX, I wouldn't have been part of the Bruin women and their first National Basketball Championship, which sparked the imagination of the press, who loved to write about UCLA's brother and sister basketball greats, thus creating nationwide momentum for women's basketball.

In his later years, Papa told a reporter that I was the one who "really got women's basketball going." What a compliment!

I feel blessed to have been in the right place at the right time, to have been part of the first Women's Olympic Basketball team, which resulted in the formation of the very first women's professional basketball league in 1978-79 (The WBL), which led to the ABL in '94-97, and ultimately the WNBA in 1997.

Equality for women is a universe away from where it was in the 70s. Our last three Secretaries of State have been women, and the post-recession Washington gang in charge of finance re-regulation is headed up by women. The commander at Paris Island, responsible for molding men into Marines is the first woman ever so appointed. But we still have a ways to go.

I am currently the only female Vice President on the operation side of the NBA, and there are only two female GMs in the MLB, where there is only one female VP. Less than three percent of all Fortune 500 companies have female CEOs, and women still earn 77cents for every dollar that a man takes home (with working moms seeing the largest wage gap).

Our dismantling of prejudice follows a predictable course. We've finally had a black president. History dictates that we'll soon have a female president. When that happens, more little girls will dream of being in leadership positions and that will be a good thing.

Experiences gained in the locker room are invaluable, later, in the boardroom. Young women who compete in organized sports benefit from the same lessons that young men benefit from. It's not surprising therefore that 80% of women in executive positions today have competed in sports growing up. The more girls there are who compete in school sports today, the less mothers there will be in the future dolling their young daughters up to compete in beauty pageants. The more girls compete in sports today, the fewer women there will be in the future whose greatest goal will be losing twenty pounds, or landing some reality TV show that capitalizes on bad behavior instead of changing the world.

While things have come a long way in terms of viewing women as equal to men, there's still a long way to go in terms of actually empowering women. Studies from the Women's Sports Foundation have shown that women become empowered by competing in sports.

A few years ago Bill Russell held a Hall of Fame Basketball Camp in Vegas. He only invited ten Hall of Famers as coaches, but his wife, Marilyn said "Well, you have to invite Annie."

So there I was with John Havlicek, Sam Jones, Jerry West, Julius Erving, Magic Johnson, Clyde Drexler, Kareem Abdul-Jabbar, and Charles Barkley, some were my longtime idols. At one of the breaks between games and stations, Clyde, Julius, and I played a friendly game of H-O-R-S-E and I won. The guys didn't mind that a woman beat them because they never saw me as being at a disadvantage to begin with.

That is my dream for the future: that the phrase "You Let Some GIRL Beat You?" becomes obsolete. The notion that women are less able than men is a no-win situation for everybody. I was fortunate to have been raised that way. The opportunities sports, and basketball in particular, have given me, along with hard work and guidance by others, have made me who I am today.

In 2010, *Time Magazine* named me, along with Billie Jean King, and eight others, including my childhood hero, Babe Didrikson Zaharias, "Top Ten Female Sports Pioneers of All Time." Yet most people still don't recognize the name Ann Meyers Drysdale. But that doesn't matter. What matters is that I know what I have achieved. And when people ask me if I think it was important that I was the first woman to have done this or that, I always tell them there were others before me who opened the door.

What matters is not that I was the first, but that I not be the last.

Halls of Fame and Awards/Honors

-1975 -'76-'77-'78 First 4X All America (male or female) in College
    Basketball

-1976 - Olympic Silver Medal Winner – Started with the First
    Olympic US Women's Basketball Team

-1975 - Part of UCLA's National Championship Team in Track and
    Field

-1977 -'78-'79 Won AAU Championships with Anna's Bananas

-1978 - Part of UCLA's National Championship Team in Basketball

-1978 - Broderick Cup Winner for Basketball (Player of the Year)

-1978 - Broderick Cup Overall Winner

-1978 - UCLA's Athlete of the Year

-1978 -'79- #1 Overall pick in the WBL

-1979 -'80- Co-MVP of the WBL

-1979 - First -and Still Only- Woman to have a tryout in the NBA
    (Pacers) as a Free Agent

-1981- Cincinnati Hall of Fame

-1981-'82-'82- First Place in Women's Superstars Competition

-1981- First and Only Woman Ever Invited to Compete in the Men's
    Superstars

-1985 - International Women's Sports Foundation Hall of Fame (First
    Team Sport Athlete to be Inducted)

-1986 - Orange County Sports Hall of Fame

-1988 - UCLA Hall of Fame (First Woman to be Inducted)

-1993 - Naismith Memorial Basketball Hall of Fame

-1994 - Catholic Youth Organization Hall of Fame

-1995 - National High School Federation Hall of Fame

-1999 - Women's Basketball Hall of Fame

-1999 – Mel Greenberg Media Award

-2001 - Wooden All Time All American

-2002 - Southern California Sportscaster "Good Guy" Award

-2003 - NCAA Silver Anniversary Award

-2006 - Ronald Reagan Media Award

-2006 - California Sports Hall of Fame
-2007 - FIBA Hall of Fame -First American Woman and one of the
    first three Americans to be inducted (along with Bill Russell
    and Dean Smith)
-2007 & 2009 - General Manager of the WNBA Champion Phoenix
    Mercury
-2010 - Named "Top Business Woman" by Phoenix Business Journal
-2011 - YWCA's "Sports Leader of the Year" Award
-2012 - USBWA Named "National College Player of the Year
    Award" in honor of Ann Meyers Drysdale

Acknowledgements

I would like to first thank my parents for being such supportive and good role models. My Mom has been my rock and friend throughout my life, as she has for all her children.

My brothers and sisters-their love, support and guidance has never wavered for me in good times and bad. To Julius Erving, thank you for your kind words and always being another big brother to me. You're the BEST!

Nick Lampros, who has been my business manager, confidant, friend and is always there for me.

To all the coaches and teachers who impacted me in believing in myself and challenging me to be a better athlete and person, especially Ginny Dottl (Clark), Kenny Washington, Billie Moore, Gary Cunningham, Jim Bush, Patty Meyers, Ducky Drake, Andy Banchowski, Sue Gunter, Howie Landa, and Pat Summitt.

To all my teammates and opponents that challenged me in my career and helped make all things possible for my successes and failures. My dear friends and teammates, Juliene Simpson (my roommate who pushed me daily and even today and whom I shall always consider a dear friend), Sue Enquist, Beth Moore, Kim Bueltel, Carol Blazejowski, Lusia Harris, Nancy Dunkle, Pat Head (Summitt), Yvette Duran, Judy LeWinter, Karen Nash, Denise Corlett, Terry Condon, Monica Havelka, Debbie Ricketts, Anita Ortega, Donna Geils (Orender), Lori Allen, and SO many others! You've all left footprints in my heart.

All the teachers from my elementary schools, to Jr. High, Sonora High School, to UCLA, that helped me form my dreams and believed in me. Especially Art Friedman, Paul Tanner, Mr. Felshaw and Miss Wilson.

To all the guys that I played in pick-up games throughout my life from high school with Dale Yahnke and so many other of my brother Jeff's friends to college with guys like Wilt, Julius, Marques, Calvin and so many others. You made it fun, challenging, taught me to be tough and never back down or quit.

Thank you for not taking it easy on me and preparing me for the next level.

I'd especially like to thank Sam Nassi for his vision and unwavering conviction in having the guts to offer me a contract with the Indiana Pacer's. He went out on a limb and I hope I didn't disappoint him, his family, the Indiana Pacers, or the NBA.

The Indiana Pacers, thanks for sticking with me, even when there was so much doubt in what Sam Nassi was trying to present. A special thanks to Sandy and Bill Knapp for taking me under their wings and Davey Craig (trainer), for keeping me together during the try-outs, and to Coach Bob Leonard and his staff and players for their honesty.

My hat goes off to David Stern and Adam Silver for their tireless efforts to make the WNBA a success. Jerry Colangelo for being the first NBA owner to show his support for the league, and for the efforts and job that our first President Val Ackerman performed. To all involved with USA Basketball, thank you.

I'd like to thank with all my heart, all the Networks and stations that had the confidence in my ability and work ethic to broadcast for them. From CBS, ESPN, ABC, Prime Ticket, Sports Channel, TNT, FOX, KGMB, and mostly NBC. They have embraced me throughout the years within their family, especially with the Olympics and WNBA. Dick Ebersol has been the patriarch for so many, and I feel blessed that I have been able to work for him.

Dick Heckmann and the K2 Board, Stanley Gold and the L.A. Gear Board, Rafer Johnson and everyone associated with Special Olympics, John Hamilton and the Lott Board. And to every other board or charity that I have been associated with, you continue to amaze me with your support and the monies you raise to help so many others.

Special thanks go to all the announcers and production people I have worked with over the 30+ years in broadcasting. Your knowledge of the games and athletes has been an inspiration for me to be better behind the mike every time. I would especially like to thank Mike Breen, James Brown, Dick Enberg, Terry Gannon, Keith Jackson, Mark Jones, Chris Marlowe, Beth Mowins, Brad Nessler, Dave Obrien, Mike

Patrick, Robin Roberts, Hannah Storm, Barry Tompkins, Pam Ward, and so many others who helped make me a better broadcaster. Thank you for your hard work and dedication to the sport.

To the Women's Sports Foundation (WSF), Billie Jean King and ALL the women who were instrumental in opening the doors for me and others my age to benefit from all their courage and sacrifices. They were instrumental in the birth of Title IX. And to know that the women of this generation will understand how fortunate they are to feel empowered by what others have done for them.

Coach John Wooden (Papa) and his family, for their sacrifices of sharing their father, grandfather, great grandfather, and great, great, grandfather with so many in the world. Thank you for your friendship and kindness. And to Dr. Judith Holland, you were key to the success of so many UCLA Athletes.

Pete Newell and the Tall Women's Camp for sharing your basketball knowledge with the women and having fun doing it.

To all the Baseball Teams and Networks that my late husband Don Drysdale worked for. He found great joy and friendship in everywhere he went. Special thanks to the Angels, Chicago White Sox, and L.A. Dodgers.

To Bob Uecker—live, love, laugh is what you do. And without you, there would not have been Donnie and I. Thank you for bringing us together.

Jerry Reinsdorf and Eddie Einhorn for seeing what 2 good baseball men in the booth together could accomplish. Your undying friendship and loyalty to Don's family has been so appreciated. Thank you. And to Peter O'Malley and Terry Seidler and the Dodgers, you have ALWAYS been the "CLASS" of any organization I have been around, because you treated "everyone" like family. Thank you for embracing us in the Dodger Family with so much love and respect. You always have done things "the right way!" I will always be indebted to you.

Thank you to all the baseball players and personnel that have opened their arms to Don's children, especially Tommy (IZZY) Lasorda. All the hours in the dugout and on the field with the boys after their dad passed away. And still you and your family treat us like one of your own.

Robert Sarver and the Phoenix Mercury and Suns, thank you for your persistence in hiring me to be a part of a wonderful organization. And to have worked with Jay Parry, Amber Cox, Rick Weltz, Steve Kerr, Mike D'Antoni, Alvin Gentry, Paul Westhead, Jim Pitman, Corey Gaines, Lesley Factor and the hundreds of employees that make our jobs so much easier. Thank you to the thousands of WNBA fans and Mercury Season Ticket holders that have supported us and helped our players bring 2 WNBA titles to Phoenix.

I can't thank Don's folks, (who have since passed away) Scotty and Verna, and sister Nancy, enough for embracing me into their family. Kelly (Don's Daughter), you continue to be a guiding light for your sister and two brothers. Thank you! You are loved and appreciated.

And to Joni Ravenna, who, without her continued digging, persistence, and challenges, I don't think I could have told some of the stories that she got out of me. Thank you for your friendship Joni and never getting mad at me for saying "no" about a story. You quietly and gently persuaded me to be the best I could for you. Thank you for your everlasting patience and hours and hours of staying up to hear stories and doing rewrites. You are amazing!

To our agent, David Fugate, we thank you for your guidance and belief in the project.

To Lynn and Fred Price at Behler Publications, for having the enthusiasm to immediately say "yes" to publishing my story. I knew right away that with your forthright positive attitude that my story could be told.

Heather Riccio, how you keep me grounded with the new wave of social media. Thank you for making me look good.

And lastly, to the young girls and boys, women and men- believe in your passion, and don't let anyone tell you "you can't do something." Prove them wrong!